1 MONTH OF
FREE
READING

at
www.ForgottenBooks.com

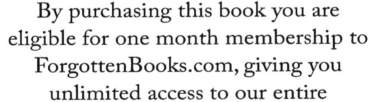

By purchasing this book you are eligible for one month membership to ForgottenBooks.com, giving you unlimited access to our entire collection of over 1,000,000 titles via our web site and mobile apps.

To claim your free month visit:
www.forgottenbooks.com/free964476

ISBN 978-0-260-69148-4
PIBN 10964476

This book is a reproduction of an important historical work. Forgotten Books uses state-of-the-art technology to digitally reconstruct the work, preserving the original format whilst repairing imperfections present in the aged copy. In rare cases, an imperfection in the original, such as a blemish or missing page, may be replicated in our edition. We do, however, repair the vast majority of imperfections successfully; any imperfections that remain are intentionally left to preserve the state of such historical works.

LIVINGSTON'S
GLOBE

Three
Finest
Tomatoes

LIVINGSTON'S
BEAUTY

THE
LIVINGSTON
SEED CO.

FAMOUS for TOMATOES

COLUMBUS,
OHIO.

Three Famous Livingston Tomatoes

Known and Grown the World Over
Each One the Leading Variety in Its Class

Livingston's Globe

The Greatest Shipping Tomato for the South

Originated With Us and Introduced in 1905. The Finest Early Purple Tomato in Existence. Very Distinct in Shape, Firm Fleshed, of Delicate Flavor. Blight Proof.

Livingston's Globe is an extra good all-round sort, of a distinct globe shape, with quite a large percentage of elongated fruits. It is a very beautiful variety, and on account of its shape one that permits of a great number of slices to be made from each fruit. It is early. We class it with the first earlies, both in our greenhouses as well as in our field trials, along with many other varieties. The fruits are of large size, and a good marketable size is retained throughout the season. It is always smooth, of firm flesh, and few seeds; ripens evenly; color, a fine glossy rose, tinged with purple, and without the slightest tinge of yellow at any stage of ripening. It is an exceedingly productive variety, having plants with many short joints, at which large clusters containing three to seven fruits are almost invariably formed. In quality there is nothing more to be desired, being mild, pleasant and of delicious flavor. There is no better variety for greenhouse growing or for early growing on stakes or trellises. Its blight-proof qualities are remarkable. May be picked quite green, will carry to distant markets in excellent shape and ripen up uniformly to meet quick and profitable sales. Pkts., 5c. and 10c.; ¼ oz., 15c.; oz., 30c.; ¼ lb., $1.00; lb., $3.25.

Warning

Not all Tomato seed called "Livingston's" is grown by Livingston's. To be sure of genuine seed grown by us, send to us direct or insist on your dealer supplying in our bags and under our registered "True Blue" seal.

Livingston's Beauty

The Greatest of All Purple-Colored Market Sorts. Strong Grower, Very Productive. First Large and Smooth Early.

Although introduced by us thirty years ago, this is still the greatest of all purple colored market Tomatoes. Hosts of "new" sorts have been brought before the public since, but not one has in any sense become a real rival of Livingston's Beauty, although our "Globe" has now surpassed it among the Southern growers. The plants make a strong growth, are hardy and bear plentifully. The fruit is produced in clusters of four to six, is large, of perfect shape, and retains its size until late in the season. It ripens early, has firm flesh of excellent quality, and the seed cells are very small. For shipping and early market it is excellent. May be picked quite green; will ripen up nicely, look well and keep in perfect condition for a week after becoming fully ripe. Pkts., 5c. and 10c.; ½ oz., 15c.; oz., 25c.; ¼ lb., 75c.; lb., $2.75.

Livingston's Stone

The Greatest Canning Tomato in the World

The Largest, Bright Red, Perfectly Smooth, High-Yielding, Best Keeping, Finest Flavored Main-Crop Variety in Existence.

Livingston's Stone is always of good size, deep through from stem to blossom end and very firm. Skin is bright scarlet, perfectly smooth and strong enough to stand shipping and long distance hauling to perfection. Flesh is very solid, and of finest flavor. Seed cells are small and few. Livingston's Stone is now recognized by all as the greatest canning Tomato. We alone supply enough seed to the leading Tomato growers every year to produce millions of plants and large quantities of Stone Tomato seeds are sold by others, but—Seed of Livingston's Stone, as introduced by us, can only be bought from **Livingston's.** Price—Pkts., 5c. and 10c.; ½ oz., 15c.; oz., 30c.; ¼ lb., 85c.; lb., $3.00.

For other varieties of Tomatoes, see pages 63 to 69.

Crop of Tomatoes Grown on Wire Trellis at True Blue Farm

The Livingston Seed Co.

Our Reference:
The Users of True Blue Seeds

IMPORTERS, GROWERS and DEALERS IN

"True Blue"
Garden, Field and Flower
Seeds

ESTABLISHED 1850

True Blue Nurseries, Trial Grounds and Greenhouses, near this City.
Kirkersville Seed Farm, Kirkersville, Ohio.
Retail Store, 114 North High and 9-11 East Long Sts.
Seed Warehouse, 59-61 East Chestnut St.

Greetings to Our Friends: *Columbus, Ohio, January 1, 1916*

We regret our good wishes for 1915 did not quite come true. However, we have much to be thankful for, especially in view of the fact that the war in Europe, with its attendant suffering, is still going on. The season of 1915 saw some very low prices in many markets for garden and farm products; and this, in addition to very short crops, has worked hardships to many of our gardener friends. It was a season of many discouragements. In our own experience of cultivating several hundred acres of land, we found this to be true. We believe the outlook for next season (1916) is, however, much brighter. There are thousands of men at work now, that were idle a year ago. The warring nations will have many things to buy besides munitions, and the United States is in the best position of any neutral country to supply them. This will give employment to a great many men all over this country. When everybody is busy, times are good.

The unfavorable season has made it quite difficult to secure ample seed stocks, but we have been quite fortunate with most varieties. There are some of the Beans, especially Wax varieties, and Onions, that may not be in sufficient supply to see us through, but we will make them go as far as possible, so as to cause as little inconvenience as we can. Our friends can be assured of our untiring efforts to secure the best of everything, that the season has produced, and we are confident the seed stocks in general will be found up to our usual high standard.

We are pleased to be able to again announce a further reduction in many varieties of Peas, also on Golden Self Blanching Celery, both in American and French grown stock. In some other sorts we have been compelled to advance prices owing to increased cost.

We have included parcel post charges, at a low average cost, in the smaller quantities offered this season, and believe it will be much more convenient to our customer.

Wishing you all a most successful season in your 1916 gardens, we remain

Yours as ever,

THE LIVINGSTON SEED CO.

A partial view of our True Blue Farms

IMPORTANT SUGGESTIONS: By carefully observing the following Rules and Directions, Mistakes and Misunderstandings will be very largely avoided.

COLUMBUS, OHIO, is a city of over 200,000 inhabitants centrally located geographically, has 17 steam railroad systems, five electric roads, which practically cover the entire country, Express Companies, Telegraph and Telephone wires in all directions, which afford us unequaled facilities for receiving orders, shipping and procuring lowest rates to all parts of the country; besides you have the assurance of getting your order in the quickest possible time.

Within Twenty-four Hours' Time we can reach two-thirds of the Population of the United States.

ALWAYS USE THE ORDER BLANK and envelope sent with this Catalogue when possible. Write plainly, keep a copy of your order, and be sure to sign your name, Post-office, County, and State every time you write to us. Extra Envelopes and Order Blanks will be sent on application, also additional Catalogues, if desired.

SEND MONEY. Remittances should always accompany the order. Remittances may be made at our risk by any of the following methods: (1st and best)—**Post-Office Order;** (2d)—**Draft on New York;** (3d)—**Express Co. Money Order;** (4th)—**Cash by express** in amounts not less than $5.00; (5th)—**Registered Letters.** When money cannot be sent by either of the first four methods, it may be enclosed in a Registered Letter. The rates charged for Post-Office Orders and Express Money Orders are now so low this is the best way to remit where they can be obtained. We will bear expenses of sending money in either of above ways when order amounts to $1.00 or over.

NO GOODS SENT C. O. D. Unless cash to the amount of one-fourth the order accompanies the same.

Seeds by Mail. Sending seeds by mail is a very important branch of our business, and we are prepared to fill orders promptly and correctly the day they are received in nearly all cases.

Our Prices. In comparing our mail prices, especially on heavy seeds, such as Peas, Beans and Corn by the pound and two pounds, and other seeds by the pound and one-fourth pound, bear in mind that we pay the postage, unless otherwise noted. Remember another thing—packets of heavy seeds like Peas, Beans, etc., quoted by some seedsmen at 5 cents per packet, postpaid, contain but a small amount of seed, allowing for the postage that it requires to mail each packet. Preferring to please customers rather than disappoint them we put up liberal 10c packets of such seeds.

ORDER EARLY. It is important to order as soon after you get the Catalogue as convenient, then you will have your seeds at hand for planting when you want them; besides if you want seeds in large quantities, they can be sent by freight much cheaper than by express. Small orders, however, can often go by express as cheaply.

SHIPPING ORDERS. When goods are to be shipped by freight or express, give plain shipping directions; otherwise we use our best judgment.

LARGE ORDERS. Any Dealer, Market-Gardener, Institution or any Individual, wishing seeds in large quantities, is requested to mail us a list of what they want and we will promptly return it to you with the very lowest prices marked. A letter of inquiry may save you dollars if you want to buy in quantity.

SMALL ORDERS. If you only want a single packet, do not hesitate to order it. We take as much pains with small orders as with large ones. Small True Blue Seed orders are sure to grow larger.

BE FREE TO WRITE US for any information pertaining to our business, and not found in this Catalogue, on a separate sheet of paper from your order, as your letter goes to the general office and your order to the Mail, Express, or other departments.

WE URGE Customers to inform us promptly on the arrival of orders if anything proves otherwise than expected. We aim to make friends of our customers, and mail orders receive the same careful attention that customers do over our counters, but we are only human, and errors sometimes (though not often) occur. When they do we are willing and anxious to rectify them.

OUR SEED ANNUAL. Please show this Seed Annual to your friends, and if you should receive an extra copy be kind enough to hand it to some neighbor interested in seeds, who will be pleased to get it. We will be glad to send a copy free to any of your friends likely to want seeds, in this or any other country. In return we will ask you to speak a good word for us to your friends and neighbors. An order this season, no matter how small, secures our Catalogue for next season as soon as issued.

CHANGE OF ADDRESS. If you have changed, or intend to change your address, please let us know, and we will change it on our books, so that you will receive our Seed Annual, at your new postoffice.

If you have Rural Mail Delivery be sure to give the Name and Number of your Route, if necessary, when ordering.

GUARANTEE. Complaints made that seeds are not good should quite as often be attributed to other causes, as to the quality of the seeds. There are contingencies continually arising to prevent the very best seeds always giving satisfaction, such as sowing too deep, too shallow, in too wet or too dry soil; insects of all descriptions destroying the plants as soon as, or before, they appear; wet weather, cold weather, frosts; chemical changes in the seeds induced by temperature, etc. Soil preparation for the reception of seed is very important. If not properly done, seed with very high germination is bound to perish. For all these reasons it is impossible to guarantee seeds under all circumstances, and, while we exercise the greatest care to have all seeds pure and reliable, we give no warranty, expressed or implied, as to description, quality, productiveness or any other matter of any Seeds, Bulbs, or Plants we send out, and we will not be in any way responsible for the crop. If the purchaser does not accept the goods on these terms, they are at once to be returned. We test all our seeds before sending them to our customers, and should they fail to grow, if promptly and properly tested by the customer, will replace the same amount or give value in others. We cannot afford, knowingly, to send out seeds doubtful as to vitality or purity, and you can get no better stocks of any seedsman, even though he deceitfully professes to warrant seeds, which frequently covers nothing but the amount paid for the seeds. If you do not think so inquire into the extent of the warranty and you will ascertain that your warrants are not crop protection. A guarantee from an irresponsible seedsman is of no value whatever.

Setting Tomato Plants at our Kirkersville Seed Farms

WE give below a Parcel Post rate table for the convenience of those wishing goods sent by mail in larger quantities than are quoted "postpaid" herein. Bear in mind however that we pay the postage or express charges, unless otherwise noted, on flowering bulbs up to and including dozen lots, and on all seeds up to and including pounds (Beans, Corn and Peas two pounds). The price on other items does not include prepayment of this charge except as noted.

The rate for Seeds, Bulbs, Plants and Books is 1 cent for each two ounces up to 8 ounces regardless of distance. Over 8 ounces the pound zone rate applies	Local Zone City of Cols. and its rural routes Postage required.	1st Zone Not over 50 miles from Columbus Postage required.	2nd Zone 51 to 150 miles from Columbus Postage required.	3rd Zone 151 to 300 mi. from Columbus Postage required.	4th Zone 301 to 600 mi. from Columbus Postage required.	5th Zone 601 to 1000 mi. from Columbus Postage required.	6th Zone 1001 to 1400 mi. from Columbus Postage required.	7th Zone 1401 to 1800 mi. from Columbus Postage required.	8th Zone Over 1800 miles from Columbus Postage required
Over 8 oz. up to 1 lb.	5c	5c	5c	6c	7c	$0.08	$0.09	$0.11	$0.12
Over 1 lb. up to 2 lbs.	6c	6c	6c	8c	11c	.14	.17	.21	.24
Over 2 lbs. up to 3 lbs.	6c	7c	7c	10c	15c	.20	.25	.31	.36
Over 3 lbs. up to 4 lbs.	7c	8c	8c	12c	19c	.26	.33	.41	.48
Over 4 lbs. up to 5 lbs.	7c	9c	9c	14c	23c	.32	.41	.51	.60
Over 5 lbs. up to 6 lbs.	8c	10c	10c	16c	27c	.38	.49	.61	.72
Over 6 lbs. up to 7 lbs.	8c	11c	11c	18c	31c	.44	.57	.71	.84
Over 7 lbs. up to 8 lbs.	9c	12c	12c	20c	35c	.50	.65	.81	.96
Over 8 lbs. up to 9 lbs.	9c	13c	13c	22c	39c	.56	.73	.91	1.08
Over 9 lbs. up to 10 lbs.	10c	14c	14c	24c	43c	.62	.81	1.01	1.20
Over 10 lbs. up to 11 lbs.	10c	15c	15c	26c	47c	.68	.89	1.11	1.32
Over 11 lbs. up to 12 lbs.	11c	16c	16c	28c	51c	.74	.97	1.21	1.44
Over 12 lbs. up to 13 lbs.	11c	17c	17c	30c	55c	.80	1.05	1.31	1.56
Over 13 lbs. up to 14 lbs.	12c	18c	18c	32c	59c	.86	1.13	1.41	1.68
Over 14 lbs. up to 15 lbs.	12c	19c	19c	34c	63c	.92	1.21	1.51	1.80
Over 15 lbs. up to 16 lbs.	13c	20c	20c	36c	67c	.98	1.29	1.61	1.92
Over 16 lbs. up to 17 lbs.	13c	21c	21c	38c	71c	1.04	1.37	1.71	2.04
Over 17 lbs. up to 18 lbs.	14c	22c	22c	40c	75c	1.10	1.45	1.81	2.16
Over 18 lbs. up to 19 lbs.	14c	23c	23c	42c	79c	1.16	1.53	1.91	2.28
Over 19 lbs. up to 20 lbs.	15c	24c	24c	44c	83c	1.22	1.61	2.01	2.40
Over 20 lbs. up to 21 lbs.	15c	25c	25c						
Over 21 lbs. up to 22 lbs.	16c	26c	26c						
Over 22 lbs. up to 23 lbs.	16c	27c	27c						
Over 23 lbs. up to 24 lbs.	17c	28c	28c						
Over 24 lbs. up to 25 lbs.	17c	29c	29c						
Over 25 lbs. up to 26 lbs.	18c	30c	30c						
Over 26 lbs. up to 27 lbs.	18c	31c	31c						
Over 27 lbs. up to 28 lbs.	19c	32c	32c						
Over 28 lbs. up to 29 lbs.	19c	33c	33c						
Over 29 lbs. up to 30 lbs.	20c	34c	34c						
Over 30 lbs. up to 31 lbs.	20c	35c	35c						
Over 31 lbs. up to 32 lbs.	21c	36c	36c						
Over 32 lbs. up to 33 lbs.	21c	37c	37c						
Over 33 lbs. up to 34 lbs.	22c	38c	38c						
Over 34 lbs. up to 35 lbs.	22c	39c	39c						
Over 35 lbs. up to 36 lbs.	23c	40c	40c						
Over 36 lbs. up to 37 lbs.	23c	41c	41c						
Over 37 lbs. up to 38 lbs.	24c	42c	42c						
Over 38 lbs. up to 39 lbs.	24c	43c	43c						
Over 39 lbs. up to 40 lbs.	25c	44c	44c						
Over 40 lbs. up to 41 lbs.	25c	45c	45c						
Over 41 lbs. up to 42 lbs.	26c	46c	46c						
Over 42 lbs. up to 43 lbs.	26c	47c	47c						
Over 43 lbs. up to 44 lbs.	27c	48c	48c						
Over 44 lbs. up to 45 lbs.	27c	49c	49c						
Over 45 lbs. up to 46 lbs.	28c	50c	50c						
Over 46 lbs. up to 47 lbs.	28c	51c	51c						
Over 47 lbs. up to 48 lbs.	29c	52c	52c						
Over 48 lbs. up to 49 lbs.	29c	53c	53c						
Over 49 lbs. up to 50 lbs.	30c	54c	54c						

Insured Parcel Post

Packages up to $25.00 in value will be insured for their full value on payment of a fee of 5 cents for each package in addition to the regular post rates. Packages in value over $25.00 will be insured for their full value, but not to exceed $50.00 for a fee of 10 cents for each package in addition to the regular Parcel Post rates. If you desire your package insured, send the insurance fee in addition to the amount you send to pay for the goods—and be sure to mention same on your order.

Weight Limit

In the local, first and second zones, packages will be delivered by Parcel Post, weighing up to 50 pounds. In the third to eighth zones the weight limit is 20 pounds.

Size Limit

The size of the parcel in no case is to exceed 72 inches in length and girth combined. In other words, the circumference of the parcel at its thickest part, plus its length, must not exceed 72 inches.

Returning Goods

Should you ever find it necessary to return goods by Parcel Post, never put a letter or any money in the package, as that would make the whole shipment bear a first-class postage charge. Never seal a Parcel Post package, or place a stamp over the string. Always put your name and address in the upper left-hand corner.

Novelties and Specialties for 1916

"Sure Crop
Stringless
Wax Bean

You will find under this heading new varieties worthy of trial, and others of such value as to warrant our giving them special mention. A vast number of novelties are offered each year which, after growing on our trial grounds, prove no better than standard varieties, if as good, so that in line with our policy of furnishing the best seeds procurable we endeavor to furnish in new types, only such as have made good on our trial grounds. There are varieties which, while not new in the strictest sense of the word, are of recent introduction and demand special notice as being much superior to ordinary types, and these we hope our customers will try along with some of the novelties, all of which will prove of interest and aid in the development of a more productive garden.

"Sure Crop" Stringless Wax Bean

Plants are very thrifty and hardy. Thick, leathery leaves resist blight admirably and help this sort to stand a remarkable amount of dry weather. Sure Crop Stringless Wax is the Bean "par excellence" for dry sections. Pods average 6 inches long, are flat, thick and fleshy and entirely stringless. Pkt., 10c.; ½ lb., 20c.; lb., 30c.; 2 lbs., 55c.; ½ pk. (7½ lbs.), $1.65; pk., $3.00.

Livingston's Hardy Wax Bean

Can be Planted Early, High Quality, Stringless

You can't find a stronger or more healthy grower than this variety. It resists disease and grows in spite of unfavorable weather, and when it comes to quality they are unsurpassed in their class. We made pretty strong claims for Livingston's Hardy Wax when we first introduced it, but we haven't taken back a word that we said. It is of great value either for market or home garden. Pkt., 10c.; ½ lb., 15c.; lb., 30c.; 2glbs., 45c.; ½ pk. (7½ lbs.), $1.40; pk., $2.50.

Fordhook Bush Lima Bean

Bush Stiffly Erect, Beans Fat and Delicious

The stiffly erect bushes branch freely and bear tremendous crops. It is ready for use as early as the popular Burpee's Bush Lima, but the Beans are plumper and remain green longer. The shelled Beans are very fat, are closely packed in the pods, which shell very easily. Pods are borne in clusters of from 4 to 6, average 4 to 5 inches long and contain usually 4 tender Beans of a delightful flavor. Pkt., 10c.; ½ lb., 20c.; lb., 35c.; 2 lbs., 55c.; ½ pk. (7 lbs.), $1.25; pk., $2.25; bu., $8.50.

Kentucky Wonder Wax Pole Bean

A New Early Large Yellow Podded Sort of Finest Flavor, and Stringless

Quite similar to the Kentucky Wonder or Homestead Green Pod except in the color of pods, which in this one are light waxy yellow. It has a thick broad pod very tender, of delicious flavor and stringless. The pods often attain a length of 8 to 9 inches. It begins bearing when the vines are only a few feet in height, hence its earliness, and therefore a sort well adapted to maturing a crop where seasons are quite short. In our trial grounds, 1915, it came into bearing a week or 10 days sooner than the old variety. Pkt., 10c.; ½ lb., 15c.; lb., 25c.; 2 lbs. 50c.; ½ pk. (7½ lbs.), $1.40; pk., $2.75.

For other standard varieties of Beans, see Pages 18, 19, 20 and 21.

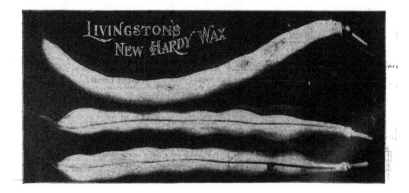

LIVINGSTON'S NEW HARDY WAX

Chinese Cabbage (Pe Tsai)

Also known as "Celery Cabbage," "Odorless Cabbage," "Chinese Lettuce," etc.

An annual introduced into this country from Shontung, China. A new vegetable for the United States, and already has about a half dozen names, all more or less appropriate. It is a species of cabbage, with a fine delicate flavor so that it might be called odorless, also resembles a stalk of celery more than a cabbage head. It is as tender as head lettuce and once introduced becomes a great favorite and is in great demand for numerous dishes such as salads, cole slaw, and having a mild and pleasant delicate flavor, it can be eaten raw, or it may be cooked, but being very tender it must be cooked quickly. Soil best suited to it is low and moist and cannot be made too rich, if finest quality is desired, but it can·be grown to fair size on any good garden soil that will grow good cabbage. If the weather should be very warm at the time of heading, tie up like Endive. Keep well watered.

For Fall or early Winter crop, the proper time to sow the seed in drills outside is early in August, depending on weather and other conditions. It is a very rapid grower, but apt to run to seed instead of heading, in hot, dry weather, therefore important to plant late. If sown outside make rows not less than 20 inches apart and the plants finally thinned to 12 or 15 inches apart. Cultivate the same as cabbage. For Winter use it is taken up before hard frost or freezing and cared for the same as cabbage in Winter. If permitted to freeze it will rot very quickly. The mode of storing is to cover with straw and a sufficient quantity·of earth·to keep out the·frost. (See illustration.) Pkt., 10c.;·½ oz., 20c.; oz., 35c.; ¼ lb., $1.10; lb., $3.75.

Danish Summer Ball-Head Cabbage

In Danish Summer Ball-Head we have a variety coming between Copenhagen Market and the regular type of Danish Ball-Head. The season of this new Cabbage is about the same as Henderson's Succession, it being a mid-season or Summer Cabbage and the good things said about Copenhagen Market can be applied to this new Cabbage of true ball-head type. Pkt., 5c.; ½ oz., 15c.; oz., 25c.; ¼ lb., 70c.; lb., $2.25.

Copenhagen Market Cabbage

Everybody who grows Cabbage is familiar with the Danish Ball-Head or Hollander, a Winter Cabbage grown for market more extensively than any other variety. When we say that in Copenhagen Market we have almost an exact counterpart except as to season, every one will know at once that we are offering a Cabbage of real merit. Copenhagen Market is an early Danish Ball-Head. It matures with the Wakefields but is of much larger size. We have tested out many varieties alongside of it and it was not only the earliest Cabbage, but every plant developed a fine solid head—all exceptionally uniform in type, averaging about 8 inches in diameter each way and weighing from 5 to 8 lbs. each. We place Copenhagen·Market in the front rank as an early Cabbage and feel sure that every one planting it will be highly pleased with the crop. Pkt., 10c.; ¼ oz., 20c.; oz., 35c.; ¼ lb., $1.10; lb., $3.50.

Danish Summer Ball-Head

For other varieties of Cabbage, see pages 23, 24 and 25.

A head of Chinese Cabbage ready for market

Copenhagen Market Cabbage

Livingston's Earliest on Earth

Livingston's Earliest on Earth

Records on our trial grounds for the past three years show it to be earliest of all including such well-known extra-early varieties as "Peep O' Day," "Golden Bantam," "Nordheims," "Premo," and all strains of Cory. Planted May 25, 1912, it was ready for market in 62 days. Retaining the sweetness and color of Golden Bantam, it is 7 to 10 days earlier. Having 10 to 12 rows of grains, gaps in the ears, so common in the 8-rowed varieties, are prevented. Length runs 6 to 8 inches in roasting-ear stage. Ears are produced on short stalks and on account of extreme earliness, late Cabbage or other crop may be easily secured on same ground the same season. Pkt., 10c.; ½ lb., 25c.; lb., 40c.; 2 lbs., 75c.; ½ pk. (6 lbs.), $1.25; pk., $2.25.

Livingston's Early Sugar

A distinct and valuable addition to the early Sweet Corns. As compared with other good early sorts, it has bigger ears with more even rows which are invariably filled well to the tip.

Ears average 8 inches long by 2¼ in diameter, have from 10 to 12 rows of deep, broad, pearly white kernels of delightfully sweet flavor which is not surpassed by any other early kind. Sixty per cent. of the stalks carry two splendid, well-developed ears which are usually placed from 2 to 3 feet above the ground. A remarkable characteristic of Livingston's Early Sugar is the exceptionally strong husk which protects the ears well from ravages of insects. Pkt., 10c.; ½ lb., 15c.; lb., 25c.; 2 lbs., 45c.; ¼ pk. (6 lbs.), 60c.; pk., $1.10; bu., $3.75.

For other varieties of Sweet Corn, see pages 30 to 32.

Livingston's New Tom Thumb Pop-Corn

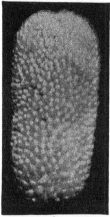

Livingston's New Tom Thumb Pop-Corn

A great many people like to grow Pop-Corn, but there is so much difference in the popping qualities of the various varieties that one hesitates to offer anything in this line unless it has real merit. In this variety we have a dwarf growing corn, a heavy yielder of attractive ears, peculiar in form, but the grain is very similar to the best strain of White Rice Pop-Corn. The photograph reproduced on this page shows exact size of the ears which run very uniform. Of a pearly white color and the grain is of excellent popping quality and of fine flavor after being popped. We recommend Tom Thumb as a Pop-Corn well worthy of a trial, believing it will give general satisfaction. Pkt., 10c.; ½ lb., 25c.; lb., 40c.; 2 lbs., 75c.

Livingston's Early Sugar

Vickery's Forcing Cucumber

Right Shape, Right Color, Long Standing

This is undoubtedly one of the finest Cucumbers for either forcing under glass or out-door cultivation. It is of the White Spine type, but the blossom end is quite blunt. The fruits are somewhat longer than Extra-Early White Spine, which is one of its parents, and the rich dark green color continues well down to the blossom end. Market gardeners will appreciate the fact that this Cucumber holds its color for a long time after being picked.

It is only such varieties as show real merit that find a place on our Kirkersville Seed Farms. Only after repeated tests in our trial grounds were we convinced that Vickery's was a good variety and one worthy of a place in the already long list of Cucumbers. Each season we now grow quite an acreage of this variety under our personal supervision and the care taken and careful selections made will be appreciated by those planting this stock.

Seed of our own growing: Pkt., 10c.; ½ oz., 25c.; oz., 45c.; ¼ lb., $1.35; lb., $5.00.

The Preferred Lettuce

A Black-Seeded Big Boston

A new variety quite similar to Big Boston except as to color of the seed, which in this variety is black. The heads are large and compact; and the leaves are claimed to be free from the slight bronze tinge on the outer edge of the leaves, which is common to the old style of Big Boston. If this has proven an objection, the Preferred should prove desirable in this respect. Pkt., 5c.; ½ oz., 10c.; oz., 15c.; ¼ lb., 50c.; lb., $1.75.

Tom Watson Water Melon

Best Quality, Best Shape, Best Shipper, Best Size, Best Appearance.

In the **Tom Watson** we have a decidedly good thing from the State of Georgia, the "home of the Water Melon," where the Watermelon grows to a greater state of perfection probably than in almost any other part of the United States.

The **Tom Watson** is an extra long Melon of attractive appearance, uniform in shape and quality. The luscious crimson flesh is "as sweet as honey," melting, and of superb flavor. The average Melon will weigh 35 to 40 pounds. It is very prolific, producing in greatest abundance the large delicious fruits. Introduced only a few years ago and has already taken a leading place with large Melon growers and shippers. Our sales of Tom Watson now exceed any other variety. Pkt., 5c.; oz., 10c.; ¼ lb., 20c.; lb., 50c. By express, not paid, 5 lbs., $1.75; 10 lbs., $3.25.

Taylor Wilson, Wicomico Co., Md., writes: "The Tom Watson Watermelon seed I got from you was the truest I ever saw. There was not a mixed one in the patch. I had the best patch of Watermelons that was around here. Everybody who saw them said they were the best they ever saw in their life and the truest Tom Watson. People asked me where I got my seed and I told them from you people. I will buy from you as long as you treat me right and will do all I can for you."

Complete List of Watermelons, pages 42 and 43.

Vickery's Forcing

Tom Watson

Special Wholesale Prices on Melon Seed in quantity

Livingston's Orange Water Melon

Livingston's Orange Water Melon

Not a new variety, but not having been catalogued for many years, we consider it worth while to bring it to the attention of our customers, as it is certainly a novelty and at the same time a nice variety for the home garden. The peculiarity of this fine Melon is that when well ripened the inner core separates from the rind, as shown in our picture, which is reproduced from a photograph of a Melon grown at our Kirkersville farms the past season. Frequently one can lift the entire heart of the Melon out of the shell or rind by carefully cutting the Melon rind only, as shown in the picture. In this case the upper half was lifted off the Melon and after the photograph was taken we lifted out the center or fleshy part complete. It will be noticed that the inner portion of the Melon quite resembles an orange after peeling, hence the name. The flesh of this Melon is of a beautiful pink shade and fine quality. It grows to a medium size, is productive and, taken altogether, is a very desirable variety. Pkt., 10c.; oz., 20c.; ¼ lb., 60c.; lb., $2.00.

For other varieties of Water Melon, see pages 42 and 43.

Gold-Lined Rocky Ford Musk Melon

It is a pleasure to be able to offer **Gold-Lined Rocky Ford.** Our stock of it is the result of several years' careful selection by a progressive grower. The shape is ideal, being slightly oval, and it is heavily netted over the entire surface. The flesh of the entire Melon is noticeably thick, fine grained and sweet. The color is green with a gold margin next to the seed cavity. Attractive, both as to outward appearance and when cut. We offer hand saved seed from selected Melons. Pkt., 10c.; oz., 15c.; ¼ lb., 45c.; lb., $1.50.

For other varieties of Muskmelon see pages 40 and 41.

Dwarf or Bush Musk Melon

This Melon grows in bush form; the stem between the joints of the vine being shorter than on the ordinary kinds. Fruit small but early and very productive. The hills can be planted as close as 2½ feet apart, leaving 2 to 3 plants to the hill. Flesh green and of fine quality. Pkt., 10c.; ½ oz., 15c.; oz., 25c.

Livingston's Ohio Sugar Musk Melon

A Green-Fleshed Tip Top

Livingston's Ohio Sugar Melon is an absolutely distinct and very superior Melon. It is the result of careful hybridizing and painstaking selection and breeding. We believe it to be absolutely the sweetest and most luscious green-fleshed cantaloupe now on the market. It is of that desirable size in demand in all markets; round, inclined to oval in shape, heavy in proportion to size because the flesh is so deep. It is distinctly ribbed and thickly netted—color of skin grey-green. Because of its firm flesh and solidity, it is a splendid shipper. Seed cavity small. It is no lottery to select a good Ohio Sugar Melon. They are all good, sweet and delicious clear to the rind. It is the rarest exception that an under-quality Melon is found. **The flesh is an attractive green of exquisite texture, sugary, juicy, tender, and entirely free from any stringiness. Handsome and uniform shape;** every Melon a good one; sweet and luscious clear to the rind. It has become a popular market and home-garden Melon. **Produces good Melons on all soils.**

Every one who tries this Melon goes into ecstacies over its captivating flavor. It has that delightfully rich aromatic flavor which is so refreshing. The vines are of luxuriant and vigorous growth, yielding bountifully through the entire season. Pkt., 10c.; oz., 20c.; ¼ lb., 60c.; lb., $2.00.

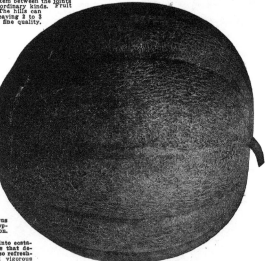

Livingston's Ohio Sugar Musk Melon

Livingston's Yellow Beauty Onion

**Produces the Hardest, Smoothest, Roundest,
Best Keeping Onion Sets of Any
Variety Known to the Trade**

Introduced by Us in 1914

Hundreds of gardeners have been depending on our Brown Beauty Onion for years. We introduced it in 1900 and prior to this it had been known locally for some time and very generally grown here. Because of its value we procured a stock and began selecting year after year and improving the strain on our farms.

Realizing the importance of a lighter colored Onion of the same qualities as Brown Beauty, we set to work to develop it and last year offered to our customers **Livingston's Yellow Beauty**, an exact counterpart of Brown Beauty, except in color, which is a bright lemon yellow. The flesh is very fine, firm and mild.

Livingston's Yellow Beauty is a medium-sized Onion, a strong grower producing in one season from the black seed a fine marketable Onion of good appearance.

Livingston's Yellow Beauty is a remarkable keeper. It remains in good marketable condition quite often up to the first of June.

Livingston's Yellow Beauty produce the finest, smoothest, hardest, best-keeping sets of any Onion grown. Market gardeners everywhere will be quick to recognize the merits of this excellent new Onion and we anticipate a very large demand for it once its merits become known. We have made the price very low for a new variety and trust that every Onion grower will try at least a small amount of this splendid variety, knowing that if once grown it will be purchased regularly as one of the really good things in the vegetable line. Pkt., 10c.; ½ oz., 15c.; oz., 25c.; ¼ lb., 75c.; lb., $2.50.

Livingston's Yellow Beauty

Mammoth Silver King Onion

**One of the Finest for Bunching, to
Follow Sets.**

A very quick growing variety which will produce fine bunching green onions, immediately following those produced from onion sets, by sowing the seed the same time the onion sets are planted. They are pure waxy white and of mild flavor. They will sell well when fully matured, but they do not keep well when grown. Try this delicious onion for using green or for stewing. You will like them. Pkt., 5c.; ½ oz., 10c.; oz., 15c.; ¼ lb., 50c.; lb., $1.75.

We are Growers of Onion Seed in Some of the Leading Sorts

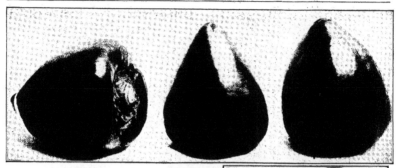

Sweet Salad Pepper

This new Pepper is an improvement on the Spanish or Pimento type. This one is large, very smooth, uniform in shape and size. The fruits are a beautiful dark green ripening to a rich scarlet. Flesh sweet, very solid, thick and of fine texture. This is a great Pepper for canning, because of its lack of pungency, and its firm, thick flesh which permits of its being scalded and peeled. Delicious with salad or stuffed, or can be eaten from the hand.

We have tested out several varieties of this type of Pepper and find this one best of all, and predict that it will become very popular. Pkt., 10c.; ½ oz., 30c.; oz., 50c.; ¼ lb., $1.75; lb., $6.00.

Livingston's Prolific Yellow Pepper
A New Variety Distinct from all others
Very Early, Very Productive, Very Mild

Introduced by Us in 1914. **(See Illustration Along Side)**

Immensely productive, of bright yellow fruits of the most convenient size for stuffing. Comes into bearing much sooner than the mammoth sorts, and is the surest crop of all. It may be used for stuffing while yet green. We secured a small amount of the seed of this variety some years ago from one of our gardener customers and after carefully selecting it so as to produce fruits true to type, we offered it for the first time in 1914.

On account of the mildness and thick walls of Livingston's Prolific Yellow Pepper, it is one of the finest for use in salads or pickles. Pkt., 10c.; ½ oz., 25c.; oz., 45c.; ¼ lb., $1.35; lb., $4.50.

Tomato Shaped Pepper (Pimento)
Very Thick Meated and Mild
(See Illustration Below)

The evry popular variety used extensively by the Spanish people in their Pimento salads. It is a thick meated variety of mild flavor, being brilliant red flesh and is very productive. Pkt., 10c.; ½ oz., 20c.; oz., 35c.

Livingston's Prolific Yellow Pepper

A. H. Powell, Licking Co., O., writes: "Your Yellow Prolific Pepper is the best yellow Pepper I have ever seen, and also the earliest. I picked Peppers on the fourth day of July and continued picking until the frost came. They are also the most prolific Peppers I have ever seen."

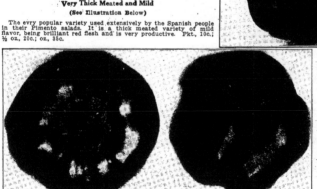

Quite Content Pea

Largest Podded of Any. Season Same as Telephone

This variety has created a sensation by its vigor and size, being by all odds the largest Pea in existence. In spite of its size it possesses all the merits of such varieties as Alderman or Telephone and its season is about the same—perhaps a little later. Vines average four to five feet high and the foliage is most luxuriant. The pods, which are usually produced in pairs, are simply immense, being from five and a half to six inches in length and each pod contains from nine to eleven large Peas of fine quality. It is a good cropper. Pkt., 15c.; ½ lb., 20c.; lb., 35c.; 2 lbs., 60c.; ½ pk. (7 lbs.), $1.25; pk., $2.25.

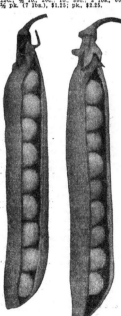

Buttercup

Buttercup Pea

A Grand New Medium Early Pea
An Improved Carters Daisy

In this grand variety we have a large podded Wrinkled Pea comparing in size and quality with Telephone, Boston Unrivaled and Alderman, but the vines, while very thrifty and vigorous, only grow from 16 to 20 inches high and bear great crops of big pods filled with deliciously flavored Peas. In season, Buttercup comes between Premium Gem and Telephone, hence valuable as a market variety. Buttercup is a few days earlier than Carter's Daisy, and is fast supplanting this old standard variety. A much better cropper and the pods fill quicker. Pkt., 15c.; ½ lb., 20c.; lb., 35c.; 2 lbs., 60c.; ½ pk. (7 lbs.), $1.25; pk., $3.15; bu., $8.00.

For general list of Garden Peas, see pages 50, 51, 52.

Pioneer

Pioneer Pea

Dwarf, Dark Green Pods and Peas

A new large podded early Wrinkled Pea of great promise. The vines are extremely vigorous, growing fifteen to eighteen inches high, dark green and produce a wonderful crop of dark green pods which are filled with big Peas of delicious flavor. It is one of the earliest Wrinkled Peas, coming about the same season as Gradus, but a heavier cropper. Try this one in place of Laxtonian, which we cannot supply, in quantity, this season. Pkt., 15c.; ½ lb., 20c.; lb., 35c.; 2 lbs., 60c.; ½ pk. (7 lbs.), $1.25; pk., $2.25; bu., $8.50.

Peter Pan Pea

A very promising new early sort with big pods and peas. See outside cover for illustration in color.

A fine new early sort having large pods filled with peas of highest quality. It has vigorous growing large dark foliage standing about 15 to 18 inches in height. The Peter Pan Pea is the "last word" in this class of large podded dwarf growing dark green foliage, pods and peas. Price per packet, 15c.; 2 for 25c.

Livingston's First in Market Pea

This splendid extra early variety can be sown even while the ground is yet quite cold. The quality is not quite as sweet as the big wrinkled green sorts, but coming so early and the pods always well filled they are highly appreciated. Order a few of Livingston's First in Market for sowing at the same time you set out your Onion Sets or make your very first early garden beds, and you will want some every season. Pkt., 10c.; ½ lb., 15c.; lb., 25c.; 2 lbs., 50c.; ½ pk. (7½ lbs.), 75c.; pk., $1.40; bu., $5.25.

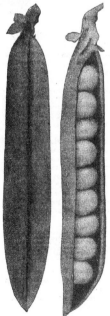

Peter Pan

Four New Spencer Sweet Peas

Margaret Atlee

2625—The largest and finest Sweet Pea yet introduced. First Prize American Sweet Pea Society at Philadelphia and Silver Medal, National Sweet Pea Society of Great Britain.

Margaret Atlee is a rosy salmon-pink on a creamy-buff ground; a rich, soft color, and extremely attractive, both as individual flowers and in the bunch. The standard is large and wavy and inclined to double, under favorable conditions. The wings are e q u a l l y large, wavy and well set. It runs almost uniformly four blossoms to the stem; well poised and graceful. In all respects it is the grandest Sweet Pea to date, either from foreign introductions or American varieties. Pkt., 20c.

Illuminator

2627—In color it is perfectly distinct from all other varieties and has been pronounced the most glorious Sweet Pea ever seen. It might be described as a rich glowing cerise-salmon, with an indication of bright orange suffusion which marvelously scintillates and glistens under bright sunlight; under artificial light the flowers appear to be a glowing orange-scarlet. Uniformly of large size and great substance. The flowers are most perfectly formed, and well placed on long stout stems, frequently in "fours." Of vigorous g r o w t h, the vines carry a rich profusion of blooms. Pkt., 15c.

New Spencer Sweet Pea Margaret Atlee

Our Great Collection of 7 Superb Spencer Sweet Peas for 25c., postpaid.

A complete general list of Spencer varieties and Our Spencer Mixture are fully described on pages 112 and 113.

Miss J. C. Burgen, Erie Co., N. Y., writes: "Regarding a small sample of Sweet Peas which you sent me this Spring, I want to say they are the handsomest Sweet Peas I ever saw. The red, white and pink ones blossomed nearly all double with three flowers on nearly every stem. No one has anything like them that I have seen."

King White

2626—Undoubtedly the best white now in cultivation. Too much cannot be said in praise of this unique new white Spencer. It has all the first-class qualities which go to form Sweet Pea perfection. It is remarkable for the "glistening immaculate purity of the whiteness" and the perfect finish of the flower. While of truly gigantic proportions, the flowers are most exquisitely finished in every detail. King White has such marvelous substance —which might almost be termed "leathery"—that it is entirely free from the objectionable reflexing habit so generally found in the standard of other whites. The grand flowers are borne almost invariably in "fours" upon stout stems of great length. The bold, widely expanded standard is waved exquisitely, while the wings, also well w a v e d, a r e beautifully placed. The plants are exceptionally vigorous in growth with distinctive rich green foliage, and wonderfully profuse in bloom for a long season. Pkt., 15c.

Wedgwood

2628—This beautiful novelty is likely to become quite as popular in the Sweet Pea world as the famous china is among connoisseurs. Wedgwood is a unique shade of lovely light blue and completely eclipses such varieties as Flora Norton Spencer, Princess Mary, Southcote Blue and Zephyr. The flowers, of good size and substance, are well waved in both standard and wings; they are borne almost uniformly in four-flowered sprays upon long stout stems. Wedgwood is a color long sought for in Sweet Peas and will be eagerly welcomed by all lovers of this beautiful annual. Pkt., 15c.

Miss F. H o l z h a u e r, Wood Co., Ohio, writes: "I had a most beautiful flower bed last year, the seeds coming from Livingston's. I was very much pleased."

Shell-pink Rochester Aster

Salvia New Ostrich Plume

2385—This new variety is the most beautiful of Salvias of recent introduction. The habit of this Salvia resembles that of the Splendens type, but produces a Plume quite similar in form to Ostrich Plume Celosia. One Plume alone is a bouquet itself, quite a per cent of the flowers are double and this is the only Salvia up to the present time that is double. The color is somewhat different from all other Salvias, being of a rich, glossy, dark scarlet. By very careful selection and severe roguing for the past three seasons, this variety now runs very true to type. Pkt., 20c.

New White Oriental Poppy

(See Illustration Alongside)

2334—It is the most distinct "Break" that has yet been made in Oriental Poppies, it being a pure satiny white with a bold crimson blotch at the base of each petal, unquestionably the most important addition to the list of hardy perennial seeds for the season of 1916. Like most hybrids the seedlings are liable to vary somewhat in color, but a good percentage can confidently be expected to come true. Pkt., 25c.

Miss May Miller, Fairfield Co., Ohio, writes: "The flowers from your mixed bedding Petunias and mixed Phlox seed last year were the most beautiful I ever saw."

Mrs. E. C. Hartwell, Worcester Co., Mass., writes: "Your Foxgloves and Pinks got first prize at our flower contest, blossoms from seed sown last Spring, so there are several people very anxious for your catalogue, to buy perennial seeds for next Summer's show."

New Aster

Vick's Shell Pink Rochester

(See Illustration Alongside)

1493—In this Aster we have another color added to the already popular Rochester type. The color, as the name indicates, is of a soft shell-pink, one of the most popular colors in Asters. The flowers are large and are supported on long, stiff stems. The long narrow petals are twisted and curled, making a very rich effect. The introducers of this grand new variety believe that as soon as it has been given a trial, it will take its place as one of the leading Pink Asters. Pkt., 25c.

New Cardinal Climber

1598—A new annual climber of the Ipomea or Morning Glory family. It is a wonderfully vigorous grower, climbing 20 feet in a season from seed sown in the Spring. The foliage is beautifully cut and is very graceful. The flowers are very brilliant, being a fiery scarlet, the individual blooms being about 1½ inches across and produced in clusters of 5 to 7. It flowers very profusely the entire Summer, and bids fair to take a place as one of our best annual climbers, having attracted much attention wherever grown. It should be planted in a warm sunny location in good soil and will then give a good account of itself. Pkt., 15c.

Mrs. W. L. Lemon, Yakima Co., Calif., writes: "I received the Blue Ribbon on Asters last year. Had saved the seed for several years, having started with your collection. Please send me your very best."

New White Oriental Poppy

Livingston's Choice Cactus Dahlias

This splendid type is one which instantly arrests the attention of the observer because of the unique forms and charming shades which obtain in flowers of its class. These characteristics are in themselves sufficient to explain its rapid strides in popularity with each passing year.

Countess of Lonsdale

This is probably the freest bloomer of all the Cactus varieties. Its color is an exquisite shade of rich red, suffused with salmon and with just a suspicion of apricot at the base of the petals, a color very difficult to describe. Very symmetrical in form. 20c. each; $2.00 per dozen.

Kriemhilde

A beautiful shell pink gradually shading to a creamy white in the center. It has proved extremely popular as a cutting variety, since it is a very pleasing form on long straight stems and keeps a long time after being cut. 20c. each; $2.00 per dozen.

Pius X

A large snow white, very double with a slight sulphur tint. This is a superb variety; a strong grower and a free bloomer; very superior in both form and habit. 20c. each; $2.00 per dozen.

J. B. Briant

Large rich golden yellow of immense size—a splendid flower for exhibition purposes. The petals are long, narrow and beautifully incurved with a scarcely perceptible tint of pink on the tips. 20c. each; $2.00 per dozen.

T. G. Baker

One of the grandest Cactus dahlias of the yellow shades ever introduced. It is a beautiful clear yellow without a suspicion of another intruding shade. An exceptionally large variety, and the flower is very symmetrical and finely formed. 20c. each; $2.00 per dozen.

Standard Bearer

An intense, rich and fiery scarlet of perfect form, and while not one of the latest introductions, is still a prime favorite because of its habit of profuse bloom. It is one of the very best. 20c. each; $2.00 per dozen.

Type of Cactus Dahlia

Special Cactus Dahlia Offer

OF VARIETIES LISTED ON THIS PAGE

Countess of Lonsdale—A rich red, suffused with salmon.

Kriemhilde—A beautiful deep rose.

Pius X—An unusually fine white.

J. B. Briant—Golden yellow, tipped pink.

T. G. Baker—A beautiful clear yellow.

Standard Bearer—Bright pure scarlet, a splendid variety.

Any one of the above, 20 cents each.

To encourage liberal plantings of this beautiful type of Dahlia we offer one each of the six sorts described on this page for $1.00, postpaid.

New Canna Firebird

The best red-flowered, green-leaved Canna

Claimed by many to be the very best red-flowered, green-leaved Canna today. The flowers are borne in immense trusses, on tall stalks well above the leaves. They are of splendid form, round and shapely. The petals measure 2½ inches and over across, and the color is a clear glistening scarlet without any streaks, spots or blotches. We have tested many varieties during the past 30 years and have never seen one that surpassed it. Each, 50c.; doz., $5.00.

Gustave Gompper Canna

Finest Golden Yellow

A splendid variety having golden yellow flowers of large size and great substance. The lower petals are splashed with carmine. Grows to a height of 3½ to 4 feet; with stiff, erect stems and immense flower spikes. Each, 20c.; doz., $2.00.

For complete list of Cannas see pages 118 and 119.

New Canna Firebird

Mrs. Frank Pendleton

BULBS BY PARCEL POST

Gladioli Bulbs weigh about 7 lbs. per 100, and if wanted by mail, include enough to cover postage in your remittance. See page 3.

Gladioli

These are the most attractive and easiest grown of all Summer flowering bulbs. Sorts offered below are most used on the cut-flower market. You can plant Gladioli any place—in beds with other plants, among trees and shrubs, in fact they grow in all kinds of soil and produce long spikes of beautiful flowers. Be sure and include the following varieties in your orders:

Mrs. Frank Pendleton

Salmon Pink with Deep Red Throat

Flowers are very large and well expanded; of a lovely flushed salmon-pink with brilliant carmine or deep red blotches in throat, presenting a vivid contrast of orchid-like attractiveness. It is of lemoine in form and effect, the stems take up the water freely and opens up perfectly nearly every flower after being cut and placed in water. Price, each, 20c.; doz., $2.10, postpaid; $15.00 per 100.

Peace

White with Pale Violet Shading

A magnificent variety which produces large flowers. Color white, with light violet shadings on lower petals. A splendid late blooming sort. Each, 20c.; doz., $1.85; 25 for $4.00; 100 for $13.00.

Panama

Fine Deep Pink Variety

A new seedling of America which resembles the parent variety in every way except that it is a much deeper pink. A grand variety which evokes words of praise wherever exhibited. Spike very long with flowers and well arranged. Price, each, 10c.; doz., $1.10, postpaid; $7.50 per 100.

Niagara

Cream Blending with Canary Yellow

Resembles "America," flowers somewhat larger, measuring 4½ inches across. In color a delightful cream shade with the two lower inside petals blending to canary yellow. The throat is splashed with carmine, and the lower ends of the outside petals are also blushed with carmine. The stamens are purple and the stigmas pale carmine, this little addition in the coloring relieving the creamy effect of the petals. Flower spike very erect and stout with broad, dark green foliage. Price, each, 10c.; doz., $1.00, postpaid; $7.00 per 100.

One each four finest Gladiolus, 50c., postpaid.

For complete list of Gladiolus see page 123.

E VERY sort included represents the best of its class and many high-priced novelties of real merit make this collection doubly worth while. The demand for this collection started years ago when we would get orders from people for a dollar's worth of vegetable seeds—the best we could do. Many are not familiar with the merits of the different sorts offered in this Catalog and for those we get up this collection the best we know how.

From year to year we change it. Obsolete sorts are dropped, new varieties of better character added, and we firmly believe that a better collection than ours cannot be bought at as low a price anywhere in this country.

At the same time its price is the only cheap thing about it. Full-sized packets, such as we supply to the most critical trade on regular orders, go into the collection. Six of the sorts named below retail for 10 cents each. The remaining 26 packets you buy for 40 cents in this collection. For good measure we throw in an ounce of Nasturtiums or

an ounce of Livingston's Fine Mixed Sweet Peas, and the whole comes to you by mail delivered free at your door.

The reason why we sell this collection at such a low price is twofold: We can put up the boxes before the Spring rush starts, get thousands of them ready so that, when the order comes, all that needs to be done is to wrap the box, affix postage stamps and out it goes—always the same day we get the order. This popular priced collection also gives new customers an opportunity to try a large assortment of "true blue" seeds at a moderate cost. Our margin of profit on this collection is smaller than on anything else we sell; yet we consider each collection sold a good investment which, in time, will bring us increased business.

Please do not ask us for any discount in connection with an order for our Dollar Collection and any special offers in this Catalog do not apply to or cannot be taken advantage of in connection with it. No changes can be allowed.

Here is what One Dollar will buy:

32---Full-Sized Packets as Follows for Only One Dollar---32

1 Beans—Dwarf, Valentine.
2 Beans—Dwarf, Kidney Wax.
3 Beet—Detroit Dark Red. Very early and tender.
4 Beet—Edmand's Blood Turnip. Very tender, long keeper.
5 Cabbage—All Head Early. Flat heading sort.
6 Cabbage—Danish Ball-head. Solid, tender.
7 Celery—Giant Pascal. Early; good flavor.
8 Cucumber—Klondyke. Dark green, shapely pickle.
9 Cucumber—Livingston's White-Spine. Best slicer.
10 Sweet Corn—Columbus Market. Large early.
11 Sweet Corn—Livingston's Evergreen. Early and sweet.
12 Lettuce—Big Boston. Tender. Large headed sort.
13 Lettuce—Black Seeded Simpson. Finest Early Curled.
14 Lettuce—Prize Head. Fine heading sort.
15 Water Melon—Sweet-Heart. Quality very delicious.
16 Musk Melon—Rocky Ford. Green flesh. Early sweet.

17 Musk Melon—Tip Top. Salmon flesh; delicious.
18 Onion—Yellow Globe. Best for general crop.
19 Onion—Red Globe. Fine; good keeper.
20 Pepper—Ruby King. Large, sweet and prolific.
21 Parsnip—Hollow Crown. Large and extra sweet.
22 Parsley—Moss Curled. Very fine green variety.
23 Peas—Little Marvel. Early, sweet, prolific.
24 Peas—Thomas Laxton. Large pods, full of sweet peas.
25 Radish—Cincinnati Market. Great favorite for early.
26 Radish—Rosy Gem. Fine, bright red; early.
27 Radish—Livingston's Pearl. Fine, long, white variety.
28 Squash—Giant Golden Summer Crookneck.
29 Squash—Hubbard. Fine for Winter use.
30 Tomato—Livingston's Favorite. Fine red variety.
31 Tomato—Livingston's Beauty. No better purple sort.
32 Turnip—Purple-Top White Globe. One of the best.

Free With each order for OUR GREAT DOLLAR VEGETABLE COLLECTION the buyer may select one ounce of either Livingston's Fine Mixed Sweet Peas, or one ounce of Livingston's Top Notch Mixture of Tall Nasturtiums. With each collection we enclose a helpful leaflet of cultural directions—The Vegetable Garden.

A Partial View of Our Trial Grounds

Livingston's TRUE BLUE Vegetable Seeds

In this department may be found all that is best in Vegetables—except our novelties and specialties for 1916—carefully described from actual observation. We have rigidly excluded all worthless varieties, omitted an endless number which are out of date, and avoided the offering of same varieties under different names. General instructions as to planting and growth, while reliable, will not apply equally to all sections, as some allowance must be made for difference in latitude. Cultural directions will be found on most of our packets. We also send free to customers, on application, a very helpful leaflet—**THE VEGETABLE GARDEN**—which contains valuable information.

Spargel Asparagus Esparragos

It can be grown in any good garden soil, but does best in sunny, moist soil. To grow plants from seed, sow in drills about one inch deep in rows one foot apart. Keep the soil mellow and free from weeds; during the Summer thin out, and the following Spring plants may be set in the permanent bed. Set the plants one foot apart each way, ten inches below the surface, spreading the roots well apart. Cover with about three inches of soil and as plant grows fill in the trench. Annually, after cutting, the bed should be given a liberal top dressing of manure, ashes and salt, which should be thoroughly cultivated into the soil. As soon as the tops turn yellow in the Fall they should be cut and removed from the beds, and just before Winter cover the beds with four inches of coarse strawy manure or leaves, which should be removed in the Spring. A bed 6x10 feet is ample for an ordinary family, and when well established is good for 20 years. One ounce of seed will sow 60 feet of drill. About 400 plants to the ounce.

Leaflet with Cultural directions free to customers.

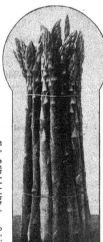

"True Blue" Seeds are "quality seeds." Our trial grounds prove to us every year that our strains are as good as the best and better than many good strains. Still, every year we learn and try to produce better seeds than those offered the year before.

Columbian Mammoth White—A distinct variety producing shoots which are white and remain so as long as fit for use. Vigorous and robust in habit; grows large shoots. Needs no earthing up. Pkt., 5c.; oz., 10c.; ¼ lb., 25c.; lb., 65c.

Early Argenteuil—Earlier, larger and better than the good old Colossal. Flavor superb. Pkt., 5c.; oz., 10c.; ¼ lb., 25c.; lb., 75c.

Donald's Elmira—Good reliable, mammoth variety of very fine quality. Pkt., 5c.; oz., 10c.; ¼ lb., 25c.; lb., 65c.

Palmetto—Large, dark green variety of vigorous growth, having pointed tips. Early. Pkt., 5c.; oz., 10c.; ¼ lb., 20c.; lb., 60c.

Conover's Colossal—Large and rapid grower of excellent quality. Pkt., 5c.; oz., 10c.; ¼ lb., 20c.; lb., 60c.

Carolina Queen—This comes from the Carolinas, where Asparagus has been grown as a special market crop for a long period of time. Earliness, great productive power, immense stalks when sprouting, rust resistance, superb quality, handsome appearance, are some of its qualities. The stalks are very pretty, being creamy white with pink heads. The flavor is delightful. Pkt., 5c.; oz., 16c.; ¼ lb., 35c.; lb., $1.25.

ASPARAGUS CULTURE

A book giving all possible details as to Growing, Soil, Marketing, Canning, etc., for home use or market. 150 pages, 5x7. Cloth, 50c., postpaid.

For Asparagus Roots, see page 70.

Livingston's Extra Selected Beans

Our strains of Beans are exceptionally fine. They are produced by the best growers in this country, who make a specialty of Beans and Peas. The fields are carefully rogued each year, the seed is hand picked, so that our stock will be found first-class.

Packets of Beans, put up to sell at 5c., postpaid, contain too small a quantity. We, therefore, put up **Liberal Sized Packets at TEN CENTS. Bean Prices** include postage, up to two pound quantities. If the larger quantities are wanted sent by mail it will be necessary to remit additional amount at the Parcels Post rates. Refer to page 3 for rates.

Two pounds (one quart) will plant 100 feet of drill; 1 to 2 bushels to the acre.

Habas nanas Dwarf or Bush Beans Buschbohnen

All varieties of Bush Wax and Green Pod are very short crop this season. Please name your second choice.

Wax Podded Varieties

Livingston's Yellow Pencil Pod

Although hardy, it is stringless, tender and of fine quality. Pods smooth, perfectly round and as straight as a lead pencil. In points of vigor, hardiness and prolificacy it is unsurpassed. Pkt., 10c.; ½ lb., 15c.; lb., 30c.; 2 lbs., 50c. By express, not paid, ½ pk, (7½ lbs.), $1.15; pk., $2.25; bu., $8.50.

Prolific German Black Wax

Pencil Pod Strain—Pods are long, fleshy, round, waxy yellow, solid and tender; very early. Pkt., 10c.; ½ lb., 20c.; lb., 35c.; 2 lbs., 60c. By express, not paid, ½ pk. (7½ lbs.), $1.50; pk., $2.75.

Brittle Wax

An extra-early hardy variety; long, round, meaty pods of rich golden yellow; very productive. Pkt., 10c.; ½ lb., 20c.; lb., 35c.; 2 lbs., 60c.

Davis White Wax

Very productive, white-seeded, rustless, string or snap variety. The dry white Beans are good for cooking purposes. Pkt., 10c.; ½ lb., 20c.; lb., 35c.; 2 lbs., 60c.

Wardwell's Kidney Wax

Immensely productive. One of the handsomest Wax Podded Beans. Early; vine medium, erect, hardy, productive. Pods long, broad, flat, brittle and of a delicate waxy yellow. Very attractive market sort. Pkt., 10c.; ½ lb., 15c.; lb., 30c.; 2 lbs., 50c. By express, not paid, ½ pk. (7½ lbs.), $1.30; pk., $2.50; bu., $9.50.

New Kidney Wax

Pods are flat, but thick and fleshy. They average 6 to 7 inches in length, are borne in large clusters and make the finest show on the market bench on account of their rich lemon-yellow color and straight, handsome shape. In quality unsurpassed. Is brittle and stringless at all stages of development. Pkt., 10c.; ½ lb., 15c.; lb., 30c.; 2 lbs., 50c. By express, not paid, ½ pk. (7½ lbs.), $1.30; pk., $2.50; bu., $9.50.

Round Pod Kidney Wax

Pods are round. Plants grow strong and sturdy, with long, round, handsome stringless pods of large size, very solid and full of meat; crisp, brittle. Wonderfully early and productive and has become very popular. Pkt., 10c.; ½ lb., 15c.; lb., 30c.; 2 lbs., 50c. By express, not paid, ½ pk. (7½ lbs.), $1.30; pk., $2.50.

Keeney's Rustless Golden Wax

A strong grower; free from rust. Pods meaty and well filled, semi-round, rich yellow, fine quality; **entirely stringless.** Pkt., 10c.; ½ lb., 15c.; lb., 30c.; 2 lbs., 50c. By express, not paid, ½ pk. (7½ lbs.), $1.30; pk., $2.50; bu., $9.00.

Improved Golden Wax

Grennell's. One of the best strains of Golden Wax. Hardy, prolific, of best quality; pods long, straight, thick, and vines very erect. Pkt., 10c.; ½ lb., 15c.; lb., 30c.; 2 lbs., 50c. By express, not paid, ½ pk. (7½ lbs.), $1.15; pk., $2.25.

Green Podded Bush Beans

Hopkins Earliest Red Valentine

One of the earliest and most prolific round green podded Beans. Comes into bearing earlier than the old stock of Valentines, is a wonderful producer and a perfect shipper. It has remained in a perfect condition for nearly two weeks after picking. Pkt., 10c.; ½ lb., 15c.; lb., 25c.; 2 lbs., 40c. By express, not paid, ½ pk. (7½ lbs.), $1.00; pk., $1.75; bu., $6.50.

Extra-Early Round Pod Red Valentine

Usually ready to pick in 35 days after planting. Pods round, thick, fleshy, of fine quality; one of the most profitable sorts for market. Pkt., 10c.; ½ lb., 15c.; lb., 25c.; 2 lbs., 40c. By express, not paid, ½ pk. (7½ lbs.), $1.00; pk., $1.75; bu., $6.50.

G. W. Tyler, Manatee Co., Fla., writes, June 8, 1914: "I am glad to say that I always get good results from your seeds. Thanking you for your promptness, I am, yours truly."

Full Measure

A very desirable round-podded variety with pods six to seven inches long, which are solid, meaty, brittle and stringless. It is a little later than Stringless Green Pod and is a splendid Bean for home or market use. Pkt., 10c.; ½ lb., 15c.; lb., 25c., 45c. By express, not paid, ½ pk. (7½ lbs.), $1.00; pk., $1.75.

Livingston's Round Six Weeks

Extra-early; strong grower and abundant cropper. Pods green, very fleshy, free from strings when young. Pkt., 10c.; ½ lb., 15c.; lb., 25c.; 2 lbs., 40c. By express, not paid, ½ pk. (7½ lbs.), $1.00; pk., $1.75; bu., $6.50.

M. Davis Harrod, Green Co., Ohio, writes, Oct. 24, 1914: "I am still picking Snap Beans; I got a peck of your Green Pod Stringless Beans and planted them July 23d, and started picking Beans, September 5th, and up to the present writing have picked 950 pounds of Snap Beans."

For Bean Nitragin, "the Best Inoculator," see Page 75.

Green Podded Beans (Continued)

Prices of beans include postage up to and including 2 pounds.

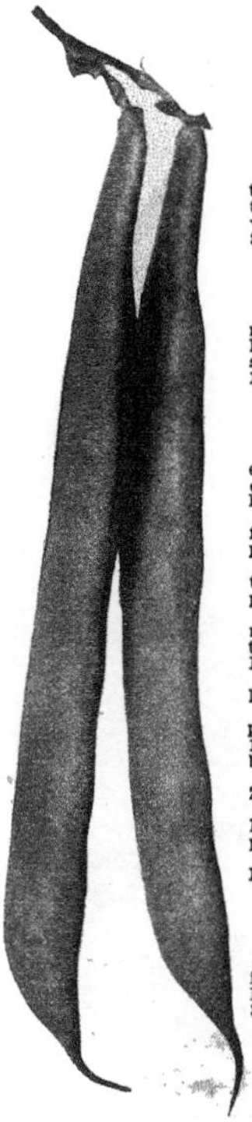

Bountiful

Bountiful

(See illustration)—A green pod Bush Bean, which comes into bearing very early and continues throughout the season. Pods beautiful rich green, very thick, broad, long and uniform; meaty, tender, fine quality; absolutely stringless. Good shell Bean for Winter use. A splendid market variety. Pkt., 10c.; ½ lb., 15c.; lb., 30c.; 2 lbs., 50c. By express, not paid, ½ pk. (7½ lbs.), $1.30; pk., $2.50; bu., $9.00.

Stringless Green Podded

One of the finest extra-early Beans in cultivation and one that has held its place in spite of many new introductions for which superior qualities were claimed. It produces in profusion long, straight, round, deeply saddlebacked pods early in the season. The pods are absolutely stringless at all stages of growth, brittle, tender and of real good flavor. Pkt., 10c.; ½ lb., 15c.; lb., 30c.; 2 lbs., 55c. By express, not paid, ½ pk. (7½ lbs.), $1.50; pk., $2.75.

Giant Stringless Green Pod

Has a much larger pod than Stringless Green Pod, or about one-third larger than the Valentine—average 5 inches long. Full and fleshy, extremely crisp and absolutely stringless; very early and prolific. Pkt., 10c.; ½ lb., 15c.; lb., 30c.; 2 lbs., 55c. By express, not paid, ½ pk. (7½ lbs.), $1.50; pk., $2.75.

Refugee or **1000-to-1**—Fine quality, medium late. Prolific; nearly round. Our strain is extra fine. Pkt., 10c.; ½ lb., 15c.; lb., 30c.; 2 lbs., 50c. By express, not paid, ½ pk. (7½ lbs.), $1.10; pk., $2.00; bu., $7.00.

Extra Early Refugee—Hardy; an abundant bearer. Ten days earlier than Refugee or 1000-to-1. Pkt., 10c.; ½ lb., 15c.; lb., 30c.; 2 lbs., 55c. By express, not paid, ½ pk. (7½ lbs.), $1.15; pk., $2.25.

Hodson "Green Podded"—Entirely unaffected by rust or blight; an exceptionally strong and robust grower; enormous yielder, often producing 50 to 60 pods to the plant. A little later than Refugee or 1000-to-1. Excellent shipping sort. Pkt., 10c.; ½ lb., 15c.; lb., 25c.; 2 lbs., 45c. By express, not paid, ½ pk. (7½ lbs.), $1.00; pk., $1.75.

Dwarf Horticulture—Speckled Cranberry. Splendid for Shell Beans. Pkt., 10c.; ½ lb., 15c.; lb., 30c.; 2 lbs., 50c. By express, not paid, ½ pk. (7½ lbs.), $1.30; pk., $2.50.

Black Valentine—Very hardy; resists unfavorable weather and disease. Long, straight, green pods of fair quality; enormously productive. Ready for market in 50 days from sowing. Pkt., 10c.; ½ lb., 15c.; lb., 30c.; 2 lbs., 50c. By express, not paid, ½ pk. (7½ lbs.), $1.30; pk., $2.50; bu., $9.00.

Improved Navy, or **Boston Pea Bean**—Very productive variety. Pkt., 10c.; ½ lb., 15c.; lb., 25c.; 2 lbs., 45c. By express, not paid, ½ pk. (7½ lbs.), 85c.; pk., $1.50; bu., $5.00.

White Marrow—Good green or dry. Standard soup Bean. Pkt., 10c.; ½ lb., 15c.; lb., 25c.; 2 lbs., 45c. By express, not paid, ½ pk. (7½ lbs.), 85c.; pk., $1.50; bu., $5.00.

White Kidney, or **Royal Dwarf**—Pkt., 10c.; ½ lb., 15c.; lb., 25c.; 2 lbs., 45c. By express, not paid, ½ pk. (7½ lbs.), 85c.; pk., $1.50; bu., $5.00.

Bush Lima Beans

These varieties are of true Bush or Dwarf form, growing but 18 to 20 inches high, without supports. About two weeks earlier than the Pole Lima Beans. Sure croppers. Abundant bearers until frost. Plant in rows 2 to 3 feet apart and a foot apart in the rows.

Burpee's Improved

This has uniformly larger pods than Burpee's Bush Lima, while the pods contain more Beans which are thicker and remain green even in the dry stage. The plants are very prolific, bearing pods in clusters of from 5 to 7. The individual pods average 5 to 6 inches long and contain from 5 to 7 Beans. The Beans are exceedingly thin-skinned and of delightful flavor. They almost "melt in your mouth," to use a popular expression. Pkt., 10c.; ½ lb., 15c.; lb., 30c.; 2 lbs., 55c. By express, not paid, ½ pk. (7 lbs.), $1.25; pk., $2.25; bu., $8.50.

Fordhook

The Fordhook is entirely distinct in habit of growth. The stiffly erect bushes branch freely and bear tremendous crops. It is ready for use as early as the popular Burpee's Bush Lima, but the Beans are much plumper and remain green much longer. The shelled Beans are very fat, are closely packed in the pods, which shell very easily. Pods are borne in clusters of from 4 to 6, average 4 to 5 inches long and contain usually 4 tender Beans of a delightful flavor. Pkt., 10c.; ½ lb., 15c.; lb., 30c.; 2 lbs., 55c. By express, not paid, ½ pk. (7 lbs.), $1.25; pk., $2.25; bu., $8.50.

New Wonder or Quarter Century

Pods about the same as Burpee's Bush Lima; Beans slightly smaller; a few days earlier and fully as productive. A sure cropper. Very true to bush form. An immense yielder. Pkt., 10c.; ½ lb., 15c.; lb., 25c.; 2 lbs., 45c. By express, not paid, ½ pk. (7 lbs.), $1.00; pk., $1.85; bu., $7.00.

Burpee's Bush Lima—Bushes are of stout growth, branching so vigorously that each plant makes a large bush. Immense yielder of well-filled pods of large Beans of luscious flavor. Pkt., 10c.; ½ lb., 15c.; lb., 25c.; 2 lbs., 45c. By express, not paid, ½ pk. (7 lbs.), $1.00; pk., $1.85; bu., $7.00.

Henderson's Bush Lima—Compact bush form, and produces large crops. Delicious flavor. Beans are smaller than above sorts. Pkt., 10c.; ½ lb., 15c.; lb., 25c.; 2 lbs., 45c. By express, not paid, ½ pk. (7 lbs.), 90c.; pk., $1.75; bu., $6.00.

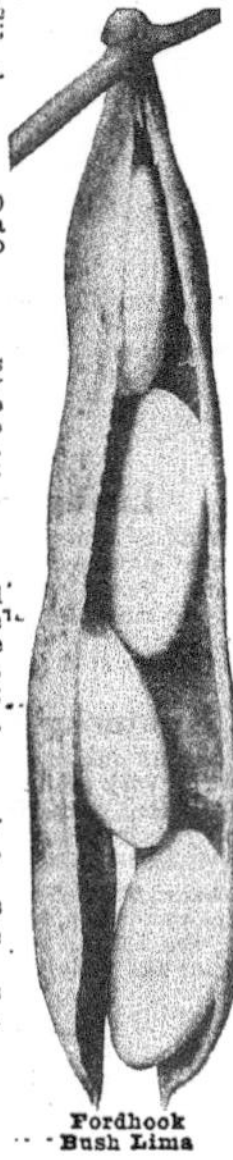

Fordhook Bush Lima

"Bean Nitragin" increases the yield. For full directions see page 75 of this catalogue.

Pole Lima Beans

Lima Beans will not grow until the weather and ground are warm. If planted before, they are almost sure to rot in the ground. See cultural directions for Pole Beans. **Prices on beans include postage up to and including two pounds.**

Early Leviathan

One week earlier than many other Pole Limas. Of superior quality. Wonderfully productive. The ideal Pole Lima. Being earlier than most other varieties, it will prove a boon to thousands of growers. Earliness is often obtained at the sacrifice of other valuable features, but in this variety we claim superiority, not only in this respect, but in size of Bean and pod and enormous productiveness. Pkt., 10c.; ½ lb., 15c.; lb., 25c.; 2 lbs., 45c. By express, not paid, ½ pk. (7 lbs.), $1.00; pk., $1.85; bu., $7.00.

Siebert's Early

One of the very best for market gardeners. The result of a number of years' selecting to largest green Beans and easily opening pods. Very productive, hardy and vigorous. Produces pods early, and continues to the last of the season. The great Beans are of immense size, but so tender and succulent that they shrink in drying to about the size of the original White Lima. Pkt., 10c.; ½ lb., 15c.; lb., 25c.; 2 lbs., 45c. By express, not paid, ½ pk. (7 lbs.), 85c.; pk., $1.60; bu., $6.25.

Carpenteria Large Green-Seeded

An excellent variety with many unique characteristics. The original "sport" plant was discovered in a field of the "Burpee-Improved" Bush Lima, from which the **Carpenteria Green-Seeded Pole Lima** inherits many good points. Vines are of strong, vigorous growth, setting many pods which are closely filled with large, fat Beans, much thicker than those of the ordinary Pole Limas. Pods contain 3 to 4 Beans, which retain the green tint in the dry state—a sure indication of fine quality. Pkt., 10c.; ½ lb., 15c.; lb., 25c.; 2 lbs., 45c. By express, not paid, ½ pk. (7 lbs.), $1.00; pk., $1.75; bu., $6.50.

King of the Garden

Vigorous grower, pods containing five to six large Beans, which are of fine quality. The vines grow strong and yield heavily. A very fine variety. Pkt., 10c.; ½ lb., 15c.; lb., 25c.; 2 lbs., 45c. By express, not paid, ½ pk. (7 lbs.), $1.00; pk., $1.75; bu., $6.50.

Dreer's Improved

Beans thick, sweet and tender; of medium size. Especially good for the home garden. Very productive. Pkt., 10c.; ½ lb., 15c.; lb., 25c.; 2 lbs., 45c. By express, not paid, ½ pk. (7 lbs.), $1.00; pk., $1.75; bu., $6.50.

Sieva, or Small Lima

Early, and the small Beans are of luscious flavor. Fine sort for the kitchen garden. Pkt., 10c.; ½ lb., 15c.; lb., 25c.; 2 lbs., 45c. By express, not paid, ½ pk. (7 lbs.), 85c.; pk., $1.60; bu., $6.25

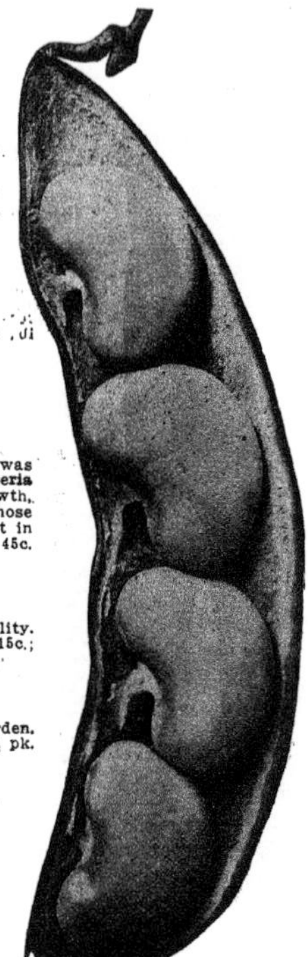

Carpenteria Large Green Seeded

Pole or Running Beans

The Pole or Running varieties are tender and should be sown two weeks later than Bush Beans. They succeed best in sandy loam, which should be liberally enriched with manure. **Two pounds will make 100 to 200 hills, according to size of the Beans.**

Kentucky Wonder Wax

See page 4.

Livingston's Royal Corn Bean

This is a fine green-podded snap Pole Bean; the pods are six to eight inches long. Stringless, very tender and delicious. Beans can be shelled green for Summer market, or left to ripen for dry Beans for Winter use. Pkt., 10c.; ½ lb., 15c.; lb., 30c.; 2 lbs., 60c. By express, not paid, ½ pk. (7½ lbs.), $1.35; pk., $2.50.

Kentucky Wonder or Old Homestead

An old favorite, with long, fleshy, deeply saddle-backed pods. Very prolific, producing an abundance of fine, stringless, crisp pods until late in the season. Of best quality. Pkt., 10c.; ½ lb., 15c.; lb., 30c.; 2 lbs., 50c. By express, not paid, ½ pk. (7½ lbs.), $1.10; pk., $2.00; bu., $7.25.

Lazy Wife—Pods 6 to 8 inches long, quite stringless; a good white Shell Bean for Winter. Pkt., 10c.; ½ lb., 15c.; lb., 30c.; 2 lbs., 50c. By express, not paid, ½ pk. (7½ lbs.), $1.10; pk., $2.00; bu., $7.50.

Powell's Prolific

A most desirable green-podded Snap Bean. Bears profusely, is quite early, and continues until frost. Very strong grower, one plant filling a pole with a mass of vines densely loaded with handsome pods. Pkt., 10c.; ½ lb., 15c.; lb., 30c.; 2 lbs., 50c. By express, not paid, ½ pk. (7½ lbs.), $1.10; pk., $2.00; bu., $7.50.

Early Golden Cluster Wax

Splendid Snap Bean. Vines strong and hardy; very early, and continues bearing until frost. Pods are golden yellow, stringless and tender. Pkt., 10c.; ½ lb., 15c.; lb., 30c.; 2 lbs., 50c. By express, not paid, ½ pk. (7½ lbs.), $1.25; pk., $2.25.

Red Speckled Cut-Short—"Corn Hill." Pkt., 10c.; ½ lb., 15c.; lb., 25c.; 2 lbs., 45c. By express, not paid, ½ pk. (7½ lbs.), $1.25; pk., $2.25.

Speckled Cranberry—Old "Bird Egg," Pkt., 10c.; ½ lb., 15c.; lb., 25c.; 2 lbs., 45c. By express, not paid, ½ pk. (7½ lbs.), $1.00; pk., $1.75; bu., $6.00.

Be sure and include a package of Bean "Nitragin" in your order. It increases the yield and adds to the quality of Beans and in fact all leguminous crops. For full directions see Page 75 of this Catalogue.

Garden Beets for Table Use

Rote Ruben   Remolachas

The soil best suited for the culture of the Beet is that which is rather light, provided it is thoroughly mixed with manure. If wanted very early, sow in hotbeds and transplant; but for main crop sow in the Spring, as soon as the ground becomes fit to work, in drills 18 inches apart, ¼ inch deep. For Winter use, the Turnip varieties may be sown as late as June and the seed covered two inches. When the plants are 3 or 4 inches in height, thin out so that they stand 3 or 4 inches apart. Keep free from weeds by frequent hoeing and hand-weeding if necessary. Before freezing weather sets in the roots may be stored in cellars or pits, same as potatoes; dry earth thrown over them before the straw is put on insures their keeping over Winter. Do not bruise them in handling. One ounce of seed will sow 50 feet of drill; 5 to 6 pounds to the acre.

CROSBY'S IMPROVED EGYPTIAN BEET

Crosby's Improved Egyptian Beet
A Money-Maker for Market Men

A very superior Beet, carefully selected for years by Mr. Crosby, a noted gardener for the Boston markets, whose aim was to secure a perfect outdoor forcing variety. The results obtained were handsome form, good size, few small tops, very small tap root, fine quality, and, above all, quick growth. The shape is very desirable, not quite so flat as the ordinary Egyptian, nor so round as the Eclipse. Takes on its turnip shape and looks well, even in the early stages of its growth, on which account it is preferred for forcing to the Globe and Half-Long varieties. May be sown outside as late as July. We have made a very fine selection of this stock for years, and we believe have it nearer the Original Crosby idea than any one in the trade. Write for prices on larger quantities.

Crosby's Improved Egyptian—Our Own Growing—Pkt., 5c.; oz., 15c.; ¼ lb., 45c.; lb., $1.50.

Edmand's Blood Turnip

Very uniform. Root is always smooth, round and handsome; top small; of good marketable size and among the best for table use. Color dark red; crisp, tender and sweet; good keeper. Pkt., 5c.; oz., 10c.; ¼ lb., 25c.; lb., 90c.

Crimson Globe

Root of medium size, very handsome, globe shape, and has a remarkably smooth surface. Both the skin and flesh are deep, rich red, fine grained, sweet and tender in all stages of growth. Small tap root; leaves are small, dark green. Pkt., 5c.; oz., 15c.; ¼ lb., 40c.; lb., $1.25.

Extra-Early Dark Red Egyptian—Very early, dark blood red, medium size, tender and sweet; the best for kitchen gardens. Pkt., 5c.; oz., 10c.; ¼ lb., 25c.; lb., 90c.

Extra-Early Eclipse—Is very early, and lasts well throughout the season. Handsome smooth, dark, globe-shaped Beet; quality very desirable; good Beet for private gardens. Pkt., 5c.; oz., 10c.; ¼ lb., 35c.; lb., $1.15.

Dewing's Improved Blood Turnip—The leading main crop variety. Roots always smooth, handsome, good size, tender and sweet. An enormous cropper. A favorite with marketmen. Pkt., 5c.; oz., 10c.; ¼ lb., 30c.; lb., $1.00.

Half-Long Blood Red—Of handsome shape, fine quality, quick growth; good for Winter use if planted late. Pkt., 5c.; oz., 10c.; ¼ lb., 30c.; lb., $1.00.

Lentz's Early Blood Turnip—A great favorite with market gardeners around New York and Philadelphia. Of a rapid growth; fine form, exceedingly sweet and delicious. Pkt., 5c.; oz., 10c.; ¼ lb., 25c.; lb., 90c.

Edmand's Blood Turnip

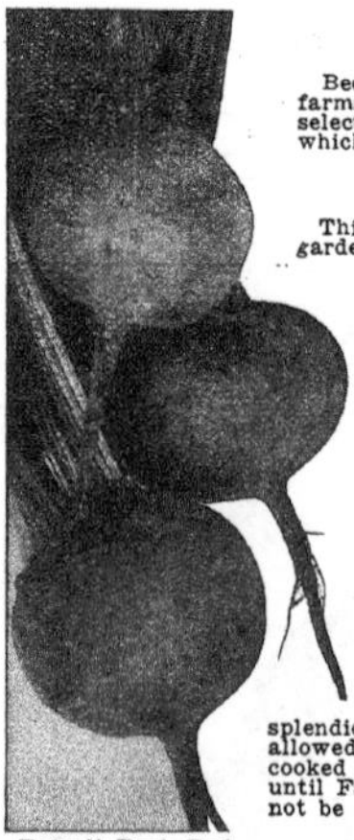

Garden Beets for Table Use. (Continued)

Beets are one of our great specialties and we grow acres of them for seed at our Kirkersville farms, first growing the roots from seed, holding these over and then making a very careful selection of the roots in the Spring, when ready to plant. This we have been doing for years, which enables us to offer a very superior strain of Beet Seed.

Detroit Dark Red

This superb variety is probably the most popular deep red Turnip Beet, not only for market gardeners, but for home use. It is also one of the best for canning, making a strikingly handsome product, far superior to that obtained from any other variety. Its small top, early maturing and splendid shape and color have made it a favorite. Top small, upright growing, so that the rows may be close together; leaf stem and veins dark red, blade green; root globular and very smooth (see illustration); color of skin dark blood red; flesh deep, bright red, zoned with a darker shade, very crisp, tender and sweet, remaining so for a long time. Very uniform in shape, color and quality. Pkt., 5c.; oz., 15c.; ¼ lb., 40c.; lb., $1.25.

Howard H. Hoover, Oklahoma, writes: "The Edmund's Blood Turnip Beets were the finest I ever saw. They were smooth and large. All the seed obtained of you has been satisfactory."

Bastain's Early Turnip

The largest of the turnip-shaped Beets. Tender and sweet; is somewhat lighter in color than other sorts. Pkt., 5c.; oz., 10c.; ¼ lb., 25c.; lb., 75c.

Long Dark Blood Red—A good keeper of good size, flesh dark blood red. Pkt., 5c.; oz., 10c.; ¼ lb., 30c.; lb., $1.00.

Swiss Chard or Spinach Beet

A peculiar variety of Beet, of which the leaves only are used. It does not make a large root, but the leaves are splendid "greens" when cut young, and are equally delicious when allowed to mature. The broad, white leaf-stalks or mid-ribs are cooked and served like Asparagus. Produces continually from July until Fall. Can be had throughout the Summer when Spinach cannot be grown. Pkt., 5c.; oz., 10c.; ¼ lb., 30c.; lb., $1.00.

Detroit Dark Red

Swiss Chard Lucullus

An improvement over the common variety. The plants grow from 2 to 2½ feet tall and consist, when fully developed, of about a dozen creamy white, attractively curled leaves. These leaves are carried on broad, thick stalks, about 12 inches long. Take the leafy portion of the plant and cook it like Spinach. Prepare the stalks as you would Asparagus. Pkt., 5c.; oz., 10c.; ¼ lb., 30c.; lb., $1.15.

Mangel-Wurzels

An ever-increasing acreage is being planted to stock Beets, because of the wonderful results from feeding them. Fattening, breeding and milk cattle do equally well on them. About one-fourth of the daily rations should bet of roots. Sow in rows 2½ to 3 feet apart as soon as the ground can be thoroughly worked. Cover seed about 1 inch, making ground firm over the seed. When 4 inches high, thin to 8 inches apart. Six pounds sow one acre.

Mammoth Long Red

Also called Norbiton Giant, Jumbo Mangel, Colossal, etc.—A favorite with the farmer and dairyman; large, well-formed; blood-red color; very nutritious; a big cropper. Pkt., 5c.; oz., 10c.; ¼ lb., 15c.; lb., 50c. By express, not paid, lb., 40c.; 10 lbs., $3.75.

Golden Tankard

Very productive and sweet; flesh yellow, tops and neck very small; easily pulled. Especially relished by sheep and cows. Pkt., 5c.; oz., 10c.; ¼ lb., 15c.; lb., 50c. By express, not paid, lb., 40c.; 10 lbs., $3.75.

Yellow, or Orange Globe

Very productive; easily pulled; fine keeper; spherical shape; orange-yellow color. Pkt., 5c.; oz., 10c.; ¼ lb., 20c.; lb., 55c. By express, not paid, lb., 40c.; 5 lbs., $1.75.

Golden Giant Intermediate

(Yellow Leviathan, or Mammoth Yellow) —Beautiful russet yellow; skin smooth; flesh white, firm, sweet; productive; easily pulled; good keeper. Pkt., 5c.; oz., 10c.; ¼ lb., 15c.; lb., 50c. By express, not paid, 40c.; 5 lbs., $1.75.

Albert Schmidt, Philadelphia, writes! "Your Crosby's Egyptian Beet seed purchased from you were very early, and all that would be desired as far as eating was concerned."

Sugar Beets

Sugar Beets are not as heavy yielders as the Mangels, but contain a large amount of sugar. They are excellent for feeding cows.

Vilmorin's Improved White

Greatly esteemed by sugar manufacturers, and one of the finest for stock feeding. Pkt., 5c.; oz., 10c.; ¼ lb., 15c.; lb., 60c.

Lane's Imperial

Especially good for stock feeding. Large, smooth, fine grained and very sweet. Pkt., 5c.; oz., 10c.; ¼ lb., 15c.; lb., 50c.

Klein-Wanzleben

This splendid Sugar Beet is one of the greatest milk-producing roots known. The yield is not quite equal to Mangels, yet the feeding value is superior. Contains the greatest amount of sugar of any. Pkt., 5c.; oz., 10c.; ¼ lb., 15c.; lb., 50c.

Giant Half-Sugar White

Yield nearly as much per acre as Mangel Wurzels, and the roots are of much higher nutritive value. Roots grow partly out of ground and are easily harvested. Pkt., 5c.; oz., 10c.; ¼ lb., 15c.; lb., 45c.

Giant Half-Sugar Rose

Similar to above, only rose colored. Pkt., 5c.; oz., 10c.; ¼ lb., 15c.; lb., 45c.

J. H. Small, North Carolina, writes: "We have purchased seeds from you for the past three years, and find them very satisfactory, especially Cucumber and Beet seeds. They are very fine and are largely used by my neighbors who gladly voice my sentiments."

W. C. Davis writes: "The Crosby's Egyptian Beet I got of you did excellently well for me. I raised nice Beets, good for market, sold at sight. Your seeds always prove good for me."

Jay Carpenter, New York State, writes: "Those Crosby Beets were very fine. All about the same size, and the earliest I had."

Giant Half Sugar

Brocoli Broccoli Spargelkohl

This plant is very closely allied to the Cauliflower, the variation being very slight. It is generally considered rather more hardy, however. In growing Broccoli, a seed bed should be prepared and the seed sown in May. The plants will be ready to transplant late in June or early in July, and should be set in very rich, mellow ground, in rows about 2½ feet apart, leaving 18 inches between the plants. In cool, moist Fall weather, it thrives well.

Early Large White—Heads medium size, close and compact. One of the most certain to head. Pkt., 10c.; oz., 30c.; ¼ lb., $1.00; lb., $3.75.

Early Purple Cape—Rather hardier sort; greenish purple heads; good flavor. Pkt., 10c.; oz., 30c.; ¼ lb., $1.00; lb., $3.75.

Brussels Sprouts

Col de Bruselas   Rosenkohl

A species of the Cabbage family, which produces miniature heads from the sides of the stalk. These heads are a great delicacy, boiled in the same way as Cauliflower. The seed should be sown about the middle of May, in a seed bed, and the plants afterwards set in rows 2 feet or more apart, and cultivated like Cabbage. This vegetable does not require extremely high cultivation, however. It is ready for use late in autumn after the early frosts. Keep bottom leaves trimmed off.

Improved Dwarf—Produces compact sprouts of the finest quality; a good keeper. Pkt., 5c.; oz., 20c.; ¼ lb., 50c.; lb., $1.75.

Pride of Denmark—A fine new variety, growing about 3 feet tall. Sprouts develop along entire stalk at one time, lower ones being as good as those at top. Pkt., 10c.; oz., 35c.; ¼ lb., 90c.; lb., $3.00.

Borecole, or Kale—See Kale, page 36.

Pride of Denmark Brussels Sprouts

Col repollo Livingston's High-Bred Cabbage Seed Weisskraut

Cabbage requires deep, rich, mellow soil, high manuring and good culture to obtain fine, solid heads. For early use, sow seeds of the early kinds in the hot-beds or in a box in the house the last of January or early in February; transplant into the open ground in April, in rows 2 feet apart and 18 inches in the row; or sow a bed of seed outside as soon as the soil can be worked. Transplant in about four weeks. For second early Cabbage, sow in April and transplant in May. For late Cabbage, sow in May and transplant in July in rows 3 feet apart and 2 feet in the row. In transplanting, it is important that plants be set down to the first leaf, so that the stem may not be injured in case of frost. Be careful not to cover the heart of the plant. Hoe every week and stir the soil deep. As they advance in growth draw a little earth to the plants until they begin to head. To prevent splitting or bursting, go frequently over the ground and push every Cabbage that appears about to mature over sideways, which will break some of the roots and check its growth. To prevent attacks of the cabbage fly on small plants, dust thoroughly with plaster, air-slacked lime or wood ashes. For cabbage worm, try Hammond's Slug Shot. **One ounce of seed produces about 2500 plants. Four ounces will grow enough plants to set an acre.**

Chinese Cabbage (Pe Tsai), Celery-Cabbage, Odorless Cabbage, etc. Something new. See page 5.

Early Jersey Wakefield

Early Jersey Wakefield

Many market gardeners consider this the very best Early Cabbage in cultivation. Certainly deserving of its great popularity. Grown extensively for market and shipping. Its merits are many, among which are large heads for an early sort, small outside foliage and uniformity of crop. Pyramidal in shape, having a blunted or rounded peak; very solid, fine texture and sweet. The seed we offer is first-class, sure to give satisfaction. Pkt., 5c.; ½ oz., 15c.; oz., 25c.; ¼ lb., 80c.; lb., $2.75.

Large Charleston Wakefield

A selection from Early Jersey Wakefield, only it is about one week later than that popular early variety and grows much larger heads, often averaging 8 to 10 pounds. As solid as Early Winningstadt. There are immense quantities grown in the South for Northern markets. Pkt., 5c.; ½ oz., 15c.; oz., 25c.; ¼ lb., 75c.; lb., $2.50.

All-Season (Vandergaw)

Greatly improved strain of Early Dwarf Flat Dutch. Heads very large, round, solid and of fine quality, keeping as well as the Winter sorts. Remarkable for its ability to stand hot sun and dry weather. Planted late—a choice Winter sort. Pkt., 5c.; ½ oz., 15c.; oz., 25c.; ¼ lb., 80c.; lb., $2.75.

Copenhagen Market

A splendid new extra-early round-headed sort which matures as early as the Wakefields and is of much larger size. Each plant forms a perfect, tightly folded head, averaging five to eight pounds in weight and about eight inches in diameter each way. The compact growth of the plant, the solidity of the head, its excellent flavor, and extreme earliness—all combine to make Copenhagen Market one of the most meritorious Cabbages that have come to our notice in a decade. See also page 5. Pkt., 10c.; ½ oz., 15c.; oz., 30c.; ¼ lb., $1.00; lb., $3.50.

Eureka First-Early

In comparison with Early Jersey Wakefield, Eureka First Early is heavier, hardier, earlier, and has flat head. Forms head fit for market 5 days earlier than Early Jersey Wakefield. Its shape and excellent table qualities make it a favorite with consumers. Pkt., 5c.; ½ oz., 15c.; oz., 25c.; ¼ lb., 80c.; lb., $2.75.

Early Spring

As early as Early Jersey Wakefield. Will yield one-third more than any other extra-early Cabbage on same area. Plant 21 inches apart and you have 13,000 per acre. Has the peculiarity of heading firmly even before fully grown. Also flat-headed, making it valuable for extra-early market or home use. Pkt., 5c.; ½ oz., 15c.; oz., 25c.; ¼ lb., 80c.; lb., $2.75.

Early Winningstadt

(The Old Standby)—Well known and popular Cabbage. In season very close to Early Jersey Wakefield. Heads large, decidedly conical. Solid, even in Summer; almost worm-proof, because so hard. A very sure header. Pkt., 5c.; ½ oz., 15c.; oz., 25c.; ¼ lb., 75c.; lb., $2.50.

Glory of Enkhousen

It is very early and large, always extremely solid and fine ribbed—more so than any other kind. Once known, it will hold its own with the market gardeners and home growers alike. In our judgment it excels in flavor all varieties known to us. It is an exceedingly tender, fine grained and as a cropper no early Cabbage will approach it. Planted side by side with Early Jersey Wakefield, under the same conditions, the former produced heads of marketable size five to six days earlier, and in size fully double that of the Early Jersey Wakefield. Glory of Enkhousen Cabbage is more solid and better flavored and keeps in fine condition much longer. It is very dwarf and compact, allowing of close planting. Heads fine, ball-shaped, and with few outside leaves. Size ideal for marketing. An extra good cropper on account of extra size over many other first early sorts. Pkt., 5c.; ½ oz., 15c.; oz., 30c.; ¼ lb., 85c.; lb., $3.00.

Henderson's Early Summer

About 10 days later than the Early Jersey Wakefield, but, being fully double the size, may be classed with best large Early Cabbages. Equal in weight to most of late varieties; may be planted nearly as close as Early Jersey Wakefield. Keeps long time without bursting. Heads round. Pkt., 5c.; ½ oz., 10c.; oz., 15c.; ¼ lb., 50c.; lb., $1.75.

Glory of Enkhousen

Early Dwarf Flat Dutch

Excellent second early variety, producing fine, large heads. Highly valued for its fine quality and ability to resist heat. Heads very solid, broad, round, flattened on top, tender and fine-grained. Pkt., 5c.; ½ oz., 10c.; oz., 20c.; ¼ lb., 70c.; lb., $2.25.

Fottler's Short-Stem Brunswick

Rapid grower; large, solid heads, few outside leaves; planted early, is ready for use in July; planted late, is a choice Winter sort. Pkt., 5c.; ½ oz., 10c.; oz., 20c.; ¼ lb., 65c.; lb., $2.00.

Surehead

Very reliable header; large, round, flattened heads, and is remarkable for its certainty to head; good keeper and shipper. It is very sweet flavored, has but few loose leaves, keeps well, and, as a Cabbage for the kitchen garden, is unequaled. Pkt., 5c.; ½ oz., 10c.; oz., 20c.; ¼ lb., 70c.; lb., $2.25.

Succession

About one week later than the Henderson's Early Summer, but nearly double the size, while it can be planted nearly as close, its outer leaves being unusually short. A very sure header. Pkt., 5c.; ½ oz., 15c.; oz., 25c.; ¼ lb., 80c.; lb., $2.75.

All-Head Early

All-Head Early

A thoroughbred sort of remarkably uniform size and shape and sure heading qualities. Deep, flat heads, solid and uniform in color, shape and size. In tenderness unsurpassed. For Winter use, sow in July. By reason of its compactness, 1000 more heads can be obtained from an acre than of many other good-sized varieties. Pkt., 5c.; ½ oz., 15c.; oz., 25c.; ¼ lb., 75c.; lb., $2.50.

The Volga (No. 20)

This variety is of the greatest uniformity. In a field of several acres frequently not a single plant shows any variation from a true and valuable type. In some respects it is a vegetable wonder, as the heads are about equal in size and shape, weighing from 12 to 15 pounds each, round as a ball, the largest measuring about 12 inches in diameter either way. Unlike most varieties, the heads are perfectly solid, and the stem does not run up into the head; the flesh is exceedingly firm, tender and white. In respect to hardiness, we have never seen a type which would favorably compare. This type will mature its heads fully two weeks earlier than any of our late-growing kinds. Pkt., 5c.; ½ oz., 15c.; oz., 25c.; ¼ lb., 75c.; lb., $2.50.

Autumn King or World Beater

One of the finest strains of late Cabbage. It produces regular, even heads of enormous size; a great cropper on account of few outside leaves. Pkt., 5c.; ½ oz., 10c.; oz., 15c.; ¼ lb., 50c.; lb., $1.75.

Volga

Danish Ball-Head (Tall Stem)

Hard as a Rock—Heavy as Lead
Greatest Weight in Smallest Space

This splendid variety is well known for its remarkable solidity and grand keeping qualities. So great has been the demand among the users of Cabbage for this fine-grained sort as to render its importation from Denmark a most profitable enterprise for the vegetable dealer. The heads are very heavy and superb in quality. The extra weight, in limited space, will be appreciated by those who grow for distant markets, ship in car loads and sell by weight. This variety has been sold under a number of different names, such as "Hollander," "German Export," "Dutch Winter," etc., but the correct name is "Danish Ball-Head." Pkt., 5c.; ½ oz., 10c.; oz., 15c.; ¼ lb., 50c.; lb., $1.75.

Danish Ball-Head (Short Stem)

The head is quite similar to the above, but has shorter stem. Less outer foliage and better able to resist blight. Stands hot weather better than the tall stem. Pkt., 5c.; ½ oz., 10c.; oz., 15c.; ¼ lb., 50c.; lb., $1.75.

Danish Summer Ball-Head—New, see page 5 ·

Large American Drumhead

A superior Fall and Winter variety; large heads. Pkt., 5c.; ½ oz., 10c.; oz., 15c.; ¼ lb., 50c.; lb., $1.75.

Livingston's Premium Flat Dutch

Years ago we set out to build up a strain of Large Late Flat Dutch Cabbage that would be better than any other on the market, and now we have it in our **Livingston's Premium Flat Dutch. Our purpose has been to weed out every objectionable point, and to fix firmly every good quality.** It produces many tons to the acre, because of its solidity and compact, snug manner of growth. Unlike most large sorts, it is solid to the heart. Our stock seed is always grown from heads (not from stalks after the heads are taken off), fully developed and perfect in every respect. This strain has no superior. **The heads are large and very solid; open white, are crisp and tender, and sure to head.** Grown largely by marketmen on account of its good shipping qualities. Pkt., 5c.; ½ oz., 10c.; oz., 20c.; ¼ lb., 70c.; lb., $2.25.

Livingston's Ideal Winter

(See illustration.) A few days earlier than Livingston's Premium Flat Dutch, and one of the most magnificent strains of Late Flat Dutch known today. By persistent selection, year after year, it has been brought to a state of perfection rarely attained. The large, solid heads, the low, short stems, the absence of useless foliage, uniformity of size and shape, reliability for heading, and long-continued selection mentioned above, all combine to make this the **Ideal Cabbage for profit.** Pkt., 5c.; ½ oz., 10c.; oz., 20c.; ¼ lb., 65c.; lb., $2.00.

Danish Ball-Head Cabbage

Louisville Drumhead

About Cincinnati and Louisville it has been grown for more than 40 years. Heads very large and solid; a sure header; will stand without bursting almost the entire Summer. For Winter use, sow late in the season. Pkt., 5c.; ½ oz., 10c.; oz., 15c.; ¼ lb., 50c.; lb., $1.75.

Col de Milan Savoy Cabbages Wirsingkohl

The Savoy or Curly Cabbages are of exceptionally fine flavor and quality, and should be more generally cultivated. They are particularly adapted for private use, where quality rather than quantity is considered. Most delicious after frost.

Small Early Savoy

Best early dwarf Savoy; heads firm, solid, and beautifully crimped; finest quality. Pkt., 5c.; ½ oz., 10c.; oz., 20c.; ¼ lb., 65c.; lb., $2.00.

Improved American Savoy

Superior to the ordinary Drumhead Savoy offered under different names. Heads large and finely curled; short stalk; a compact grower; sure header; keeps well. Best for main crop. Pkt., 5c.; ½ oz., 15c.; oz., 25c.; ¼ lb., 75c.; lb., $2.50.

Repollo colorado Red Cabbages Rotkraut

Danish Ironball (Red)

As round as a ball and as hard as iron—those are the two leading characteristics of this elegant new sort. Heads grow to a large size, averaging 8 inches in diameter, of rich purplish color throughout. Pkt., 10c.; ¼ oz., 15c.; oz., 25c.; ¼ lb., 80c.; lb., $2.75.

Extra-Early Blood Red Erfurt

Earliest and reddest. Pkt., 5c.; ½ oz., 10c.; oz., 20c.; ¼ lb., 70c.; lb., $2.25.

Mammoth Rock Red

Heads as large as Large Late Flat Dutch; deep red to center. Highly recommended. · Hard as a rock. Pkt., 5c.; ½ oz., 15c.; oz., 25c.; ¼ lb., 80c.; lb., $2.75.

Livingston's Ideal Winter

J. B. Anderson, Jefferson Co., O., writes: "I have grown the Livingston's True Blue Seeds for twenty-five years and I find by experience for myself they are getting better all the time and I want no other. My friends tell me I get one-third of a crop more on less ground than they do, so I expect to give you all my orders."

W. E. Coffin, Calcasieu County, La., writes as follows: "I have been using your seeds for quite a while and beg to say they have given the best of satisfaction, and have never received a single package of any kind of seed but what has germinated and grown fine."

Livingston's Earliest Cauliflower

Cauliflowers

Coliflor   Blumenkohl

Cauliflowers delight in a rich, moist soil, and in dry seasons should be abundantly watered, especially when heading. Sow the seed in the hotbed in January or February, and transplant the plants 2 or 3 inches apart in boxes or in another hotbed, until such time as they are safe to be planted in the open ground. Set the plants in the field 2 feet by 15 inches apart. If properly hardened off, they are seldom injured by being planted out too early. When heading, tie the outside leaves loosely over the head to protect it from the sun. Cauliflowers should be kept constantly growing, as the crop may be injured if growth is checked at any time. **One ounce produces from 1500 to 2000 plants.**

Livingston's Earliest

Our grower in Denmark spares no pains or expense with this stock. For wintering in cold-frames it can not be excelled and it does equally well for a Fall crop if planted late and treated the same as late Cabbage. Livingston's Earliest Cauliflower should take the place of many of the late varieties on account of its fine texture, pure white heads, and large, uniform size. A most compact grower and sure header. Market gardeners throughout the country are perfectly satisfied with it.

Price (under our **True Blue Seal**), ⅛ size pkt., 15c.; pkt., 25c.; ¼ oz., 85c.; oz., $3.00; ¼ lb., $10.00.

Danish Perfection

A new variety which comes to us highly recommended. It is similar in growth to Livingston's Earliest, but is even earlier, coming eight to ten days ahead of it, on the introducer's grounds. It is extremely uniform in type, the heads very solid and the introducers state that the leaves fold so closely about the head that it blanches very little, trouble on the part of the grower. We believe it is well worthy of trial on the part of those growing Cauliflower. ½ size pkt., 15c.; pkt., 25c.; ¾ oz., 80c.; oz., $2.75; ¼ lb., $10.00.

Dry-Weather Cauliflower

(Also known as **Danish Giant** and **Gilt-Edge**.) This is a fine, large, heavy variety that matures about a week later than Livingston's Earliest Cauliflower. It is especially adapted for growing in dry locations on account of its large leaves, which furnish greater protection to the heads. To secure a large crop of the best solid heads it is essential that the ground be well enriched and most thoroughly cultivated during the growing season. ⅛ size pkt., 15c.; pkt., 25c.; ¼ oz., 75c.; ½ oz., $1.40; oz., $2.50; ¼ lb., $8.50.

Livingston's Green-House Forcer

For a great many years we have realized that a variety of Cauliflower that would grow in a small space, and, at the same time, combine all the good qualities of our best sorts would be greatly appreciated by every one who forces this vegetable under glass. Livingston's Green-House Forcer is unexcelled for this purpose. ½ size pkt., 15c.; pkt., 25c.; ¼ oz., 85c.; oz., $3.00.

Henderson's Early Snowball

One of the best types of Cauliflower on the market. Its compact habit of growth renders it a very profitable variety to force under glass, and it does well for late planting, as well as for early crops. It is a sure header. ½ size pkt., 15c.; pkt., 25c.; ¼ oz., 75c.; ½ oz., $1.40; oz., $2.50; ¼ lb., $8.50.

Veitch's Autumn Giant

Heads are beautifully white, large, compact. Pkt., 10c.; ¼ oz., 25c.; oz., 50c.; ¼ lb., $1.50; lb., $5.50.

Extra-Early Dwarf Erfurt

Dwarf habit, compact growth; short outside leaves. Can be planted 20 inches apart. Pkt., 25c.; ¼ oz., 75c.; ½ oz., $1.40; oz., $2.50; ¼ lb., $8.50.

Large Late Algiers

Popular with canners and market gardeners. Ample foliage protects the heads well, which remain a long time fit for use. Pkt., 10c.; ¼ oz., 30c.; oz., 75c.; ¼ lb., $2.00.

A. J. Shanabruck, of Stark County, Ohio, writes as follows: "Your seeds are high, but I want them. I know what I am getting. Your Coreless Tomatoes are out of sight. Melons, Peas, Peppers, Beans, and all seeds that I have been using for over twenty years are just what you claim them to be without any mistake."

Danish Perfection

Zanahorias Carrots Mohren

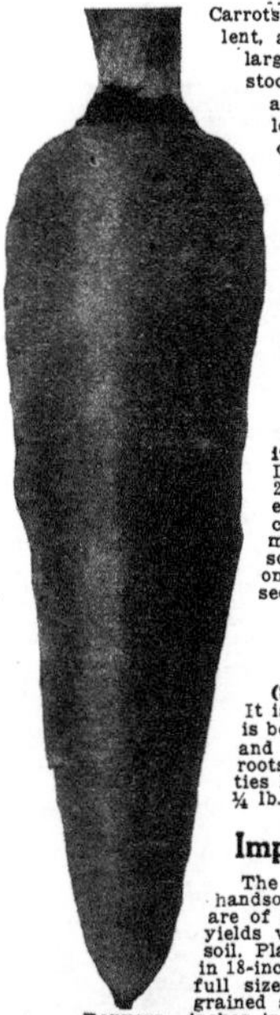

Carrots are not appreciated as they should be. Their table qualities are excellent, and as a food for stock they are surpassed by few root crops. The larger varieties produce large crops and are relished by all kinds of stock. They are especially valuable when fed to dairy cows, producing an increased flow of rich milk and imparting a beautiful golden yellow to the butter. We urge a more general use of the Carrot among our customers, knowing its great value will be appreciated when better known. Like other root crops, it flourishes best in a well-enriched sandy soil, deeply tilled, and if plowed the Fall before so much the better. Sow in early Spring in drills 15 to 18 inches apart, finally thinning the plants to 3 or 4 inches. If sown early on a moist soil, a half-inch is deep enough to cover the seed. The seed is slow to germinate. Keep clean by frequent hoeing and weeding. If neglected, the young plants are easily smothered, and the crop is lost. **One ounce sows 100 feet of drill. 4 pounds sow one acre.**

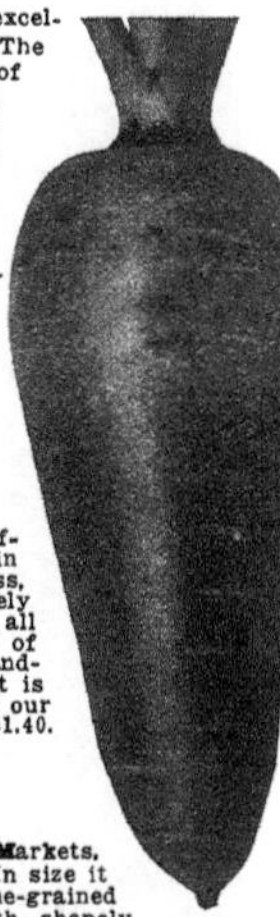

Improved Danvers Half-Long

The best for general crop. Will yield the most per acre. Most profitable for market gardeners; stump-rooted. This variety originated in Danvers, Mass., where the raising of Carrots is made a special business, 20 to 30 tons per acre being no unusual crop. It is now grown largely everywhere on account of its productiveness and adaptability to all classes of soils. Tops medium size, roots deep orange, large but of medium length tapering uniformly to a blunt point. Smooth and handsome flesh; sweet, crisp and tender. Although of medium length, it is one of the largest yielders. We take extra pains in the selection of our seed stock. It is second to none. Pkt., 5c.; oz., 15c.; ¼ lb., 40c.; lb., $1.40.

Improved Chantenay

(See illustration)—A Popular and Profitable Sort to Raise for City Markets. It is about 6 inches long, thick through and decidedly stump-rooted. In size it is between the Oxheart and Danvers. The flesh is a deep orange red, fine-grained and of a splendid flavor. It is very early and always produces smooth, shapely roots. Its fine appearance finds for it a ready market; its splendid table qualities keep it in demand. Our strain of seed is unsurpassed. Pkt., 5c.; oz., 15c.; ¼ lb., 50c.; lb., $1.75.

Chantenay

Improved Long Orange

The standard late variety; very handsome and uniform in shape; roots are of deep orange color, good flavor; yields very heavily. Requires a deep soil. Plants should stand 6 inches apart in 18-inch drills for roots to attain their full size. The roots are smooth, fine grained and very large, growing to 12 inches in length and 3 inches in diameter. For feeding milch cows it is very valuable, as it increases the flow of milk and imparts to the butter a rich golden hue. Pkt., 5c.; oz., 10c.; ¼ lb., 25c.; lb., 90c.

Danvers

Livingston's Early Market

A very choice strain. Tender, fine-grained flesh. An enormous producer; handsome, medium stumped roots. Considered by many to be the best table Carrot, because of its quality and shape; free from core and of a deep golden yellow color. Can be sown very thick, and consequently well adapted for frame culture. A most excellent forcer. Pkt., 5c.; oz., 15c.; ¼ lb., 40c.; lb., $1.25.

Saint Valery, or Intermediate

A thick, intermediate smooth variety; an English sort. It very much resembles the Danvers Carrot in both general shape and size. The color is a rich orange red, and of fine flavor. The roots grow very uniform; a most desirable Carrot for private gardens or market purposes. Pkt., 5c.; oz., 15c.; ¼ lb., 40c.; lb., $1.25.

Earliest French Forcing

The earliest small round variety, much used for first early forcing in hot beds. Color reddish orange, and bunches very nicely; used largely for market, as well as kitchen garden. Quality the best. Pkt., 5c.; oz., 20c.; ¼ lb., 50c.; lb., $1.75.

Oxheart, or Guerande

Intermediate length; is fully 3 to 5 inches in diameter; quality extra good. Some sorts require digging, but the Oxheart can be easily pulled. It is especially adapted to shallow soils, where the longer sorts would not thrive as well. Pkt., 5c.; oz., 10c.; ¼ lb., 25c.; lb., 90c.

Nantes Half-Long

(Stump-Rooted)—Sweet and fine flavored; almost without a core; very fine grained; excellent for the home garden or market. One of the finest in quality and handsomest in shape of the medium-sized sorts. Pkt., 5c.; oz., 10c.; ¼ lb., 30c.; lb., $1.00.

Early Scarlet Horn

For forcing and early garden use; flesh deep orange, fine grained; agreeable flavor; small top, stump rooted. Pkt., 5c.; oz., 15c.; ¼ lb., 40c.; lb., $1.25.

Carrots for Stock Feeding

Too much cannot be said in praise of the Carrot as a wholesome addition to the Winter feed for stock, apart from its great value as a vegetable for table use. The splendid roots make a most desirable change of feed for your cattle when given in connection with grain and dry fodder. Plant plenty of Carrots for all purposes. Ask for prices in larger quantities.

Improved Short White—Very large, half-long roots; pearly white. It is the heaviest cropper known. Pkt., 5c.; oz., 10c.; ¼ lb., 30; lb., $1.00.

Large White Belgian—Standard for field culture. Pkt., oz., 10c.; ¼ lb., 20c.; lb., 75c.

W. C. Clon, Tuscarawas Co., O., writes: "I have used your seeds for over 20 years and always found them very satisfactory."

J. F. DeBerry, Manatee Co., Fla., writes August 9, 1915: "I have used your seeds almost exclusively for 16 years and have always found them good and true to name and type. I lost part of my crop two or three different times by getting seeds or plants from some of my neighbors, but I never use seed any more unless they have the name of Livingston on the package."

Jacob J. Mayer, Allegheny Co., Pa., writes: "We have had a very successful season, with good crops from True Blue seeds."

Special prices on Carrot Seed in quantity.

Apio **Choice Celery Seed** Sellerie

One Ounce of Seed Produces 2,000 Plants. Cultural Leaflet Free to Customers

Celery Culture

Celery can be successfully grown with but little labor, in any good garden soil, by using plenty of well rotted manure with a liberal sprinkling of coarse salt worked into it, and this mixture should be put into the trenches, working it well into the soil, at least two weeks before the plants are transplanted into them. It delights, however, in low, moist, rich bottom land, or well-drained muck soil. It is usually grown as a second crop.

Growing the Plants

It is not necessary to sow the seeds in a hot-bed or cold frame, as it is apt to run to seed if started too early, but sow in the open ground as soon as it is fit to work in April, and an additional sowing or two between this date and May first, will insure a plentiful supply of good plants. Sow in rows so that it can be kept free from weeds. Prepare the soil well and cover the seed very shallow and firm the soil well after sowing; also keep very moist until the seed germinates. After coming up the plants should be partially shaded for a week or ten days, and see that the soil does not get too dry. When two inches high thin and transplant to three inches apart. To insure good "stocky" plants, the tops should be cut back, to within say two inches of the crown, when about four inches high.

Transplanting

The evening is the best time, and especially if after a shower; otherwise give them a good watering and you will lose but very few plants. Remember that it is essential that the soil be pressed firmly about each plant when set out, especially if done in a dry time; the old method of setting in deep trenches is a thing of the past. Some of our most successful growers set on the level surface, while others prefer a broad, shallow trench, only three or four inches deep. These trenches should be at least three feet apart for the dwarf, and not less than four feet for the larger sorts; set plants in single rows not over six inches apart in the trench. Transplanting is done about the middle of June for the first early, and as late as the middle of August for the latest. Keep well cultivated, and in about six weeks "handling" should begin (never do this when wet from rain or dew). This is done to make the celery grow upright. The soil is drawn to the row from each side with an ordinary hoe. Now take all the leaves of the plant in one hand and with the other draw the soil around it, pressing firmly, being careful that no soil gets between the leaves, as it is apt to cause rust, or rot the plant. In about two weeks, or as often as it is necessary to keep the leaves in this upright position, more soil should be drawn to the row.

Columbia

Golden Self-Blanching

This grand Celery is of French origin. It has the demand above all other sorts because of its many superb qualities. It has the same self-blanching habit as White Plume, but is much heavier and more compact, though not so early. Grows to good size, is very tender and free from strings, the heart large and solid, crisp, brittle, of excellent quality and very beautiful.

American grown seed from French stock seed—This has proven after repeated trials to be equal to French grown stock. Pkt., 10c.; ⅛ oz., 20c.; oz., 35c.; ¼ lb., $1.25; lb., $4.50.

French grown seed—From one of our most careful growers. Pkt., 15c.; ¼ oz., 20c.; ½ oz., 35c.; oz., 60c.; ¼ lb., $2.25; lb., $8.00.

Columbia

An early maturing sort unsurpassed in shape and quality. The plant is of medium height but very stocky and heavy. The stalks are thick, almost round, resembling in shape those of Giant Pascal; the color has in it more of the rich yellow tint of Golden Self Blanching, which variety it resembles very much in appearance. When trimmed and bunched for market. The foliage is of a distinctly light shade of green with a tinge of yellow. In season it follows in close succession Golden Self Blanching. In quality is certainly exceptionally fine, some considering it equal or even superior to either Golden Self Blanching or Giant Pascal. Pkt., 10c.; ½ oz., 20c.; oz., 35c.; ¼ lb., $1.25; lb., 4.50.

Livingston's Snowhite

It is without a rival in purity of color; crisp, tender and of good size. In vigor of growth, ease of blanching, richness of flavor and beauty of stalk, "Snowhite" is ideal. Single stalks sometimes weigh 2½ pounds and quite frequently 2 pounds. It grows solid on all kinds of soil and keeps better than a great many of the best standard varieties. We regret to report a very short crop of this excellent sort. Pkt., 10c.

Golden Self-Blanching

White Plume

Stalks and portions of the inner leaves and heart are so nearly white naturally that tying or simply drawing the soil up against the plants will complete the work of blanching. It is very ornamental. Early, of good flavor and fine texture; adapted to Fall and early Winter use; a good keeper up to the holiday season. Pkt., 5c.; ½ oz., 15c.; oz., 25c.; ¼ lb., 60c.; lb., $2.25.

Giant Pascal

Forms solid, crisp stalks of incomparable flavor. Of strong growth, producing perfectly blanched stalks when hilled up properly. Of rich, nutty flavor. Blanches very easily and is very brittle. A fine keeper, an excellent shipper, retaining color and fresh appearance a long time. A favorite with Southern growers. For mid-Winter and early Spring use, it is excellent. Pkt., 5c.; ½ oz., 10c.; oz., 15c.; ¼ lb., 45c.; lb., $1.50.

Boston Market

An excellent keeper; remarkably tender, crisp, solid. Best for light soils. Pkt., 5c.; ½ oz., 10c.; oz., 20c.; ¼ lb., 50c.; lb., $1.50.

Evan's Triumph

A splendid long keeper of extra fine flavor. Healthy, strong grower, crisp and tender. Pkt., 5c.; ½ oz., 10c.; oz., 20c.; ¼ lb., 50c.; lb., $1.50.

Dwarf Golden Heart

Solid, an excellent keeper and of fine, nutty flavor. Heart, which is large and full, is a light yellow. A showy and desirable variety for market. Pkt., 5c.; ½ oz., 10c.; oz., 15c.; ¼ lb., 40c.; lb., $1.25.

Giant Golden Heart

In quality, appearance and large size, it is one of the best. One of the best varieties for market gardeners. Pkt., 5c.; ½ oz., 10c.; oz., 20c.; ¼ lb., 50c.; lb., $1.50.

Winter Queen

Of short, stocky growth, with broad, heavy stalks. Fine for Winter use. Pkt., 5c.; ½ oz., 10c.; oz., 20c.; ¼ lb., 60c.; lb., $1.75.

Celeriac

Turnip-Rooted Celery

Sow seed the same way as for Celery. Transplant into rows 2 feet apart and 9 inches in the row. Thorough cultivation is necessary to secure good roots. Earthing up is not necessary. The roots may be cooked or used as salad.

Giant Smooth Prague—A large and smooth variety. Desirable for market; an excellent keeper. Pkt., 5c.; ½ oz., 10c.; oz., 20c.; ¼ lb., 50c.; lb., $1.50.

Giant Pascal

Corn Salad or Fetticus

A vegetable used as a salad. Sow the first opening of Spring in rows 1 foot apart and it is fit for use in six or eight weeks.

Large Leaved—Pkt., 5c.; oz., 10c.; ¼ lb., 25c.; lb., 75c.

Collards

A plant of the Cabbage family. It is well adapted to the South, enduring extreme heat; excellent for greens.

True Southern, or Georgia—Pkt., 5c.; oz., 10c.; ¼ lb., 30c.; lb., 90c.

Berro Cress or Pepper-Grass Kresse

A well-known pungent salad; can be used alone or with lettuce. Requires to be sown thickly, (covering very lightly) at frequent intervals, to keep up a succession, as it soon runs to seed.

Water Cress

Well-known hardy perennial aquatic plant. Is easily grown along margins of ponds and streams, where it increases both by spreading of roots and seeding. Has a pleasant, pungent flavor. Growing Water Cress should prove a profitable enterprise where the conditions are favorable. Pkt., 10c.; ½ oz., 20c.; oz., 35c.; ¼ lb., $1.25; lb., $4.00.

Extra Curled

(Pepper Grass)—May be cut two or three times. Pkt., 5c.; oz., 10c.; ¼ lb., 25c.; lb., 75c.

Upland Cress

This is a hardy perennial; stays green nearly the whole year; ready for use in the Spring before any other salad. Eaten like Lettuce or boiled like Spinach. Sow in April in rows 1 foot apart. Pkt., 5c.; oz., 15c.; ¼ lb., 50c.; lb., $1.50.

Dandelion

Sow in May or June, in warm, rich soil, in drills half an inch deep and 18 inches apart. Some of the plants will be ready for use in September, balance the following Spring. Make delicious greens. **One ounce will sow 150 feet of drill.**

Large-Leaved—Leaves fully double the size of the common Dandelion. Years of the most careful cultivation have developed a very fine strain of seed. Pkt., 10c.; ½ oz., 25c.; oz., 40c.; ¼ lb., $1.25.

Maiz dulce Corn, Sweet or Sugar Speise Mais

The Sweet or Sugar Corn Varieties, being liable to rot in cold or wet ground, should not be planted until May, or when the soil has become warm and dry. For a full supply for the table during the entire season, plant every ten days or two weeks until the last week in July, in hills 2x3 feet apart for the early kinds, and 3x3 feet for the large late sorts. Some plant in rows 3½ feet apart and 8 inches apart in the rows. Give frequent and thorough cultivation all the season. **Two** pounds of seed corn plants 200 to 300 hills; 15 to 18 pounds will sow an acre.

SWEET CORN PRICES in quantities up to and including 2 pounds include prepayment of postage. If the larger quantities are wanted sent by mail, it will be necessary to remit additional amount at the Parcels Post rates. Refer to page 5 for rates.

Extra Early Golden Bantam

One of the finest. The ears are from 6 to 7 inches long, eight rowed, filled with broad, sweet, golden yellow kernels of a delightful flavor. It may be planted from ten days to two weeks earlier than most Sweet Corns, as it is not as apt to rot as many of the softer kinds. It is as early as the Cory and of much better flavor. It is always good, whether planted in the Spring or during the Summer. We confidently advise all lovers of a real good Sweet Corn to give "Golden Bantam" a trial. The way to find out how good it is is to try it; and while you are about it, plant enough, or you'll surely be sorry when you begin to eat it. Pkt., 5c.; ½ lb., 15c.; lb., 25c.; 2 lbs., 45c. By express, not paid, ½ pk. (6 lbs.), 65c.; pk., $1.15; bu., $4.00.

Livingston's Early Sugar
(See Page 6 for Full Description)

This is a remarkably fine early variety; a heavy cropper producing large ears for so early a variety, and a great drouth resister. The ears have such a thick husk that they are rarely troubled by worms and are of fine appearance and excellent flavor. Pkt., 10c.; ½ lb., 15c.; lb., 25c.; 2 lbs., 45c. By express, not paid, ½ pk. (6 lbs.), 60c.; pk., $1.10; bu., $3.75.

Golden Bantam

Extra-Early Premo

A "sixty-day" Sweet Corn that combines all the merits of the leading varieties, and is superior to many of them in size, quality and yield. Premo can be planted fully as early as the Adams, for the young plants withstand slight frosts, while the other varieties are tender. The stalks grow about 5 feet high, and are very vigorous, generally bearing two well-developed ears to the stalk. Pkt., 5c.; ½ lb., 15c.; lb., 25c.; 2 lbs., 45c. By express, not paid, ½ pk. (6 lbs.), 60c.; pk., $1.10; bu., $3.75.

Peep-O'-Day—The stalks of Peep-O'-Day Corn grow from 3½ to 4½ feet high and bear from 2 to 3 ears each. The foliage is light green and, being small, stalks will stand very close planting. Have the rows just far enough apart to admit of thorough cultivation. Pkt., 5c.; ½ lb., 15c.; lb., 25c.; 2 lbs., 40c. By express, not paid, ½ pk. (6 lbs.), 60c.; pk., $1.10; bu., $3.50.

Extra-Early Adams—Same size, type and style as next below. Hardiest and earliest Corn. It is not a Sugar Corn, but is grown for early use. Ears short; kernels very white. Pkt., 5c.; lb., 10c.; 2 lbs., 20c. By express, not paid, ½ pk. (7 lbs.), 60c.; pk., $1.00; bu., $3.50.

Early Adams—Similar to Extra-Early Adams; ear somewhat larger, but not quite so early; is good for early table use. Like the above, is hardy, and can be planted early. Pkt., 5c.; ½ lb., 15c.; lb., 25c.; 2 lbs., 40c. By express, not paid, ½ pk. (7 lbs.), 60c.; pk., $1.00; bu., $3.50.

Mammoth White Cory—This new strain is as early as the original Extra-Early Cory, with ears of larger size, and kernels more compact. Cob and kernel are pure white. Pkt., 5c.; ½ lb., 15c.; lb., 25c.; 2 lbs., 45c. By express, not paid, ½ pk. (6 lbs.), 60c.; pk., $1.10; bu., $3.75.

Extra-Early Cory—Red Cob—One of the earliest varieties. Large ears, considering size of stalk; small red cob, well filled up with handsome and very sweet kernels. Pkt., 5c.; ½ lb., 15c.; lb., 25c.; 2 lbs., 40c. By express, not paid, ½ pk. (6 lbs.), 60c.; pk., $1.25.

Extra-Early Cory—White Cob—Identical with Extra-Early Cory, except color; the cobs are white. Pkt., 5c.; ½ lb., 15c.; lb., 25c.; 2 lbs., 45c. By express, not paid, ½ pk. (6 lbs.), 60c.; pk., $1.10; bu., $3.75.

"4 Best" Sweet Corns for Home Gardens

This collection will supply the table continuously throughout the entire season: **Peep-O'-Day** (extra early), **Columbus Market** (early), **Country Gentleman** (main crop), **New White Evergreen** (late). One large pkt. each of above, 15c.; ½ lb. each, 45c.; 1 lb. of each, 85c. postpaid.

Sweet Corn for Fodder

Sow thickly in drills or broadcast at the rate of 2 to 3 bushels per acre. Express not paid. Peck, 65c.; bu., $2.25.

Mr. E. D. Bland, Louisiana, writes: "Your 'Volga Cabbage' has proved to be a decided acquisition to our Winter Cabbage crop, making the finest heads carried to this market. At this writing, am still cutting from the field, every plant making a fine head."

Wholesale prices on larger quantities of Sweet Corn on request.

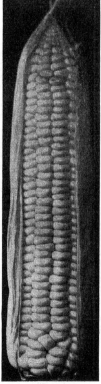

Premo

Livingston's Earliest on Earth

(See Page 6 for Full Description)

This is without doubt the earliest of all Sweet Corns, and possesses the quality which has made Golden Bantam so popular. It is about ten days earlier than the latter, but has a little smaller ear. Be sure and try it. Pkt., 10c.; ¼ lb., 25c.; lb., 40c.; 2 lbs., 75c. By express, not paid, ½ pk. (6 lbs.), $1.25; pk., $2.25; bu., $8.00.

Kendel's Early Giant

(See illustration)—The ears are large, measuring 8 to 9 inches long, thick through; with ten or more rows of plump and purest white kernels, that are of most deliciously sweet flavor. It is several days earlier than Shaker's Early, which gives it the distinction of being an early and at the same time a large-eared variety. Gardeners report this Sweet Corn ready to use in sixty days when grown on sandy soil, and in seventy-two days on heavy ground. We first offered Kendel's Giant Sweet Corn to our customers some ten years ago, and it has given the greatest satisfaction ever since to both market gardeners and home gardeners alike. Owing to our skillful selection year after year, Kendel's Early Giant has become a much more valuable sort than when first introduced. Pkt., 5c.; ¼ lb., 15c.; lb., 25c.; 2 lbs., 45c. By express, not paid, ½ pk. (6 lbs.), 65c.; pk., $1.15; bu., $4.00.

Shaker's Early

This fine Corn is a splendid market variety, being large and well formed. It comes in a little later than the "first earlies," being a good variety to plant for mid-season. Pkt., 5c.; ¼ lb., 15c.; lb., 25c.; 2 lbs., 40c. By express, not paid, ½ pk. (6 lbs.), 55c.; pk., 90c.; bu., $3.25.

Early Minnesota

White cob and kernels. Pkt., 5c.; ¼ lb., 15c.; lb., 25c.; 2 lbs., 45c. By express, not paid, ½ pk. (6 lbs.), 60c.; pk., $1.10; bu., $3.75.

Columbus Market

Ready for table with the second earlies, such as Crosby's Early, Shaker's Early, etc., but is fully twice as large as any of them. The ears carry an average of 16 rows of fine large, deep, white and very sweet grains, which are second to none in tenderness and flavor. The stalk is very strong, sturdy and of only medium height; the leaves broad and dark green in color, a habit of growth which gives it great endurance during a dry time. Especially adapted for early trucking; also very desirable for the home garden. Pkt., 5c.; ½ lb., 15c.; lb., 25c.; 2 lbs., 45c. By express, not paid, ½ pk. (6 lbs.), 60c.; pk., $1.10; bu., $3.75.

Livingston's Broad-Grained

Very Broad and Sweet

For a number of years this variety has been closely selected to produce the broadest possible grains, and at the same time to retain its depth of grain and splendid quality. The grains are simply enormous when in the roasting ear stage. For those who enjoy running a knife blade down through the rows of grains before eating, Livingston's Broad-Grained Sweet Corn is unexcelled; there is no dodging of the knife about these big grains. The ears are of the eight-rowed type and 7 or 8 inches long. It matures very soon after the Extra Early varieties. Pkt., 5c.; ¼ lb., 15c.; lb., 25c.; 2 lbs., 45c. By express, not paid, ½ pk. (6 lbs.), 65c.; pk., $1.15; bu., $4.00.

Kendel's Early Giant

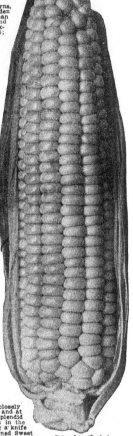

Columbus Market

Mammoth Late Sugar

Produces larger ears than any other Sugar Corn, and of good quality; a rich and very sweet late variety. Pkt., 5c.; ¼ lb., 15c.; lb., 25c.; 2 lbs., 45c. By express, not paid, ½ pk. (6 lbs.), 65c.; pk., $1.15; bu., $4.00.

Black Mexican

One of the sweetest varieties; color when in roasting ear, purple and white; also a fine late sort. Pkt., 5c.; ¼ lb., 15c.; lb., 25c.; 2 lbs., 45c. By express, not paid, ½ pk. (6 lbs.), 65c.; pk., $1.25; bu., $3.75.

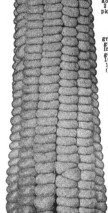

Sweet Corn (Continued)

Narrow Grained Evergreen

Narrow Grained Evergreen

A selection of Stowell's Evergreen retaining its large size and productiveness and adding the delicious sweetness of Country Gentleman. There will be less trouble for the canners to get the farmer to grow Narrow Grained Evergreen on account of increased yield. The Market Gardener should find ready sale for this large, medium late sort. We believe our stock of it will be found superior to much that is offered. We intend growing it on our own farms, making very careful selections of planting stocks each season. Get started using some of this variety this season. You will be pleased. Pkt., 5 cts.; ½ lb., 15c.; lb., 25c.; 2 lbs., 45c. By express, not paid, ½ pk. (6 lbs.), 65c.; pk., $1.15; bu., $4.00.

Livingston's Evergreen (Red Cob)

Our old original variety, introduced by us in 1860, and now a general favorite for family use, as well as market purposes. It is a first-class second-early sort. Productive, large, well-filled ears, with broad kernels and small cob, filled well over tip. Pkt., 5c.; ½ lb., 15c.; lb., 25c.; 2 lbs., 40c. By express, not paid, ½ pk. (6 lbs.), 60c.; pk., $1.00; bu., $3.50.

Livingston's Evergreen (White Cob)

This is our old Livingston's Evergreen (described above), with a white cob. Pkt., 5c.; ¼ lb., 15c.; lb., 25c.; 2 lbs., 40c. By express, not paid, ½ pk. (6 lbs.), 60c.; pk., $1.00; bu., $3.50.

Early Evergreen

An early strain of Evergreen Sweet Corn must be of great value. This variety resembles the Stowell's Evergreen, but is ready for use much earlier, and remains in good condition equally as long. The ears grow to a good size, usually about 7 inches long, and contain from 16 to 18 rows of deep, sweet grains. Pkt., 5c.; ½ lb., 15c.; lb., 25c.; 2 lbs., 45c. By express, not paid, ½ pk. (6 lbs.), 60c.; pk., $1.10; bu., $3.75.

Stowell's Evergreen

A favorite with canners and market gardeners for late use and especially for the kitchen garden. Ears large, kernels very deep, tender and of most delicious sweetness; very productive. Pkt., 5 c.; ½ lb., 15c.; lb., 25c.; 2 lbs. 40c. By express, not paid, ½ pk. (6 lbs.), 60c.; pk., $1.00; bu., $3.50.

White Evergreen

This is a high-bred, pure-white type of the ever-popular Stowell's Evergreen. From one pure white-grained ear, accidentally discovered some years ago, it has developed by careful selection. Stalks very vigorous, 6 to 7 feet high. The ears are uniformly very large and well filled. When in the green state both cob and kernel are white as snow. Pkt., 5c.; ¼ lb., 15c.; lb., 25c.; 2 lbs., 45c. By express, not paid, ½ pk. (6 lbs.), 60c.; pk., $1.10; bu., $3.75.

Country Gentleman

One of the Richest Flavored of all the late varieties. As a table Corn this variety stands unrivaled, and without doubt is the most luscious of all varieties of Sweet Corn. The plump, pearly-white kernels are of great depth, most delicious, and the flavor will delight an epicure. We have selected this sort for many years and are especially proud of our strain. It comes, as true to type as any we have ever seen. Ears average 9 inches long by 2 inches in diameter and are typical "shoe-peg," appearance. Pkt., 5c.; ½ lb., 15c.; lb., 25c.; 2 lbs., 45c. By express, not paid, ½ pk. (6 lbs.), 60c.; pk., $1.10; bu., $3.75.

Livingston's Evergreen

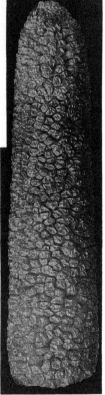

Country Gentleman Sweet Corn, ½ Natural Size

Livingston's Select Cucumber Seeds

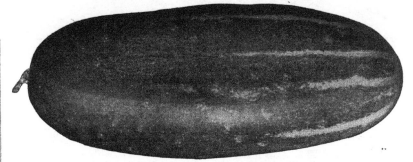

Livingston's Select Extra-Early White Spine

How to Grow Cucumbers

As soon as the weather has become settled and warm, plant in hills 4 to 6 feet apart each way, with 8 to 10 seeds in a hill; cover one-half an inch deep, smoothing the hill off with the hoe. When the plants are out of danger of insects, thin out to three or four plants to a hill. The seed may also be sown in rows 6 feet apart, with the seed every few inches in the row. When danger from bugs is past, they must be thinned out to 3 or 4 feet apart. This latter way of planting insures a good "stand," as the bugs cannot take all of them. Four or five moth balls placed in a dish or pan and set close to the hill are said to drive away bugs. For pickles, plant from 1st of June to 1st of August. The fruit should be gathered when large enough for pickling, whether required for use or not, as, if left to ripen on the vines, it destroys their productiveness. Cucumbers forced under glass turn yellow quickly; sometimes from overfeeding, and often from the use of manures that are quick acting; on this account cow manure is preferred to horse manure. One ounce of seed will plant about 50 hills; one to two pounds to the acre.

Livingston's Selected Davis Perfect

By using this variety gardeners can produce out-of-door Cucumbers that will sell in the market for hothouse forcing varieties. The shape is ideal. It is almost seedless one-third of its length from the stem, and the few seeds that are contained in its blossom end when in eating condition are so small and tender that they are hardly noticeable. Most important of all, it does not lose its dark, rich color when grown outdoors. It is hard to tell the difference between it and a hothouse cucumber. Pkt., 5c.; oz., 15c.; ¼ lb., 35c.; lb., $1.25.

Improved Long Green

Long and crisp; one of the very best for the family garden; also popular and reliable for pickles. Extra choice stock grown on our own farms—Pkt., 5c.; oz., 15c.; ¼ lb., 35c.; lb., $1.10.

Livingston's Select Extra-Early White Spine

This private strain we have had over thirty years, and it is the most thoroughbred, uniform and shapely variety known, not only for first early, but for general crop as well.

Excels in earliness, often ready for slicing when other sorts are only pickles. In purity it is unequaled. Vines are vigorous growers. The very best for slicing, and make choice pickles, straight and smooth; a great bearer; keeps green much longer than the yellow varieties; no sort excels it in crispness and flavor. Every market gardener knows how difficult it is to secure pure cucumber seed, and as this sort is remarkably free from mixture we are sure it will be quickly appreciated. Pkt., 5c.; oz., 15c.; ¼ lb., 35c.; lb., $1.25.

Livingston's Evergreen Pickling

(Introduced by us in 1890.) Generally admitted to possess every qualification required in a perfect pickling Cucumber. Exceptionally productive. One grower says it bears "four to one" compared with many standard sorts. It is a very strong grower, extra-early, and bears firm, crisp fruits, which are excellent for slicing also. We devote the greatest care to the selection of this seed stock. Pkt., 5c.; oz., 15c.; ¼ lb., 35c.; lb., $1.25.

Livingston's Emerald

(Introduced by us in 1897)—We were eight years in perfecting this variety which represents a dark-green Cucumber that will hold its color. It is strictly an evergreen, retaining its color until quite ripe, making it very attractive. The plant sets early, and its vigorous vines abound in long, straight, handsome fruits of the most desirable qualities. As a slicer the flesh is perfectly crisp and tender, and the flavor most pleasing. The young fruit is dark green, straight, slender and almost spineless; makes an excellent pickle, and when ripe none excel it for making sweet pickles. It is not excelled for beauty in color and form. Excellent shipping variety. Pkt., 5c.; oz., 15c.; ¼ lb., 35c.; lb., $1.25.

Livingston's Selected Davis' Perfect Cucumber

Klondike

Excellent strain of White Spine, remarkable for the uniformly dark green skin of its shapely fruits. Popular with Southern planters for shipping to the Northern markets. Pkt., 5c.; oz., 10c.; ¼ lb., 25c.; lb., 90c.

Westerfield Chicago Pickling—Popular with Chicago gardeners. Medium length, slightly pointed at ends; very large; prominent spines; deep green. Pkt., 5c.; oz., 10c.; ¼ lb., 30c.; lb., $1.00.

Jersey Pickling—Intermediate between Long and Short Green. Long, slender, cylindrical; crisp and tender. Pkt., 5c.; oz., 10c.; ¼ lb., 30c.; lb., $1.00.

Green Prolific, or Boston Pickling—Of uniform growth, seldom too large for pickling; immensely productive. Pkt., 5c.; oz., 10c.; ¼ lb., 25c.; lb., 90c.

Extra-Long, or Evergreen White Spine—Averages longer than other strains. Extra fine shape and quality; makes a good pickle; used extensively for growing under glass. Pkt., 5c.; oz., 15c.; ¼ lb., 35c.; lb., $1.25.

Arlington Improved White Spine—For market use and pickling it is superior to the old White Spine. Pkt., 5c.; oz., 10c.; ¼ lb., 30c.; lb., $1.00.

Extra-Early Russian—Small, extra-early, hardy; productive, good for small pickles. Pkt., 5c.; oz., 10c.; ¼ lb., 30c.; lb., $1.00.

Early Frame, or Short Green—A popular early variety of medium size and good shape; good for small pickles. Pkt., 5c.; oz., 10c.; ¼ lb., 25c.; lb., 90c.

Nichol's Medium Green—Introduced by us in 1883. Color dark green; flesh crisp and tender; medium size; straight and smooth; a real handsome and prolific variety. Pkt., 5c.; oz., 10c.; ¼ lb., 30c.; lb., $1.00.

Early Green Cluster—Short and prickly; bearing in clusters; prolific; fine for bottling. Pkt., 5c.; oz., 10c.; ¼ lb., 30c.; lb., $1.00.

Cool and Crisp—The beautiful green color is all that can be desired. Excellent for pickling or slicing. Pkt., 5c.; oz., 10c.; ¼ lb., 25c.; lb., 90c.

Frame and Forcing Cucumbers

Used in greenhouse growing, for which they are especially adapted.

Rawson's Hothouse

A very fine strain of Cucumbers for forcing. It is an improvement on the White Spine, the fruit being about two inches longer and darker green in color. Pkt., 10c.; ½ oz., 25c.; oz., 45c.; ¼ lb., $1.35; lb., $5.00.

The "Vickery" Forcing

See Page 7 for Full Description

A very fine strain of the White Spine type; is longer than the ordinary White Spine and holds its rich, dark green color well down to the blossom end; immense cropper. A choice variety for hothouse growers; also hard to excel for out-door cultivation. Pkt., 10c.; ½ oz., 25c.; oz., 45c.; ¼ lb., $1.35; lb., $5.00.

Rollison's Telegraph—Grows about 18 inches long; bright green, and is almost seedless. Pkt. of 15 seeds, 25c.

Early Fortune

A fine new variety of White Spine type; the fruit is of uniform size and shape and is of very firm texture, thus permitting long distance shipping. The skin, which is dark green, holds its color remarkably well and therefore remains in slicing condition longer than some of the other standard sorts. Pkt., 5 oz., 10c.; ¼ lb., 30c.; lb., $1.00.

Cumberland—Is of the hardy, White Spine type. The pickles differ from all other hardy sorts in being thickly set with fine spines over almost the entire surface. During the whole period of growth the form is very straight and symmetrical, thus being as choice for slicing as for pickles. Pkt., 5c.; oz., 10c.; ¼ lb., 25c.; lb., 85c.

Curious Cucumbers

Serpent, or Snake Cucumber—A great curiosity. Interesting for children or for exhibition. The Cucumbers grow curled up like a snake, with head protruding; sometimes several feet in length. Pkt., 10c.; ½ oz., 15c.; oz., 25c.

Gherkins (True West India)—Used only for pickles. Pkt., 5c.; oz., 15c.; ¼ lb., 45c.; lb., $1.50.

"Lemon" Cucumber—A new and desirable variety, having a strong resemblance to a lemon in its size, shape and color. It has a thin skin. The crispness, tenderness and sweetness are all that could be desired, and it seems to lack the bitterness of the common Cucumber. Pick just as it turns yellow. Pkt., 10c.; ½ oz., 15c.; oz., 25c.

Japanese Climbing—Vines, extra strong; being a climbing sort, can be grown on trellises or other supports; valuable in small gardens. Very prolific, from 40 to 50 fruits having been counted on single plants. The Cucumbers are long and of fine flavor. Pkt., 5c.; ½ oz., 10c.; oz., 15c.; ¼ lb., 40c.; lb., $1.25.

Arlington White Spine

Berenjena Egg-Plant Eierpflanze

Sow seeds in hotbed or warm greenhouse in March or early in April; if no hotbed is at hand, they may be grown in any light room where the temperature will average 75 degrees. When plants are two inches high, or have formed two rough leaves, transplant them into beds and set 3 or 4 inches apart. Keep beds closed and very warm, shading from direct rays of the sun and giving an abundance of water until the ground is warm and all danger from frost and cold nights is past; then harden the plants by gradual exposure to the sun and air, and increase the supply of water; transplant to the open ground late in May or June, into warm, rich soil, 2 to 3 feet apart each way, according to the richness of the ground. When about a foot high, draw the earth up to the stems. Care should be used in cutting the fruit so as not to disturb the roots of the plants. **One ounce of seed produces about 1000 plants.**

Livingston's Mammoth Purple
(See illustration below of typical fruits grown on "True Blue" trial grounds)

This splendid variety we have obtained by years of the most careful selection and extra cultivation, beginning with a true strain of New York Improved Large Purple. We now have the finest strain of Mammoth Purple Egg-Plant obtainable. It is quite early for such a large sort, a sure cropper, and entirely spineless. The plants are large, vigorous and very productive. The fruit is uniform in color and shape, very large, usually 6 to 8 inches in diameter, but sometimes specimens are grown measuring 10 inches. Skin a handsome dark purple, smooth and glossy. Flesh white, of superior quality. **Selected Seed**—Pkt., 10c.; ½ oz., 20c.; oz., 35c.; ¼ lb., $1.00; lb., $3.50.

Florida High Bush

Black Beauty

From ten days to two weeks earlier than the purple varieties, and of rich, lustrous, purplish black color, and is a distinct sort and a favorite where known. The plants are remarkably healthy in their growth and yield an abundance of large fruits. The fruit is very attractive in appearance. This variety is entirely spineless. Quality the very best. Pkt., 10c.; ½ oz., 15c.; oz., 25c.; ¼ lb., 90c.; lb., $3.25.

New York Improved Large Purple

A leading variety; fruit very large, oval-shaped, smooth, deep purple; flesh white and of good quality. The seed we offer is a very fine strain of this popular sort. Pkt., 10c.; ½ oz., 15c.; oz., 25c.; ¼ lb., 90c.; lb., $3.25.

Florida High Bush

A large fruited purple sort; very popular with Southern growers. Fruit is held well off the ground. A splendid shipper and finds ready sale. The plant is vigorous, quite productive, drought resisting and stands wet weather well. Pkt., 10c.; ½ oz., 15c.; oz., 25c.; ¼ lb., 90c.; lb., $3.25.

Mr. E. Bushyager, Pennsylvania, writes: "I took first premium on Egg Plants grown from your seed, weighing over four pounds, and no special effort made to grow them. They were still growing when cut."

Mr. A. J. Goddard, Florida, writes: "I planted your Mammoth Purple Egg Plant last season. They were the finest Egg Plant I ever saw. Every fruit a beauty and of large size."

Livingston's Mammoth Purple Egg Plant

Kale, or Borecole

Breton   Blatterkohl

Kale, or German Greens, do not form heads, but furnish an abundance of pretty curled leaves that are highly prized as food. Sow from the middle of April to the beginning of May; transplant and cultivate like Cabbage. Will endure considerable frost without injury. **One ounce of seed sows 200 feet of drill. 4 pounds sow an acre.**

Dwarf Green Curled, German Greens, or Sprouts. (See illustration) —Is very dwarf and spreading. The leaves are beautifully curled and of a bright green color. Quite hardy. Pkt., 5c.; oz., 10c.; ¼ lb., 25c.; lb., 75c.

Siberian Kale—Dwarf growth, bluish green leaves. Sow in September, in rows a foot apart, and cultivate the same as Spinach; very hardy and makes an excellent Spring green. Pkt., 5c.; oz., 10c.; ¼ lb., 25c.; lb., 75c.

Ask for Special Prices on Large Quantities of Kale Seed.

Dwarf Green Kale
Growing in Our Trial Grounds

Herbs

Sweet Pot, Culinary, and Medicinal

Herbs delight in a rich, mellow soil. Sow in early Spring in shallow drills 1 foot apart; cover lightly with fine soil, and when up a few inches thin out, or transplant into prepared beds. Care should be taken to harvest properly. Do this on a dry day, just before they come into full blossom; dry quickly in the shade, pack closely in bottles or dry boxes to exclude the air. Varieties in the list marked with an (*) are perennials.

	Pkt.	Oz.		Pkt.	Oz.
Anise	5c	10c	*Rosemary	5c	35c
*Balm	5c	15c	*Rue	5c	25c
*Caraway, lb., 75c.	5c	10c	Saffron	5c	10c
*Catnip, or Catmint	5c	30c	Summer Savory...	5c	10c
Coriander, lb., 60c.	5c	10c	Sweet Basil......	5c	10c
*Fennel, Sweet.....	5c	10c	Sweet Marjoram..	5c	15c
*Horehound	5c	20c	*Thyme	5c	35c
*Lavender, Sweet..	5c	20c	*Winter Savory...	5c	25c
Peppermint 10c		...	*Wormwood	5c	25c

Dill—This herb is used in large quantities in the making of Dill Pickles; also for flavoring vinegar. Pkt., 5c.; oz., 10c.; ¼ lb., 25c.; lb., 85c.

Sage—Sow in rich ground and thin out the plants to stand 15 inches apart. Used for flavorings and dressings. Pkt., 5c.; oz., 15c.; ¼ lb., 50c.; lb., $1.50.

Endive

Endivien Salat   Endibia o Escarola

For an early crop, sow in April in drills 15 inches apart, and later thin the plants to stand 12 inches apart in the row. The main sowings are made in June and July. When nearly full grown, gather up the leaves and tie them by their tips to blanch them. **One ounce of seed will sow 150 feet of drill.**

Fine Green Curled—Hardiest variety; the most desirable for home use or market garden. Deep green leaves, beautifully cut and curled; easily blanched. (See illustration.) Pkt., 5c.; oz., 15c.; ¼ lb., 35c.; lb., $1.15.

Large Green Curled—A hardy, vigorous growing variety with bright deep green leaves. The dense mass of deeply divided leaves formed in the center blanches very readily to rich creamy white. Pkt., 5c.; oz., 15c.; ¼ lb., 35c.; lb., $1.25.

Broad Leaved Batavian—Broad, thick and slightly wrinkled leaves; forms very large heads, which are much used in soups. Pkt., 5c.; oz., 10c.; ¼ lb., 30c.; lb., $1.00.

Gourds

Useful Sorts for the Kitchen-Garden

Gourds are rapid growing and very interesting annual climbers, with ornamental foliage, odd and singular-shaped fruit; being tender, they should not be planted until all danger from frost is over.

Livingston's Extra Fine Mixture of Gourds—A splendid mixture of Gourds, including all the ornamental kinds, both large and small, of various shapes and colors. Pkt., 5c.; ½ oz., 20c.; oz., 35c.

Separate varieties of Gourds are listed on page 99.

Kohl Rabi, (Turnip-Rooted Cabbage)

Col rabano o Nabicol   Kohlrabi

When young and tender they are fine for table use; when matured, they keep splendidly and are excellent for feeding stock. For early use, sow in hotbed, transplant and cultivate like Early Cabbage. For Winter use, plant the middle of June or first of July outdoors in rows 18 inches apart, transplanting or thinning out to 8 inches apart in the rows. **One ounce of seed sows 200 feet of drill.**

Earliest White Vienna—Greenish white outside, with clear white flesh within. Smooth, short leaf; good for forcing; fine in quality. Pkt., 5c.; oz., 20c.; ¼ lb., 50c.; lb., $1.50.

Earliest Purple Vienna—Same in every respect as the Earliest White Vienna, except in the outside color. Pkt., 5c.; oz., 20c.; ¼ lb., 60c.; lb., $2.25.

Leeks

Puerro   Porree oder Lauch

Broad Scotch, or London Flag—A hardy kind; large strong plants with broad leaves. Cultivation the same as for Onions. Pkt., 5c.; oz., 15c.; ¼ lb., 50c.; lb., $1.50.

Large Musselburgh (Carentan or Scotch Champion)— Favorite market sort of enormous size; large, broad leaves; flavor is very mild. Pkt., 5c.; oz., 15c.; ¼ lb., 50c.; lb., $1.50.

Endive—Fine Green Curled

Select Big Boston

Lechuga # Livingston's Superior Lettuce Seed Salat

One Ounce Will Produce About 3,000 Plants

For early Spring use, sow in a seed bed in September or October, and protect through the Winter in cold-frames, or in the South with leaves or litter; or sow in a hot-bed in early Spring. Lettuce plants may also be started very successfully in the house in boxes which are about 4 inches deep. Make soil very fine and firm. Mark off into rows 2 inches apart and ¼ inch deep, into which sow the seed quite thinly; cover with blotting or brown paper fitted into the top of the box. First saturate the paper with water and keep moist until the seed germinates; then remove. Expose the young plants gradually to the light. As soon as the ground outside is dry and warm so that it can be well worked, set out the plants 8 inches apart in the rows. For a later supply, sow seeds in the garden every two weeks from the middle of April until July, choosing varieties according to their heat-resisting qualities. Sow very thinly in rows 18 inches apart, covering seed ¼ inch deep with fine soil, and when well up thin to 12 inches apart in the rows. **One ounce of seed sows 100 square feet; plants 120 feet of row, produces 3,000 plants.**

Selected Big Boston (White Seeded)

(See illustration of 3 typical heads above.) A very desirable large variety for forcing in cold-frames and for outdoor planting. Plants large, hardy, vigorous. Leaves broad, smooth, thin, of a light green color. One of the most popular sorts in the South for shipment to Northern markets. It forms good-sized heads and does particularly well during the cool Fall and Spring months. Heads of a pleasing light-green color, firm and of superior quality. When grown in cold-frames, the heads are not as tight as when grown outside. One of the best market varieties we know. Pkt., 5c.; ½ oz., 10c.; oz., 15c.; ¼ lb., 35c.; lb., $1.25.

The Preferred

A Black-Seeded Big Boston

This variety resembles the old type of Big Boston, but the heads average somewhat larger and the seed is black. It is a fine, early, large heading sort, and is especially adapted to outdoor culture as it withstands hot weather remarkably well. The outer leaves of this variety, however, do not have the bronze tinge of the old Big Boston. Be sure to include at least a packet of this grand, new Lettuce in your order this season. Pkt., 5c.; ½ oz., 10c.; oz., 15c.; ¼ lb., 50c.; lb., $1.75.

Defiance Summer

(Perpignan)—Very long standing and one of the finest large growing Cabbage varieties. Large, solid heads that are very slow in running to seed. The leaves are a beautiful bright green. Pkt., 5c.; ¼ oz., 10c.; oz., 15c.; ¼ lb., 35c.; lb., $1.25.

California Cream Butter

Extra fine sort of this type, forming splendid, large, compact heads in cool weather. Heads round and solid; outside green; within the leaves a rich, creamy yellow color; most delicious and buttery in taste. Pkt., 5c.; ½ oz., 10c.; oz., 15c.; ¼ lb., 35c.; lb., $1.25.

Wonderful (New York)

This splendid mammoth heading and long-keeping variety has been grown to weigh 6 lbs. to the head; frequently weighs 2 or 3 lbs. Heart is solid, of light green color, very sweet, tender and crisp. Long standing, perfect heads may be cut from the same bed for many weeks. Pkt., 5c.; ½ oz, 10c.; oz., 15c.; ¼ lb., 45c.; lb., $1.50.

Wonderful Lettuce

Iceberg

A beautiful Lettuce, with large, curly leaves of a bright, light green, with a very slight reddish tinge at the edges. Handsome heads, unusually solid because of the natural tendency of the large, strong leaves to turn in, which also causes thorough blanching. Crisp, tender and fine flavor. Pkt., 5c.; ½ oz., 10c.; oz., 15c.; ¼ lb., 35c.; lb., $1.25.

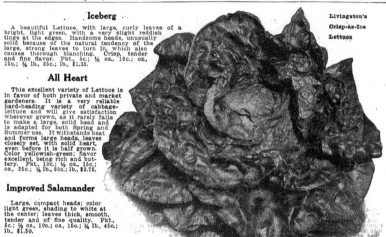

Livingston's
Crisp-as-Ice
Lettuce

All Heart

This excellent variety of Lettuce is in favor of both private and market gardeners. It is a very reliable hard-heading variety of cabbage-lettuce and will give satisfaction wherever grown, as it rarely fails to make a large, solid head and is adapted for both Spring and Summer use. It withstands heat and forms large heads, leaves closely set, with solid heart, even before it is half grown. Color yellowish-green; flavor excellent, being rich and buttery. Pkt., 10c.; ½ oz., 15c.; oz., 25c.; ¼ lb., 80c.; lb., $2.75.

Improved Salamander

Large, compact heads; color light green, shading to white at the center; leaves thick, smooth, tender and of fine quality. Pkt., 5c.; ½ oz., 10c.; oz., 15c.; ¼ lb., 45c.; lb., $1.50.

Mammoth Black-Seeded Butter

Heads large, solid, blanching to white at center; leaves smooth, thick, brittle, tender and extra fine flavored. Long standing. Pkt., 5c.; ½ oz., 10c.; oz., 15c.; ¼ lb., 35c.; lb., $1.25.

Deacon

This Lettuce does not grow as large as some sorts, but has few outside leaves; grows very solid; delicious buttery flavor. Center of head blanches to bright yellow shade; very crisp and tender, remaining so for long time, even in hot weather. One of the finest Summer sorts. Pkt., 5c.; oz., 15c.; ¼ lb., 35c.; lb., $1.25.

Livingston's Crisp-as-Ice

(Introduced by us in 1895)—A most beautiful, attractive Lettuce of the cabbage type. The heads are solid, of immense size when well grown, and so exceedingly crisp, tender and brittle as to fully warrant the name, Livingston's Crisp-as-Ice. The glossy leaves are thick, nicely crimped and curled; the outside leaves are beautifully variegated with dark bronze and green. The heads, when cut open, have a rich, creamy yellow heart. A superior family and home market Lettuce. Pkt., 5c.; ½ oz., 10c.; oz., 15c.; ¼ lb., 50c.; lb., $1.75.

Prize Head

Mammoth heads; even the outer leaves are crisp and tender; light green, tinged with brownish red. Superb flavor; very hardy; very fine for home use; too tender to ship any great distance. Pkt., 5c.; oz., 15c.; ¼ lb., 25c.; lb., $1.25.

May King

This remarkable variety has proven itself capable of satisfying the most exacting requirements that could be made on an early outdoor Lettuce. It is not easily affected by cold or wet weather, grows very quickly and produces, even in poor soil, splendid globular heads very early in the Spring. Pkt., 5c.; ½ oz., 10c.; oz., 15c.; ¼ lb., 45c.; lb., $1.50.

Early White Cabbage

This old reliable variety is very tender, has large, solid, greenish white heads and stands the heat extremely well. Pkt., 5c.; oz., 15c.; ¼ lb., 35c.; lb., $1.25.

Improved Hanson

None more reliable for outdoor cultivation. Heads grow to a remarkable size, resembling that of a flat cabbage. Extremely slow to run to seed. Outer leaves are bright green, inner leaves white and deliciously sweet, tender and crisp. In our trial grounds with dozens of other sorts, it withstood Summer heat among the best. The stock we offer is unsurpassed and gives entire satisfaction. Pkt., 5c.; ½ oz., 10c.; oz., 15c.; ¼ lb., 45c.; lb., $1.25.

Improved Hanson Lettuce

Selected Strain of Grand Rapids—as tested in "True Blue" Trial Grounds

Selected Grand Rapids

Especially adapted for greenhouse culture in Winter; also a good Lettuce to sow outside early in the Spring for family use.

Grand Rapids does not form a head, but makes large, compact bunches of light, attractively curled and fringed leaves. It grows very rapidly and keeps in good marketable condition for a long time after cutting. We take special pains to have our strain of Grand Rapids very true to type and are selling some of the largest greenhouse Lettuce growers their supply annually. Pkt., 5c.; ½ oz., 10c.; oz., 15c.; ¼ lb., 45c.; lb., $1.50.

Livingston's "Bon Ton" Lettuce

Livingston's "Bon Ton"

(See illustration)—This fine variety is of the Simpson Lettuce type, but comes almost absolutely uniform and true. It has a beautiful light green outer head, changing to a rich cream shade at the heart. The leaves are just enough wrinkled to make them beautiful, yet not enough so as to render it difficult to prepare them for the table. It is especially adapted for local markets and family gardens, but for shipping it is not so good on account of its exceeding crispness. Pkt., 5c.; ½ oz., 15c.; oz., 25c.; ¼ lb., 75c.; lb., $2.50.

Early Curled Simpson

A leading early sort; does not head, but forms a compact mass of curly leaves of yellowish green. Matures early; generally grown in cold-frames and as an early crop. Very tender and most crisp. Pkt., 5c.; ½ oz., 10c.; oz., 15c.; ¼ lb., 45c.; lb., $1.50.

Black-Seeded Simpson

Is very popular among market gardeners, and fine for the home table. Forms a large, loose head. Its nearly white, curly leaves are large, thin, very tender and of good quality. Pkt., 5c.; ½ oz., 10c.; oz., 15c.; ¼ lb., 45c.; lb., $1.50.

Denver Market, or Savoy Lettuce—An early head-lettuce for forcing or open ground. Heads are large, solid and of a desirable light green. Leaves are beautifully marked and blistered; crisp, tender and delicious. Pkt., 5c.; ½ oz., 10c.; oz., 15c.; ¼ lb., 45c.; lb., $1.50.

Celery Lettuce, Trianon Cos

This variety is the finest of the Cos or blanching sorts. The long, narrow leaves, which form solid heads, like Early Jersey Wakefield Cabbages, blanch and become snowy white. Excels in quality and crispness. The leaves, when blanched, are stiff like Celery, and can be eaten in the same manner. Pkt., 5c.; ½ oz., 10c.; oz., 15c.; ¼ lb., 45c.; lb., $1.50.

Livingston's Lettuce Mixture

One Sowing Produces Salad for the Season

Contains a grand assortment of decidedly distinct and excellent Lettuces. They mature early, medium and late; some curled and crimped, others produce heads. Colors range from almost pure white, through delicate shades of green and yellow to rich golden. All are delightfully fresh, crisp, tender and of excellent flavor. All sizes, from the small early to the mammoth Summer varieties. Liberal pkt., 10c.; ½ oz., 15c.; oz., 25c.

Special Lettuce Collection

One full-sized packet each of the following: Selected Big Boston, best head Lettuce; Selected Grand Rapids, early curled Lettuce; Deacon, finest "butter head" Lettuce—for 10 cents.

> If seeds are wanted in larger quantities than listed herein, send for our Special Wholesale Price.

Black Seeded Simpson

Musk Melons or Cantaloupes

Melon Almizcleno o Cantalu Zucker Melonen

A rich, sandy soil and good seed are absolutely necessary for success in raising the best Musk Melons. The seed should not be planted until the ground has become dry and warm; plant in hills 6 feet apart each way; old, well-rotted manure should be thoroughly mixed with the soil in each hill and in liberal quantity. Put six to ten seeds in the hill, and when danger from insects is past, leave three or four of the strongest plants only. Musk or Cantaloupe Melons may also be sown in rows, that are made about 6 feet apart, and when the plants are well up thinned to stand in hills 5 to 6 feet apart, just before the plants begin to run. This method insures a good stand of plants in spite of the bugs. If the plants grow very rank, the tips of the leading shoots should be pinched off when about 3 feet long. Cultivate often and not deep. One ounce of seed will plant 60 hills; 2 to 3 pounds will sow an acre.

Yellow-Fleshed Melons

Livingston's Tip-Top

(Introduced by Us in 1892)

TIP-TOP IN QUALITY—TIP-TOP IN APPEARANCE—TIP-TOP IN PRODUCTIVENESS

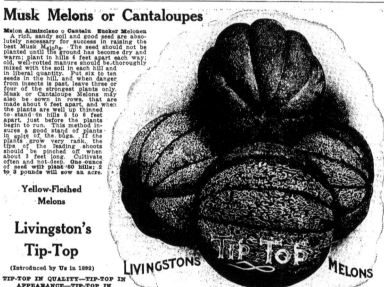

LIVINGSTONS TIP TOP MELONS

This splendid melon has "held its own" for many years against all introductions in the melon line, and no yellow-fleshed melon of which we have any knowledge compares with it in good qualities. The testimony of all who have used **Tip Top** is that every melon produced, whether big or little, early or late, is a good one—sweet, juicy, finest flavor, firm (but not hard) fleshed, and eatable to the outside coating. Its appearance on the market is very attractive—sells on sight. Customers soon learn to pick them out and will have no other variety. Fruit of large size, and flesh attractive bright salmon in color; nearly round, evenly ribbed, moderately netted, very productive. (See illustration.)

PRICE—(Under our True Blue Seal), Superior Stock—Pkt., 5c.; oz., 15c.; ¼ lb., 45c.; lb., $1.50.

G. C. Borcherding, Jackson Co., Ind., writes: "I have a very fine lot of Tip Top Melons—10 acres as good as ever was grown."

Emerald Gem

Ripens early; medium size; nearly round; flesh a delicate light salmon color, very thick, fine grained, and very few melons can compare with it in superb flavor. The rind is thin, dark green, ribbed, slightly netted. One of the best for home use. Pkt., 5c.; oz., 15c.; ¼ lb., 35c.; lb., $1.25.

Burrell Gem

A superior new orange-fleshed shipping melon. Of splendid flavor, sweet and aromatic; oblong in shape, smoothly rounded ends, closely netted and slightly ribbed, dark green skin. The rind is thin, but tough; flesh exceptionally deep rich salmon-orange color. Fruits average 6 by 4 inches. Very fine for marketing. Pkt., 5c.; oz., 10c.; ¼ lb., 25c.; lb., 85c.

Paul Rose (Petoskey)

A successful cross of the Osage with the Netted Gem, which combines the sweetness of the one with the fine netting of the other. A large size Netted Gem with deep orange flesh. Early as the Netted Gem. Adapted to shipping in baskets. Originated with an extensive grower of Northern Michigan. Pkt., 5c.; oz., 10c.; ¼ lb., 30c.; lb., $1.00.

Surprise

Fruit medium to large size, oval, distinctly ribbed, covered with slight patches of netting; skin light yellow. Flesh salmon color. Pkt., 5c.; oz., 10c.; ¼ lb., 30c.; lb., $1.00.

Osage, or Miller's Cream

A favorite salmon-fleshed variety. Large, oval, slightly ribbed and netted; skin is very dark green. Flesh is very thick and sweet flavored, most delicious to the rind. The whole crop is very even and fruit extra heavy, owing to this thickness of the flesh. A great favorite for both market purposes, and the home garden especially. Pkt., 5c.; oz., 15c.; ¼ lb., 35c.; lb., $1.25.

Hoodoo

The vine is quite vigorous, resisting blight better than most other sorts, and is very productive. The fruits vary slightly in shape, averaging nearly round, quite like the Netted Gem. The netting is distinctive in being exceptionally dense and fine, and it extends over practically the entire surface. The rind, although thin, is so very firm that the melons arrive in distant markets in perfect condition. Flesh very thick, highly colored, of finest texture and delicious flavor. Pkt., 5c.; oz., 10c.; ¼ lb., 30c.; lb., $1.00.

The Davis Grand

"The Grand" is 10 to 14 days earlier than the Osage, under the same conditions. It is salmon-fleshed, and is of remarkably uniform in size; the color and flavor of flesh are very fine. It sets fruits near the roots, has a more vigorous vine and therefore resists disease better than most sorts. Fruits average about 6 inches in diameter. Extra choice seeds, saved by the originator especially for us. Pkt., 5c.; oz., 10c.; ¼ lb., 30c.; lb., $1.00.

Banana

Very odd; 18 to 21 inches long. Yellow flesh, blending from bright green to rich salmon. Fragrant, and one of the most delicious of melons. Early. Pkt., 10c.; oz., 15c.; ¼ lb., 45c.; lb., $1.50.

Green-Fleshed Musk Melons

Livingston's Ohio Sugar

The Green Fleshed Tip-Top

Every one who tries this Melon goes into ecstasies over its captivating flavor. It has that delightfully rich aromatic flavor which is so refreshing. For full description of this grand variety see page 8. Pkt., 10c.; oz., 20c.; ¼ lb., 65c.; lb., $2.00.

Burpee's Netted Gem

This very early Cantaloupe melon is one of the most delicious in the whole list. Small and round in shape. Firm, green flesh. Sweet and luscious clear to the rind. Pkt., 5c.; oz., 10c.; ¼ lb., 30c.; lb., $1.00.

Livingston's Market

Has beautiful, close netting; a most vigorous grower; very hardy, withstands drought, blight and bugs remarkably well. Very prolific, uniform in size and has a long fruiting season. Green fleshed; of splendid flavor. Pkt., 5c.; oz., 10c.; ¼ lb., 30c.; lb., $1.00.

Rocky Ford

An improved Netted Gem Melon with sweet, green flesh. In the hands of the Rocky Ford (Colorado) growers it has made that state famous in Eastern markets for melons of unequaled quality. Pkt., 5c.; oz., 10c.; ¼ lb., 30c.; lb., $1.00.

Livingston's Rose Gem

A Fine Green-Fleshed Shipping Musk Melon Named and Introduced by Us in 1896

In shape it is more oval than the original strain, which gives it additional strength to stand long-distance shipping. One of the best and most profitable extra-early melons in existence for market gardeners and shippers, being especially adapted to basket-shipping. Pkt., 5c.; oz., 10c.; ¼ lb., 30c.; lb., $1.00.

Delicious Gold Lined Rocky Ford

An Improved Rocky Ford

Gold Lined Rocky Ford is the result of several years' careful selection. Superior to ordinary type of Netted Gems in size, shape and quality. For full description, see page 8. Pkt., 10c.; oz., 15c.; ¼ lb., 45c.; lb., $1.50.

Extra Early Hackensack

Produces melons two weeks earlier than the well-known Hackensack; heavily netted, and has light green flesh of most delicious flavor; a splendid Cantaloupe melon. Its shape and solidity admit of its being packed very closely in crates for shipment, and it will keep in good condition for several days after picking. Large, fine form; grown also for the home garden very extensively. Pkt., 5c.; oz., 10c.; ¼ lb., 30c.; lb., $1.00.

Acme, or Baltimore Nutmeg

Has a beautiful, heavily netted, green skin; good size; shape is oval, slightly ribbed; flesh thick, green, very finely flavored, smooth. Pkt., 5c.; oz., 10c.; ¼ lb., 25c.; lb., 75c.

Long Island Beauty

A splendid variety, on the style of the Extra-Early Hackensack, but slightly more ribbed. It is of very superior quality, with green flesh. Pkt., 5c.; oz., 10c.; ¼ lb., 25c.; lb., 85c.

Extra-Early Green Citron

The largest of the very early nutmeg melons. Form nearly round; fairly netted; flesh green; quality very fine. Pkt., 5c.; oz., 10c.; ¼ lb., 30c.; lb., $1.00.

Dwarf or Bush Musk Melon

A new and novel variety. Grows in true bush form. For full description, see page 8. Pkt., 10c.

Some Other Good Musk Melons

We can always supply the following varieties at the uniform price of: Pkt., 5c.; oz., 15c.; ¼ lb., 45c.; lb., $1.50 (except where otherwise noted): Perfection, Hackensack, Early Green Nutmeg, and Jenny Lind.

Special Melon Offer

Three of Livingston's Introductions—Tip Top, Rose Gem, and Livingston's Market. One regular packet of each, 10 cents, postpaid.

Write for Special Prices on larger quantities of Musk Melon Seed

Geo. C. Short, Adams Co., Ohio, writes, March 8th: "I have been buying seeds of you regularly for about 20 years and they have always given entire satisfaction. The Hoodoo muskmelon is the finest thing I have ever found."

Livingston's Rose Gem

Sandias **Water Melons** Wassermelonen

Special Prices to Large Growers Who Mention Quantities Required

A light, sandy soil, with good exposure to the sun, is the best situation to plant Water Melons. The ground should be prepared deep, but receive shallow cultivation. Hoe often and very thoroughly. If extra-large Water Melons are desired, for exhibition purposes, leave but one or two on a single vine. Plant in hills 8 to 10 feet apart each way, with a very generous shovelful of well-rotted manure mixed with the soil in each hill. If commercial fertilizer is used, it should contain a large percentage of ammonia and potash. Plant eight or ten seeds in each hill and finally, when danger from insects is past, thin out to three strong plants. Owing to the large size of Water-Melon seeds, the ounce size packets are about right for small gardens. One ounce of seed will plant 20 to 30 hills; four or five pounds will plant an acre.

Tom Watson

An extra long Melon of attractive appearance, uniform in shape and quality. The luscious crimson flesh is "as sweet as honey," melting, and of superb flavor. The average Melon will weigh 35 to 40 pounds and measure about 25 inches long and about 12 inches in diameter. It is very prolific, producing in greatest abundance the large delicious fruits. (See illustration of specimen fruit.) We have great faith in the **Tom Watson** and believe it is one of the very best Water Melons ever offered. Introduced only a few years ago and has already taken a leading place with large melon growers and shippers. Pkt., 5c.; oz., 10c.; ¼ lb., 20c.; lb., 50c. By Express, not paid, 5 lbs., $1.75; 10 lbs., $3.25.

Tom Watson

New Chilian Water Melon

A new white seeded Melon of fine quality, with a reputation already established in the Pacific States, and will, no doubt, become very popular elsewhere when it is better known. Fruits medium size, nearly round or slightly oblong, skin rich, deep green, indistinctly mottled and striped with a lighter shade. Flesh bright red; remarkably fine grained, firm and sweet, quality second to none. A good shipping Melon and keeps exceptionally well. Pkt., 5c.; oz., 10c.; ¼ lb., 25c.; lb., 75c.

Livingston's Orange

Not a new variety, but quite novel and well worth a trial. For full description, see page 8. Pkt., 10c.; oz., 20c.; ¼ lb., 60c.; lb., $2.00.

Florida Favorite

A splendid oblong Melon; ten days earlier than Kolb's Gem. Skin dark green, slightly mottled with still deeper shade; flesh dark red and of the finest flavor and quality. We have a splendid stock of this Melon to offer, at an exceedingly low price. Pkt., 5c.; oz., 10c.; ¼ lb., 15c.; lb., 50c.

Livingston's Nabob

Named and Introduced by Us in 1895.

The Best for Home, Market and Shipping. Deep Red Flesh. Crisp, Sparkling, Deliciously Sweet—A Melon for all sections; equally valuable for Northern or Southern States. Vines hardy, vigorous, healthy and productive; fruit large and heavy (weighing 30 to 60 lbs.), resembling the Kolb Gem in shape, but differing in color, being peculiarly mottled, rather than striped. Rind, thin and very firm; fruit keeps a long time, and is not excelled in shipping qualities; seeds dark buff or dun color; flesh the deepest scarlet, firm, solid and of richest flavor. Does equally well on different soils, in various climates and under unfavorable as well as favorable conditions. Every one praises its many splendid qualities. Pkt., 5c.; oz., 10c.; ¼ lb., 20c.; lb., 60c.

Kleckley Sweets

This splendid Water Melon has certainly become very popular, wherever it has been thoroughly tested. It is of superb, luscious flavor. While the skin is perhaps too thin to admit of the Melons being shipped very great distances to market, it is most desirable to plant for home use or local markets. The Melons themselves are very large, oblong in form, with dark green skin, thin rind, which is very brittle. Flesh is bright scarlet, with solid heart, deliciously crisp, sugary and splendid in every way. The Melons average from 18 to 20 inches in length by 10 to 12 inches in diameter; of handsome appearance; ripens early, and is most desirable for the home garden. Pkt., 5c.; oz., 10c.; ¼ lb., 20c.; lb., 60c. By express not paid, 5 lbs., $2.00; 10 lbs., $3.50.

A. V. Garten, Posey Co., Ind., writes: "We raised the Tom Watson Melon last year for the first time and consider them a success in every way. You cannot recommend them too highly."

L. W. Pierce, Ritchie Co., West Va., writes: "But few Melons are grown in this section, but for productiveness and quality your Livingston's Nabob beats them all."

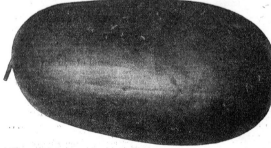

Kleckley Sweets

Watermelons (Continued)

Sweetheart

Sweetheart

A Great Producer—Splendid for Shipping—Very Popular in the South

Another variety of Watermelon, which should not be set aside on account of the many new varieties recently introduced, for it is hard to beat as to quality and productiveness, and is a splendid shipper. It is grown largely in the South for this purpose. The Melons ripen evenly, the vines are vigorous and bear many Melons of splendid size. Oval, very heavy and with a rind which is very thin but firm. In color it is a light green, slightly veined with a darker shade. The flesh is a bright red, very tender and sweet. Sweetheart remains a long time in good condition after being ripe. We have a splendid strain of seed, which will produce a very uniform crop. Pkt., 5c.; oz., 10c.; ¼ lb., 15c.; lb., 45c.

Alabama Sweets

Large, dark green Melons of oblong shape and fine quality; skin faintly netted with lighter green stripes. Flesh bright red, of delicious flavor. A good shipper. Pkt., 5c.; oz., 10c.; ¼ lb., 15c.; lb., 50c.

Georgia Rattlesnake, or Striped Gypsy

Very large, long, smooth and distinctly striped; flesh bright scarlet, very crisp and sweet. Pkt., 5c.; oz., 10c.; ¼ lb., 15c.; lb., 50c.

Halbert Honey

A very sweet, long, dark green variety. Fruits average 18 to 20 inches long, have a thin rind and deep red meat of delightfully delicious flavor; pulp entirely free from stringiness; seeds white. One of the finest for the home garden. Pkt., 5c.; oz., 10c.; ¼ lb., 25c.; lb., 75c.

Girardeau's Triumph

Large size and handsome appearance. Skin bluish-green, flesh dark red, of good quality. Pkt., 5c.; oz., 10c.; ¼ lb., 15c.; lb., 40c.

Cole's Early

Very hardy; a sure cropper for Northern states. Delicate in texture of flesh, which is dark red; rind green, striped with lighter shades, thin and very brittle; of medium size, and nearly round; matures early; especially good for home use. Pkt., 5c.; oz., 10c.; ¼ lb., 25c.; lb., 75c.

Cuban Queen

A large variety weighing 80 pounds and upwards; striped light and dark green; an enormous cropper. Pkt., 5c.; oz., 10c.; ¼ lb., 15c.; lb., 50c.

Duke Jones

(**Jones' Jumbo**)—Color of the skin is a solid dark green; flesh very bright red, particularly sweet, juicy and melting. It grows to a large size. Pkt., 5c.; oz., 10c.; ¼ lb., 15c.; lb., 40c.

Preserving Citron

Red Seeded; most desirable for preserves; flesh solid and white. Pkt., 5c.; oz., 10c.; ¼ lb., 25c.; lb., 75c.

Improved Dixie—Fruit beautifully striped; surpassed by few for shipping or table; long keeper; flesh very red, sweet and juicy. Pkt., 5c.; oz., 10c.; ¼ lb., 15c.; lb., 50c.

Fordhook Early

The earliest and best Melon of good size. Next to Cole's Early in time of ripening, but much larger. Fruit round; outer color, medium green; flesh is bright red, of fine quality. Good shipper. Pkt., 5c.; oz., 10c.; ¼ lb., 15c.; lb., 50c.

McIver's Wonderful Sugar—Large, oblong and handsome; skin shows broad bands of light green, with narrower ones of dark green. Its rose-colored flesh is crisp, very sweet and solid to the center. A choice variety. Pkt., 5c.; oz., 10c.; ¼ lb., 15c.; lb., 50c.

Phinney's Early—One of the first to ripen, of good size and very productive; oblong; rind a distinct mottled color; flesh deep red; quality excellent. Pkt., 5c.; oz., 10c.; ¼ lb., 15c.; lb., 45c.

Kolb's Gem

Probably the most extensively grown for long distance shipping of any Watermelon ever originated. The flesh is bright red and of good flavor. Melons large, of very thick, oval blocky form; skin handsomely marked in stripes of light and dark green. One of the most productive and best keeping Melons. Pkt., 5c.; oz., 10c.; ¼ lb., 15c.; lb., 45c.

Pride of Georgia—A dark green, oval variety; very fine, large, second-early sort; a good shipper and keeper. Pkt., 5c.; oz., 10c.; ¼ lb., 15c.; lb., 45c.

Round Dark Icing—One of the sweetest of all Water Melons. Very solid; thin rind; rich red flesh. Quite early and noted for its splendid quality. Pkt., 5c.; oz., 10c.; ¼ lb., 15c.; lb., 50c.

Harris' Earliest

Large, oval sort with mottled skin. Sweet, tender flesh. Pkt., 5c.; oz., 10c.; ¼ lb., 20c.; lb., 60c.

Seminole—One of the best large, long Water Melons. Early, enormously productive and of most delicious flavor. Of two distinct colors—gray and light green. Pkt., 5c.; oz., 10c.; ¼ lb., 15c.; lb., 45c.

Peerless

One of the best for home gardens and market gardeners, who deliver direct to customers. Medium size; flesh red, tender and delicious. Pkt., 5c.; oz., 10c.; ¼ lb., 15c.; lb., 50c.

Light Icing—Pkt., 5c.; oz., 10c.; ¼ lb., 20c.; lb., 60c.

Grey Monarch—Very large; oblong in shape; crimson, sweet flesh. Pkt., 5c.; oz., 10c.; ¼ lb., 15c.; lb., 40c.

Mountain Sweet—Pkt., 5c.; oz., 10c.; ¼ lb., 15c.; lb., 45c.

Special Prices to Large Users of Watermelon Seed. State quantity.

Ice Cream—True White Seeded

The Great Kitchen-Garden and Home-Market Watermelon

This old standby has too thin a rind for shipping unless packed in straw. We have sold it for many years to our extensive Scioto Valley Watermelon growers, because it has become such a great favorite with Columbus, Ohio Watermelon dealers, and consumers as well. Few varieties, if any, surpass a True Ice Cream Watermelon for quality and productiveness. Ours is not the Peerless Ice Cream, but the original type very carefully selected and is fancy stock. Of good size, medium early, fruit oblong (see illustration); rind light mottled green; bright flesh, and solid to the center; melting and delicious. Free from hard core or stringiness. An elegant sort. Seeds white. Pkt., 5c.; oz., 10c.; ¼ lb., 15c.; lb., 50c.

Ask for prices on larger quantities.

Ice Cream—True White Seeded

Okra, or Gumbo

Very wholesome. The pods, when young, make a fine soup. Plant seed after the ground is warm and dry in drills 3 feet apart, thinning the young plants to 1 foot apart. Make early and late sowings to secure a supply throughout the season. Easy to grow in any good garden soil. One ounce of seed will sow 40 feet of drill.

White Velvet

Distinct in appearance; the large pods are perfectly round, smooth, an attractive velvety white, of superior flavor and tenderness. Plant dwarf, of compact, branching growth; very prolific. Pkt., 5c.; oz., 10c.; ¼ lb., 15c.; lb., 45c.

Perkins' Mammoth

Plant dwarf; are very productive. Produces beautiful, long, slender, deep green pods, which remain tender a long time. An extra choice variety. (See illustration alongside.) Pkt., 5c.; oz., 10c.; ¼ lb., 20c.; lb., 50c.

Kleckley's Favorite

Plants are of compact growth, with many close joints. At each leaf joint develop handsome, smooth, white pods which average 6 inches long, by 1 inch in diameter. They are exceptionally fleshy and tender. Pkt., 5c.; oz., 10c.; ¼ lb., 20c.; lb., 50c.

Perkins Mammoth Okra

Mostaza **Mustard** Senf

Used as a condiment; the green leaves are used as a salad, or cut and boiled like Spinach. Cultivate same as Curled Cress or Pepper-Grass. One ounce of seed will sow 50 feet of drill.

Fordhook Fancy

The plants, of vigorous growth, have beautiful dark-green leaves. It is most productive from early Spring sowings, and stands well, even during the hot Summer months. By making several sowings a few weeks apart, a continuous growth of fresh tender leaves may be had throughout the season. Pkt., 5c.; oz., 10c.; ¼ lb., 20c.; lb., 50c.

Southern Giant Curled—Is highly esteemed in the South, where the seed is sown in the Fall and plants used early in Spring as a salad. Seeds brown. Plants are 2 feet high; enormous bunches. Pkt., 5c.; oz., 10c.; ¼ lb., 15c.; lb., 45c.

Chinese—A giant curled variety with leaves double the size of the ordinary. Pkt. 5c.; oz., 10c.; ¼ lb., 15c.; lb., 45c.

White English—Leaves are light green, mild and tender when young; seed light yellow in color. Pkt., 5c.; oz., 10c.; ¼ lb., 15c.; lb., 40c.

Brown or Black Mustard—More pungent in flavor than the White. Seed black. Pkt., 5c.; oz., 10c.; ¼ lb., 15c.; lb., 40c.

Southern Giant Curled Mustard

Seta **Livingston's Sure-Crop Mushroom Spawn** Champignonbrut

Mushrooms will usually do well almost anywhere if a fairly uniform temperature can be maintained. One pound of Spawn is sufficient for a bed 2 x 6 feet. We receive fresh Spawn several times a year from the best makers. A careful study of one of the books below will help you to be successful.

English Milltrack Spawn

(Livingston's Sure Crop)—Lb., 25c., postpaid. By express or Parcel Post, at buyer's expense; 5 lbs., 65c.; 10 lbs., $1.10; 25 lbs., $2.50; 50 lbs., $4.50.

American Pure Culture Spawn

Produced by the new grafting process from selected and most prolific varieties. Produces a crop very uniform in size and color. Per brick, 35c., postpaid. By express or Parcel Post, at buyer's expense; 5 bricks, $1.00; 10 bricks, $1.85.

MUSHROOMS: HOW TO GROW THEM—Falconer. A book of 169 pages. Cloth, price $1.00.

HOW TO GROW MUSHROOMS—A practical treatise for instruction. Paper cover, 14 pages, price 10c.

Onion Seed Growing—One of Our Specialties

Cebollas **Choice Onion Seed** Zwiebeln

About Quality in Onion Seed

It is many times better to plant no Onions at all than to sow the absolutely worthless stuff sold in so many cases and called Onion seed—and which often is purchased because it was low in price. **Strictly First Quality Onion Seed** can never be low in price. It costs a certain amount to select, sort, keep the bulbs over Winter, and again to perfection in every respect the seed is brought, the more it costs.

Owing to the exceedingly wet season, the Onion seed crop on our farms has not turned out as well as expected and it has been necessary for us to purchase a portion of our stock from Eastern growers to make up the shortage. The parties from whom we get these stocks are thoroughly reliable and we believe our customers will be well pleased with this stock.

"Profitable Onions"

IS THE TITLE OF OUR ONION BOOKLET. It tells all about the old and new method of growing large Onions from seeds, describes the finest strains of American Onions procurable and shows how we produce them. Ohiogrown Onion Seed is the finest that can be grown. Rich soil, ideal climate, constant selection and careful methods in seed production give our Onion strains the characteristics not found in the common article. Whether you raise Onions for profit or for home use, you should plant Livingston's Ohio-grown Onion Seeds for best results with this crop. Read "Profitable Onions" and learn some of "the reasons why." Free to all Onion growers.

Yellow Dutch, or Strasburg

One of the most popular varieties for yellow Onion sets. Ohio grown seed. Pkt., 5c.; ½ oz., 10c.; oz., 20c.; ¼ lb., 70c.; lb., $2.25.

Yellow Flat Danvers

A splendid extra-early yellow Onion for either market or home use. Flatter than the Select Yellow Globe Danvers; long keeper; flesh white, fine quality. Pkt., 5c.; oz., 15c.; ¼ lb., 45c.; lb., $1.50.

Select Danvers Yellow Globe

Of large size, an early and abundant cropper, very thick bulb, flat or slightly convex bottom, full oval top with a small neck and rich brownish yellow skin. We consider our strain of Globe Danvers just right for critical growers. Pkt., 5c.; oz., 25c.; ¼ lb., 80c.; lb., $2.75.

NOTE—If onion seeds are wanted in larger quantities than quoted herein, ask for our Special Wholesale Prices.

Livingston's Selected Ohio Yellow Globe Onion

The Most Perfect Strain of Yellow Globe Onions in Existence; Sure Cropper; Enormous Yielder; Long Keeper; Early

Generally admitted by seeds men and Onion growers everywhere to be the most desirable strain of Globe-shaped Onions in existence. We name it "Ohio Yellow Globe" Onion to designate it from the many strains of Globe Danvers Onion now being offered, and **we consider it to be the most valuable Yellow Onion for all markets in this country**. Besides, to Ohio growers belongs the honor of producing, by many years of painstaking care, selection and cultivation, this, **the finest strain of that extreme type of Globe** now so eagerly sought after by all the best growers, and so deservedly popular in all large Onion markets. Its main points of excellence are: **Distinct and attractive shape; handsome, bright, even color; necks very small; ripens early** and all at once. The firm, solid bulbs are **excellent Winter keepers**, and all that can be desired in size and quality; **enormous yielders**—800 bushels (standard weight) per acre are frequently grown on rich Onion land. This is a superb Onion for all classes of soil (well-enriched) and especially good for all our muck-lands, on account of its quick maturing qualities. Pkt., 5c.; oz., 25c.; ¼ lb., 80c.; lb., $2.75.

Mrs. Chas. Blackburn, Kosciusko County, Indiana, writes: "I must tell you that I had very good success with your seeds, especially your Extra Select Ohio Yellow Globe Onion. We grew for market this year and your Extra Select was a good ways ahead of all others."

Livingston's Ohio Yellow Globe

Southport Yellow Globe

Livingston's Yellow Beauty
(For Full Description, See Page 9)

Very similar except in color to our very popular Brown Beauty Onion, so well known among some of our best gardeners as one of the best for growing small, round, hard, shiny sets or medium-sized Onions from the black seed in one season, and that beats any other sort for keeping up into the Spring (often until June).

Livingston's Yellow Beauty is a bright lemon yellow sort, of very fine and firm texture, especially adapted to growing sets and Onions for late-Spring sales. Pkt., 10c.; ½ oz., 15c.; oz., 25c.; ¼ lb., 75c.; lb., $2.50.

Livingston's Brown Beauty

Grows the Hardest, Smoothest, Roundest, Best Keeping Onion Sets of any Onion on the Market. This splendid Onion was introduced by us in 1900. For nearly 40 years it has been the market gardener's favorite in the Columbus market. Our strain is of our own growing and is the result of years of expert selection and careful cultivation. For Winter and Spring sales or for home use it is hard to beat. Keeps in good shape until late Spring. Ripens early. Fine for Onion set growing. Pkt., 5c.; ½ oz., 10c.; oz., 15c.; ¼ lb., 50c.; lb., $1.75.

Australian Brown

This variety has become very popular, because of its good keeping qualities. The bulb is medium sized nearly spherical, being slightly flattened reddish brown in color and very hard and solid; rather strong flavored. Pkt., 8c.; oz., 15c.; ¼ lb., 30c.; lb., $1.25.

Southport Yellow Globe

Produces large, perfectly globe-shaped bulbs of the same size, handsome form and excellent qualities as the White Globe. The color of the skin is brownish yellow, however, while the flesh is white, fine-grained, crisp and mild. Tops die early and uniformly, insuring well ripened bulbs of good keeping qualities. Our strain is selected for slim neck and uniform ripening qualities, and will surely please the most critical. Pkt., 5c.; oz., 25c.; ¼ lb., 75c.; lb., $2.50.

Gigantic Gibralter
A Splendid Onion of the Prize-Taker Type for the South

Grown alongside of Prizetaker, this excellent type is especially noticeable on account of its bluish green, glossy foliage which resists insect attacks to a remarkable extent. Ripened bulbs greatly resemble Prizetakers in size and shape, but the skin is perhaps a little more of a straw yellow. Worthy of a careful trial. Pkt., 15c.; ½ oz., 20c.; oz., 35c.; ¼ lb., $1.00.

Prizetaker Onion Sets

These Sets make large Onions sooner than any other variety. They grow to enormous size, are quite hardy and fairly good keepers. The outside skin is rich yellow, while the flesh is white. Very mild flavored. ¼ lb., 10c.; lb., 20c.; ½ pk., 60c.; pk., $1.00; bu. (32 lbs.), $3.50.

Mammoth Prize-Taker Onion

Mammoth Yellow Prize-Taker

This is the large, beautiful Spanish variety so often seen in the fruit stores and markets of all large cities. Enormous size—14 to 16 inches in circumference. Although of such great size, it is hardy and a good keeper, as it ripens up hard and firm; very fine grained, and of mild, delicate flavor. The outside skin is rich yellow, while the flesh is white. Has produced more bushels of marketable Onions to the acre than any other variety. Our stock is True American grown seed. Pkt., 5c.; ½ oz., 10c.; oz., 20.c; ¼ lb., 65c.; lb., $2.00.

Southport White Globe

The handsomest Onion grown. Of beautiful silvery-white color, perfectly globe-shaped, uniform in size, averaging 2½ inches in diameter. Flesh firm, fine-grained and of mild, pleasant flavor. Southport White Globe as grown in the rich, black muck soil of our Kirkersville farm comes as beautiful and true to type as we have ever seen it in our thirty years of observation. Most of the bulbs are 3 inches in diameter, of true globe type, solid and with very small neck. We grow a large acreage of bulbs every year, and firmly believe that a better strain than ours does not exist. Crop of Southport White Globe is rather short with us. Pkt., 10c.; oz., 45c.; ¼ lb., $1.35; lb., $4.50.

Southport White Globe

Indiana Silver Skin

This is a strain of pure white Onion that produces round, hard Onion sets, for which we highly recommend it to you. The bulbs, when fully matured, are flat. Pkt., 5c.; ½ oz., 10c.; oz., 30c.; ¼ lb., 85c.; lb., $3.00.

White Portugal, or Silver Skin

Matures very early; rather flat in shape; mild flavor; excellent for Winter; very much esteemed for pickling when small. Pkt., 5c.; ½ oz., 10c.; oz., 30c.; ¼ lb., 85c.; lb., $3.00.

Philadelphia White Silver Skin

A good-sized white variety when full grown, and makes a most beautiful, firm, round, pearly white Onion set, for which it is very extensively grown the country over. Pkt., 5c.; ½ oz., 10c.; oz., 30c.; ¼ lb., 85c.; lb., $3.00.

Southport Red Globe

The handsomest of all the red Onions; large and of perfect shape. Red Globe is the latest of all the Southport Onions, ripening from a week to ten days after the yellows. The bulbs are remarkably uniform in shape, of a rich red color, ripen evenly and yield the largest percentage of marketable Onions. They ripen down hard and solid, keep well, and their beautiful appearance insures a ready market. Southport Red Globe will yield a heavier crop than either the Yellow or White Globe, but as a rule the two last named sorts command higher prices in the East.

Our strain of the Red Globe is absolutely unsurpassed, producing uniformly handsome, thin-necked, hard, richly colored bulbs. They measure about 2½ inches in diameter each way, are of true globe-shape and have unusually brilliant skin. Flesh pinkish white, each section showing its pink coat in form of fine lines. Pkt., 5c.; oz., 25c.; ¼ lb., 75c.; lb., $2.50.

Southport Red Globe

Large Red Wethersfield

This is a standard red variety. Large size; skin deep purplish-red; form round, somewhat flattened; flesh purplish-white. One of the best keepers. Yields enormous crops. Pkt., 5c.; ½ oz., 10c.; oz., 20c.; ¼ lb., 50c.; lb., $1.75.

Extra-Early Red

Medium size, very uniform in shape; smaller than Large Red Wethersfield, but two weeks earlier; an abundant producer; good keeper; desirable for early market. Pkt., 5c.; ½ oz., 10c.; oz., 15c.; ¼ lb., 45c.; lb., $1.50.

Livingston's Choice Onion Sets

Early green Onions are obtained much earlier by setting out sets than by sowing seed. Some of the latter, however, should be sown to follow the crop grown from the Onion Sets. Plant both Onion Sets and Seed as soon as the ground is warm and dry in the Spring.

Large Red Wethersfield

Foreign Varieties of Onions

Extra-Early White Barletta Onion—The very earliest Onion in cultivation. One of the best for pickling, being naturally quite small. Pure white, mild and delicate; adapted for table use; makes an extremely pretty bunch Onion. Pkt., 5c.; oz., 25c.; ¼ lb., 75c.; lb., $2.50.

Mammoth Silver King—Of attractive shape, with silver-white skin and flesh of most agreeable, mild flavor. It matures quite early, coming in just after the Onions grown from sets are gone. Matures to a larger size than other fl varieties. Pkt., 5c.; ½ oz., 10c.; oz., 15c.; ¼ lb., 50c.; lb., $1.75.

Earliest White Queen—A very early pure white, small, flat Onion, 1 or 2 inches in diameter; when sown early in the spring will ripen in July. Very mild flavored. Fine for pickling. Pkt., 5c.; ½ oz., 10c.; oz., 25c.; ¼ lb., 75c.; lb., $2.50.

Neapolitan Maggiajola (Italian May Onion)—A large, flat, beautiful silver-white skinned variety; one of the earliest of all and of very mild flavor. A large and handsome sort. Sells very rapidly, especially in the South. Pkt., 5c.; ½ oz., 40c.; oz., 15c.; ¼ lb., 50c.; lb., $1.75.

Our Set Prices
Our prices are based on the present market rates and are subject to market changes. It is impossible for us to make fixed prices. Lowest market prices on large or small quantities will be given on application at any time. We handle Onion Sets in large quantities. A pound of Sets is equal to a quart by measure. Order Onion Sets early.

Standard Onion Sets (Bottom Sets)
Are grown from seed sown very thick in broad, shallow furrows, and covered about half an inch deep. These are the little Onion Sets so much planted for first Onions. One bushel weighs 32 pounds.

White Onion Sets, ½ lb., 15c.; lb., 25c.; ½ pk., 50c.; pk., 90c.; bu., $4.25.

Red Onion Sets, ¼ lb., 15c.; lb., 25c.; ½ pk., 50c.; pk., 80c.; bu., $3.00.

Yellow Onion Sets, ½ lb., 15c.; lb., 25c.; ½ pk., 50c.; pk., 80c.; bu., $3.00.

White Multipliers
Pure, silvery-white, enormously productive, frequently 20 bulbs in a cluster from a single bulb. Of excellent quality and size for bunching green, or can be ripened for pickling Onions. Remarkably good keeper; very early. ½ lb., 15c.; lb., 25c.; ½ pk., 75c.; pk., $1.25; bu., $4.75 (measured).

Egyptian Winter, or Perennial Tree Onions are sold only in the Fall. See Fall Catalog regarding this variety, as Autumn is the time to set them out.

Perejil **Parsley** Petersilie

Parsley is used for seasoning soups and stews, for salads, and is also very universally used for garnishing, also for ornamental borders in the flower garden; succeeds best in a rich, mellow soil. As the seeds germinate very slowly, three or four weeks sometimes elapse before it makes its appearance. It should be sown early in the Spring. **One ounce of seed will sow about 150 feet of drill.**

Livingston's Exquisite

One of the main features in any variety of Parsley is the ornamental effect of its leaf when used for garnishing. This is a very strong point in our Livingston's Exquisite, with its very elegant and closely curled leaves of beautiful dark green, while the flavor is all that could be desired. As a pot plant for Winter decoration it is simply "exquisite." **The finest strain of Curled Parsley that has ever come under our notice.** Pkt., 5c.; ½ oz., 10c.; oz., 15c.; ¼ lb., 50c.; lb., $1.75.

Fine Double Curled

Dwarf, beautifully curled; very fine variety. Pkt., 5c.; oz., 10c.; ¼ lb., 25c.; lb., 75c.

Champion Moss Curled

More densely crimped and curled than some other sorts. Pkt., 5c.; oz., 10c.; ¼ lb., 20c.; lb., 50c.

Plain

Much used for soups and stews; rather stronger in flavor than other varieties. Pkt., 5c.; oz., 10c.; ¼ lb., 15c.; lb., 45c.

Hamburg, or Turnip Rooted

A rooted variety; the fleshy roots resemble Parsnips, and are used in u and stews. Pkt., 5c.; oz., 15c.; ¼ lb., 40c.; lb., $1.2½0 ps

Parsley—Livingston's Exquisite

H. J. Mesmer, Des Moines Co., Iowa, writes: "Your seeds have proven very satisfactory and I am well pleased with the results."

Mrs. R. J. Liggett, De Witt Co., Ills., writes: "I have bought seeds from your firm every year for forty years."

H. L. Wysor, Pulaski Co., Va., writes: "The Seeds ordered of you arrived alright and I thank you for your generous treatment. I shall hereafter purchase all my seeds from you, as I believe your goods are reliable and true to name."

J. H. Coombs, New Jersey, writes as follows: "I bought Cabbage seed from you called the Volga last year and they did fine. I put out 2,000 plants on July 20th and every one of them made a head weighing from 8 to 14 pounds. My neighbors thought they were the finest they ever saw."

Chirivia **Parsnips** Pastinake

Sow as early in the Spring as the weather will permit, in drills 15 inches apart and half an inch deep, in rich, well-manured ground, well dug. Cultivate similar to Carrots, and thin to 6 inches apart in the rows. The roots improve by being left in the ground until Spring, securing enough in pits or the cellar for Winter use. **One ounce of seed to 200 feet of drill, 5 or 6 pounds for an acre.**

Large Sugar, or Hollow Crown

(Improved Guernsey)
White, smooth, sugary, excellent flavor, easily harvested. (See illustration.) Pkt., 5c.; oz., 10c.; ¼ lb., 25c.; lb., 75c.

Long White Dutch

Roots are very long and smooth; one of the best varieties for general use. Pkt., 5c.; oz., 10c.; ¼ lb., 20c.; lb., 65c.

Livingston's Choice Peas

Chicaros o Guisantes **Livingston's Choice Peas** Erbsen

Peas mature early, when in a light, rich soil. For the general crop, a rich, deep loam, or clay, would be best. Peas thrive better if the ground has been manured for a previous crop, but if the ground is poor and requires enriching, use well-rotted manure; and for the dwarf varieties you can hardly make the soil too rich. When grown as a market crop, Peas are seldom staked or bushed, but are sown in single rows 3 to 4 inches deep, the depth depending on the time of sowing, nature of the soil, as well as the variety. Wrinkled varieties are not as hardy as the smooth sorts, and if planted early should have dry, warm soil, and not planted deep, or they are liable to rot in the ground. These wrinkled varieties are, however, the sweetest and best flavored. Rows for planting should be from 2½ to 3½ feet apart, according to the kind, soil and manner of culture desired. When grown in the kitchen garden, it is best to sow the seed in double rows, 6 to 8 inches apart, the tall sorts requiring brush. Commence sowing early varieties as soon as the ground can be worked in the Spring, and continue, for a succession, every two weeks up to end of June, discontinuing until the middle of July, when a good crop can sometimes be secured by sowing an extra-early sort. **Two pounds sow 100 feet of row; 1½ bushels for an acre.**

Livingston's First-in-Market

Excellent variety, very profitable for the gardener and shipper, because it ripens uniformly, so that almost every pod may be gathered at one picking. The pods are handsome, straight and full of medium-sized round Peas of superior quality; it is immensely productive for such an early sort. Pkt., 10c.; ½ lb., 15c.; lb., 25c.; 2 lbs., 50c.; ¼ pk. (7½ lbs.), 75c.; pk., $1.40; bu., $5.25.

Laxtonian Pea

This is a giant podded, early, dwarfed Pea—the same size and quality as Gradus, but requires no supports. We regret our crop of Laxtonian failed. And we only carried over a small quantity. The Pioneer will be found quite similar and should be given a liberal trial. We offer the Laxtonian while they last. Pkt., 15c.; ½ lb., 25c.; lb., 40c.; 2 lbs., 75c.

Thomas Laxton

Pea Prices

Our Pea Prices include postage up to and including two pounds. If any of the larger amounts are wanted sent by mail it will be necessary to remit extra to cover postage at the Parcels Post rates. See page 3 for table of rates. If for any reason you are doubtful as to the amount and will ask your Postmaster, giving the weight of your order, he will cheerfully give you the exact amount. **Ask for prices on Peas in larger quantities.**

Livingston's Selected Extra-Early Alaska

This fine Pea has become a standard extra-early market variety, and is the earliest of all blue Peas; grows about 30 inches tall; very uniform in maturing the crop; of excellent quality, and retains its desirable color after cooking. Our strain is especially fine. Pkt., 10c.; ½ lb., 15c.; lb., 25c.; 2 lbs., 50c.; ¼ pk. (7½ lbs.), 85c.; pk., $1.50; bu., $5.50.

Thomas Laxton
A Fine Wrinkled Pea

The vine grows about 3 feet high, much like that of the Gradus, or Prosperity, but more hardy and greatly more productive. Pods large, long, with square ends, similar to but larger, longer and handsomer than those of the Champion of England, and fully as uniformly well filled. The green Peas are very large, fine colored and unsurpassed in splendid quality. We are certain that this Pea needs only to be known to become one of the most popular sorts for the market gardener and home garden. Pkt., 10c.; ½ lb., 20c.; lb., 35c.; 2 lbs., 65c.; ½ pk. (7 lbs.), $1.25; pk., $2.15; bu., $8.00.

Pioneer

One of the latest introductions and bids fair to take a prominent place in the lists. For full description see page 11. Pkt., 15c.; ½ lb., 20c.; lb., 35c.; 2 lbs., 65c.; ½ pk. (7 lbs.), $1.25; pk., $2.25; bu., $8.50.

Little Marvel

This Pea has been rightly named. It is an early wrinkled Pea with all the good qualities of American Wonder, Premium Gem and Nott's Excelsior and some of its own besides. It grows about 15 inches tall and bears heavily. There is no earlier wrinkled Pea and the quality satisfies everybody. Our sales increase yearly because Little Marvel never disappoints. We hope every customer who grows Peas will buy it this year and they will thank us for suggesting it.

Large pkt., 10c.; ½ lb., 15c.; lb., 30c.; 2 lbs., 55c.; ½ pk. (7 lbs.), $1.00; pk., $1.75; bu., $6.00.

Livingston's Prolific Early Market

For length of pod, number of Peas in a pod and number of pods to a vine, this is a wonder. It is one of the smooth-seeded, extra-early varieties which can be sown the first thing in the Spring, and for the type of Pea the quality is all that can be desired. It's a bonanza for market gardeners. We first offered it in 1901 and we still offer it as being one of the really valuable varieties for first early. Try it and see if you don't agree with us. Large pkt., 10c.; ½ lb., 15c.; lb., 30c.; 2 lbs., 55c.; ½ pk. 7½ lbs.), $1.00; pk., $1.75; bu., $6.00.

Prolific Early Market

Little Marvel

Our Packets of Peas are Exceptionally Large

Potlatch

A new variety of great value, growing 15 to 18 inches high. Very large pods, measuring up to 6 inches in length. Vines and pods are a rich, dark green, and pods contain 8 to 9 immense peas. The plant is a vigorous grower, the pods being borne in pairs. It is a great producer and the quantity of Peas which shell out is surprising. One of the most promising new varieties. Pkt., 10c.; ¼ lb., 15c.; lb., 30c.; 2 lbs., 60c.; ½ pk. (7 lbs.), $1.00; pk., $1.90; bu., $7.00.

American Wonder

A leading dwarf wrinkled Pea; esteemed for earliness, productiveness, flavor and quality. Strong and robust in habit, growing about 10 inches high, and produces a profusion of good-sized pods, which are fairly packed with the finest flavored Peas. Has always been a great favorite for the home garden. Pkt., 10c.; ¼ lb., 15c.; lb., 30c.; 2 lbs., 60c.; ½ pk. (7 lbs.), $1.20; pk., $2.00; bu., $7.50.

Premium Gem

A very fine Extra-Early Dwarf Pea of Little Gem type, on which it is a decided improvement; pods are larger and more productive. Pkt., 10c.; ¼ lb., 15c.; lb., 30c.; 2 lbs., 55c.; ½ pk. (7 lbs.), $1.00; pk., $1.75; bu., $6.00.

Nott's Excelsior
(See Illustration)

This is one of the standard high-grade Peas that have established themselves with gardeners so firmly that many will take no other variety for its season. Its quality is fine and for a wrinkled Pea it is hardy and thoroughly reliable. It does not require staking and the pods ripen evenly, making it extremely valuable for home and market use. Our sales of this variety are always large. Pkt., 10c.; ¼ lb., 15c.; lb., 30c.; 2 lbs., 55c.; ½ pk. (7 lbs.), $1.00; pk., $1.75; bu., $6.00.

Nott's Excelsior

Sutton's Excelsior

Gradus or Prosperity

A Large Early Wrinkled Pea. Exceedingly Sweet, Tender and Luscious, Fairly Melting in Your Month.

(See Illustration Below)

This extra fine variety combines earliness with large size in a green wrinkled Pea. In earliness the Gradus follows closely after the First Earlies, being only two or three days later than Livingston's First-in-Market. In height, they grow about 2½ feet. The vine is very robust, bearing the handsome, large pods profusely all over the vine. The pods are long and straight; and well filled with luscious sweet peas of superb quality. No pea of recent introduction has attracted so much attention as the Gradus, or Prosperity, especially with the market men, for whom it has been a money-maker from the start. It produces most uniformly large pods, measuring 4 to 4½ inches in length, and well filled with large, handsome peas. It is certainly a very fine variety. Pkt., 10c.; ¼ lb., 15c.; lb., 35c.; 2 lbs., 65c.; ½ pk. (7 lbs.), $1.25; pk., $2.15; bu., $8.00.

Lee E. Chamberlain, Columbiana Co., O., writes March 11, 1915: "Enclosed please find my order for seeds. I have always found your seeds gave me the best satisfaction, so that I come back every spring."

Joel M. Haskins, Athens Co., O., writes March 20, 1915: "The potatoes came to hand yesterday and they are surely fine."

Gradus or Prosperity

Sutton's Excelsior

A fine wrinkled Pea quite hardy and may be planted with the hard-seeded varieties. The plants are dwarf (about 15 inches high); of vigorous growth and very productive. The quality is all that could be desired. Sutton's Excelsior produces larger and broader pods than most early varieties and it matures within a few days of Nott's Excelsior. It is a desirable variety for home and market use and is one of the varieties which is well worth growing. Pkt., 10c.; ¼ lb., 15c.; lb., 30c.; 2 lbs., 55c.; ½ pk. (7 lbs.), $1.00; pk., $1.85; bu., $6.50.

Livingston's Home Collection of the Three Best Peas for the Private Garden

The varieties contained in this collection are all superior wrinkled sorts—sweet, tender and delicious. It contains early, medium and late sorts, and will supply the table with a succession of luscious Peas for a long period.

Thomas Laxton—Bears large pods literally packed with luscious Peas early in the season.

Telephone—The largest of all late Peas and a tremendous cropper of handsome pods and peas.

Little Marvel—A fine dwarf early variety; very prolific and of excellent quality.

One 10c. packet each of **3 Best Peas, 25c.;** ½ pound each, 65c., not postpaid.

Ask for Special Prices on Larger Quantities of Peas

Buttercup

A fine new medium early sort. For full description
see page 11. Pkt., 15c.; ½ lb., 20c.; lb.; 35c.; 2 lbs., 65c.;
½ pk. (7 lbs.), $1.25; pk., $2.15; bu., $8.00.

Quite Content

A new English variety which is probably the largest
podded of all Peas. For full description see page 11.
Pkt., 15c.; ½ lb., 20c.; lb., 35c.; 2 lbs., 65c.; ½ pk. (7
lbs.), $1.25; pk., $2.25; bu., $8.50.

McLean's Advancer

The leading Pea for second-early. Excellent flavor,
very productive. This Pea is used very extensively by
market gardeners and canners on account of its great
productiveness and its exceedingly fine flavor. It is a
wrinkled variety, grows about two feet in height. Has
long pods, and well filled to the end. Ripens so uniformly that the vines can usually be picked clean in
two pickings. Pkt., 10c.; ½ lb., 15c.; lb., 30c.; 2 lbs.,
55c.; ½ pk. (7 lbs.), $1.00; pk., $1.85; bu., $6.50.

Improved Stratagem

A favorite late variety with market gardeners and
for the kitchen garden. Strong vines, immense pods,
large Peas, heavy cropper. The vines are strong, vigorous and covered with immense pods, many of which
measure nearly 5½ inches in length and containing as
high as ten large, richly flavored, wrinkled Peas. Vines
very strong and needing but slight support. The vine
branches at the surface of the soil, two generally of
equal vigor growing to a height of 2 to 2½ feet. The
quality is excellent. Pkt., 10c.; ½ lb., 20c.; lb., 35c.;
2 lbs., 65c.; ½ pk. (7 lbs.), $1.25; pk., $2.25; bu., $8.50.

Alderman   Telephone

Alderman

The Alderman is a late wrinkled variety growing four
to five feet high and bearing freely large pods of a dark
green color. These pods each contain eight or nine large
dark green Peas of unsurpassed flavor. Alderman will
eventually take the place of Telephone in markets requiring dark green pods and Peas. Pkt., 10c.; ½ lb., 15c.; lb.,
30c.; 2 lbs., 60c.; ½ pk. (7 lbs.), $1.00; pk., $1.90; bu., $7.00.

Livingston's Prolific Giant-Podded Sugar Peas

Excels all other Sugar Peas in size, productiveness and
quality. Vines are about 30 inches in height. The pods
are gigantic in size, broad, sweet and tender, extremely
fleshy and equal to the best Snap Beans for cooking pods
and all. This is a very decided improvement in Sugar
Peas. (See illustration.) Pkt., 10c.; ½ lb., 15c.; lb., 30c.;
2 lbs., 60c.; ½ pk. (7 lbs.), $1.20; pk., $2.00; bu., $7.50.

White Marrowfat

Grows 4 to 5 feet in height. Pods large, round, light
green and well filled. Excellent for Summer crop, but of
inferior quality. Pkt., 10c.; lb., 20c.; 2 lbs., 50c.; ½ pk.
(7 lbs.), 75c.; pk., $1.40; bu., $5.25.

For Nitragin Inoculator see page 75.

Carter's Telephone

The favorite late variety **for the market gardener.
Extra** large pods. Vine large, coarse leaves, height about
4 feet. The pods are very large and filled with immense
Peas. Tender, sweet and of splendid quality and flavor.
The stock we offer has been selected with great care, and
are sure will give satisfaction to the most exacting
grower. Pkt., 10c.; ½ lb., 20c.; lb., 35c.; 2 lbs., 65c.; ½
pk. (7 lbs.), $1.25; pk., $2.15; bu., $8.00.

Champion of England

An old variety, but considered by many the best tall-
growing sort. To do its best it needs support. A prolific
bearer of large pods, well filled with large wrinkled Peas.
In quality it has never been surpassed. 5 feet high. Pkt.,
10c.; ½ lb., 15c.; lb., 25c.; 2 lbs., 50c.; ½ pk. (7 lbs.),
75c.; pk., $1.40; bu., $5.00.

Livingston's Giant Podded
Sugar Pea

Pimento **Livingston's Choice Peppers** Pfeffer

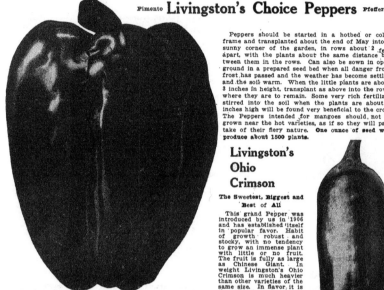

Peppers should be started in a hotbed or cold-frame and transplanted about the end of May into a sunny corner of the garden, in rows about 2 feet apart, with the plants about the same distance between them in the rows. Can also be sown in open ground in a prepared seed bed when all danger from frost has passed and the weather has become settled and the soil warm. When the little plants are about 3 inches in height, transplant as above into the rows where they are to remain. Some very rich fertilizer stirred into the soil when the plants are about 6 inches high will be found very beneficial to the crop. The Peppers intended for mangoes should not be grown near the hot varieties, as if so they will partake of their fiery nature. **One ounce of seed will produce about 1500 plants.**

Livingston's Ohio Crimson

The Sweetest, Biggest and Best of All

This grand Pepper was introduced by us in 1906 and has established itself in popular favor. Habit of growth robust and stocky, with no tendency to grow an immense plant with little or no fruit. The fruit is fully as large as Chinese Giant. In weight Livingston's Ohio Crimson is much heavier than other varieties of the same size. In flavor it is the mildest we have ever known, as the flesh, and even the seeds, may be eaten from the hand without any of the fiery sensation. Growers tell us their customers prefer it to others for making mangoes. Livingston's Ohio Crimson has been thoroughly fixed in type for years. Pkt., 10c.; ¼ oz., 25c.; oz., 45c.; ¼ lb., $1.35; lb., $4.50.

Livingston's Ohio Crimson Pepper

Mrs. A. S. Showman, Licking Co., Ohio, writes: "The Ohio Crimson Peppers I grew from seed bought from you were the largest I ever saw. People who purchased them of me on market were very anxious to know where I got the seed, and how I grew them so large."

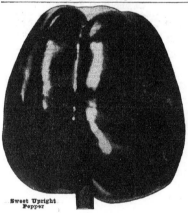

Improved Thick Long Red Pepper

Livingston's Improved Thick Long Red

A great improvement on the ordinary Long Red Cayenne. Pods of about the same length, but much thicker, and has two to three times as much meat; averaging about 1 inch in diameter at the stem end. They are grown almost exclusively for some markets. Exceedingly prolific; are very hot and have handsome bright red pods. Produced early in the season while prices are high. **See illustration of natural-sized pod.** Pkt., 10c.; ½ oz., 20c.; oz., 30c.; ¼ lb., $1.00; lb., $3.50.

Sweet Upright

This sort is more productive than the large sweet Peppers. The fruits are just the right size to serve whole, not large, about 3 inches long, 2½ inches to 3 inches across. The flesh is quite thick, mild and sweet, and the skin very tender. The color of the ripe fruit, both skin and flesh, is a rich, brilliant scarlet. Grows upright on the stem, hence its name. Pkt., 5c.; ½ oz., 15c.; oz., 25c.; ¼ lb., 75c.; lb., $2.50.

Sweet Upright Pepper

Pepper (Continued)

Livingston's Prolific Yellow

Fruits bright yellow when ripe; just right size for stuffing; very productive. Full description page 10. Pkt., 10c.; ½ oz., 25c.; oz., 45c.; ¼ lb., $1.35; lb., $4.50.

Sweet Salad

Bright red; thick fleshed; best for salads. Full description page 10. Pkt., 10c.; ½ oz., 30c.; oz., 50c.; ¼ lb., $1.60; lb., $6.

Mammoth Ruby King Pepper

Our **Mammoth Ruby King Pepper is one of the largest and finest mild Red Peppers** in cultivation. Not only is it very productive for so large a Pepper, but its splendid size and handsome appearance make it sell most readily in any market, and for the kitchen garden it is a special feature. The plants are vigorous, stocky and dwarf; very bushy, growing about 2 feet in height. They are well branched; thickly set with enormous fruits, some 4 to 6 inches long by 3 to 4 inches thick. When ripe, they are of a beautiful bright, glossy ruby red color, and are always remarkably mild and very pleasant to the taste if not grown too close to the hot varieties. They can even be sliced and eaten with salt and vinegar (like Tomatoes or Cucumbers), and are most appetizing. Pkt., 5c.; large pkt., 10c.; ½ oz., 15c.; oz., 25c.; ¼ lb., 75c.; lb., $2.50.

Giant Golden King—An exact counterpart, except in color, of the famous Ruby King. Bears large, handsome fruits of most attractive bright yellow. Flavor mild and pleasant. Pkt., 5c.; ½ oz., 15c.; oz., 25c.; ¼ lb., 75c.; lb., $2.50.

Neapolitan

This is the earliest of the large, mild red Peppers, grows about two feet high and is completely laden with fine Peppers about four inches long and four and one-half in circumference. Worthy of a place in every garden. Pkt., 5c.; ½ oz., 15c.; oz., 25c.; ¼ lb., 75c.; lb., $2.50.

Sweet Mountain

Very thin skinned, sweet and mild flavored; much used for stuffing. Pkt., 5c.; ½ oz., 10c.; oz., 20c.; ¼ lb., 70c.; lb., $2.25.

Mammoth Ruby King

Large Bell, or Bull Nose

An early variety and of mild flavor; the skin is quite thick and fleshy; of medium size; is very popular. Pkt., 5c.; ½ oz., 20c.; oz., ¼ lb., 70c.; lb., $2.25.

Long Red Cayenne—Four inches long and one-half to three-quarters inches in diameter; flesh thick and hot. Pkt., 5c.; ½ oz., 15c.; oz., 20c.; ¼ lb., 70c.; lb., $2.25.

Small Cayenne (Red Chili)—Pods 1½ to 2 inches long; very hot; used for making pepper sauce. Pkt., 5c.; ½ oz., 15c.; oz., 25c.; ¼ lb., 80c.; lb., $2.75.

Cherry Red—Fruit small, round, rich scarlet and extremely hot. Pkt., 5c.; ½ oz., 15c.; oz., 25c.; ¼ lb., 80c.; lb., $2.75.

"Red Hot" Mixture—Includes a great number of small and ornamental sorts, which are indeed just as "hot as fire." Pkt., 10c.; 3 pkts., 25c.

Mixed Mango Peppers—A choice mixture containing a very large number of varieties suitable for stuffing and mangoes. Pkt., 10c.; 3 pkts. for 25c.

Chinese Giant

(See illustration.) One of the very largest Mango Peppers. **Its mammoth size, splendid shape, beautiful rich, glossy bright red flesh and mild flavor** all lead us to speak of it in words of commendation. Its strong, bushy plants, which are literally loaded with the splendid large fruits, begin bearing quite early. Has few seeds, hence necessarily high in price. Pkt., 10c.; ½ oz., 25c.; oz., 45c.; ¼ lb., $1.35; lb., $4.50.

Mr. D. Oliphant, Pinellas Co., Fla., writes: "I wish to say that the seed I received from you was the best I have ever used. The Chinese Giant Pepper passed anything I have ever grown. It had the largest Peppers with the best flavor and the most fruits of any Peppers I have ever tried."

Chinese Giant

Livingston's Prize Winning Pumpkins
Calabazas   Speise Kurbisse

Pumpkins are not so particular in regard to soil as Melons or Cucumbers, but in other respects are cultivated in a similar manner. Sow in the month of May, when you plant your corn. Make hills, the same as you do for Squashes, but do not make the hills too close; you will find that 8 or 10 feet apart each way is best. It is preferable to grow Pumpkins in the field, and not in the garden, as they always mix badly with the Squashes and other vines. You will, of course, sow some amongst your late corn, putting in a few seeds, say, every third or fourth hill. This will give you plenty for the table, and your stock the coming Winter. **One ounce of seed will plant 15 hills; 3 to 4 lbs. plant an acre.**

Large Sweet, or Kentucky Field

Large, round, flattened, hardy and productive. 1 to 2 feet in diameter. It has thick flesh of extra fine quality and is a splendid sort for family and market use, also grown largely for stock feeding. Pkt., 5c.; oz., 10c.; ¼ lb., 25c.; lb., 75c.

Small Sweet or Sugar

This is the small, sweet Pumpkin that has made the New England States famous for their pumpkin pies. It is a very fine grained, most deliciously sweet-flavored sort. Splendid keeper. They average about 10 inches in diameter. Deep orange-yellow color. Pkt., 5c.; oz., 10c.; ¼ lb., 20c.; lb., 60c.

Mammoth Tours—Immense size, often weighs 100 pounds. Oblong, skin green; good exhibition sort or for feeding stock. Pkt., 5c.; oz., 10c.; ¼ lb., 25c.; lb., 85c.

Genuine Mammoth, or True Potiron

(King of the Mammoths, a Jumbo Pumpkin)

Form like immense Nutmeg Musk Melon with depressed ends, slightly ribbed, often 3 feet or more in diameter and weighs over 200 lbs. Salmon color; flesh bright yellow; fair quality. Pkt., 5c.; oz., 10c.; ¼ lb., 30c.; lb., $1.00.

Winter Luxury

Or **Livingston's Pie Squash** is listed and fully described among Squashes on page 55. Thick, sweet flesh of elegant flavor make this sort a universal favorite for pies. Pkt., 5c.; oz., 15c.; ¼ lb., 40c.; lb., $1.25.

Tennessee Sweet Potato—Bell shape; medium size, thick flesh, skin creamy white, fine grained, sweet, delicious. Very fine for pies. Pkt., 5c.; oz., 10c.; ¼ lb., 25c.; lb., 75c.

Large Sweet Cheese

Best for canning. Has heavy, thick sweet meat; large, round, flattened variety, with creamy-buff skin. An excellent keeper, and very productive; good quality. Pkt., 5c.; oz., 10c.; ¼ lb., 25c.; lb., 75c.

Common Yellow Field

Yankee Cow Pumpkin, or Connecticut Field—The common Yellow Field Pumpkin, so very largely cultivated by our farmers for stock feeding; very productive. Pkt., 5c.; oz., 10c.; ¼ lb., 25c.; lb., 75c.

Japanese Pie

Crooked neck; quality fine; very productive; ripens early; medium size. Excellent for pies. Pkt., 5c.; oz., 10c.; ¼ lb., $1.00.

Livingston's Pumpkin Mixture

One Sowing Furnishes Pumpkins for the Season. Especially offered to those who wish to grow a grand collection of Pumpkins for Fall fairs. **For 10c. you obtain seed of every variety in list.** Large pkt., 10c.; oz., 20c.; ¼ lb., 60c.

Rhubarb, or Pie Plant
Ruibarbo   Rhabarber

Requires a deeply cultivated and thoroughly manured soil. Sow the seed early in the Spring, in rows 1 foot apart; the second year after planting plants can be removed in the Autumn to the permanent place in the garden allotted to them. Plant the roots 2 feet apart each way. **One ounce of seed gives 500 plants.**

Victoria—In general use for market and home garden. Pkt., 5c.; oz., 10c.; ¼ lb., 30c.; lb., $1.00.

Rhubarb Roots are offered on page 70.

Large Sweet Cheese Pumpkins

Rabanitos **Radishes** Radieschen

All varieties thrive best in light, sandy loam. For early use, sow in the hotbed in February, giving plenty of ventilation, or outside in the garden, in drills, as soon as the soil is warm and dry, covering the seed about half an inch deep. Sow every two weeks from March until September, for a succession of crisp Radishes for continued use. Radishes must grow rapidly to be crisp, mild flavored and tender. We offer a very fine assortment. **One ounce of seed will plant 100 feet of drill; 8 to 10 pounds for an acre.**

Round and Olive-Shaped Sorts

Rosy Gem

(See illustration above)—One of the earliest; is perfectly globular; a rich, deep, brilliant scarlet at top, blending into pure white at the bottom, exceedingly tender and crisp; most delicious; desirable for market or home garden. A fine variety. Pkt., 5c.; oz., 10c.; ¼ lb., 25c.; lb., 85c.

Scarlet Turnip White Tip

Handsome, bright scarlet, with white tip; most attractive, quality splendid. Similar to Rosy Gem. Desirable for outside growing. Pkt., 5c.; oz., 10c.; ¼ lb., 20c.; lb., 80c.

Crimson Giant.—Pkt., 5c.

Sparkler

A splendid variety of the Scarlet Turnip White Tipped type, but showing more white, practically the whole lower part being white, while the upper half is a bright scarlet. It makes a fine show on the market bench and is of good quality. Pkt., 5c.; oz., 10c.; ¼ lb., 25c.; lb., 75c.

Scarlet Globe

This splendid globe Radish is the very finest early strain of the round, bright red Radishes. Nothing can surpass its table excellence or its beauty. The skin is a bright scarlet; flesh pure white, crisp, tender and of delicious quality. Fine for market gardeners who want a large first-early forcing Radish. Pkt., 5c.; oz., 10c.; ¼ lb., 25c.; lb., 85c.

Crimson Giant

A variety combining earliness and great size. It grows much larger than other extra-early varieties, but does not become pithy, even when fully twice as large in diameter and a week older; beautiful crimson-carmine; turnip shaped; flesh firm, crisp and tender. We recommend it for outdoor garden planting as well as for greenhouse forcing. Pkt., 5c.; oz., 10c.; ¼ lb., 30c.; lb., $1.00.

Early Scarlet Turnip

Very early, small, round Radish; entire Radish is of a rich scarlet color. This splendid variety has always been a great favorite with market gardeners and for kitchen garden alike. Pkt., 5c.; oz., 10c.; ¼ lb., 25c.; lb., 75c.

Non Plus Ultra (or Fireball)

The earliest forcing Radish in cultivation. A pretty little round Radish; deep rich scarlet in color; tops very small; crisp, tender, white flesh; a little earlier than Scarlet Globe, but not so large. Pkt., 5c.; oz., 10c.; ¼ lb., 25c.; lb., 70c.

Robert M. Dale, McLean Co., Ill., says: "Your seeds have as usual been of good germinating power, and prospects are good for a fine crop of all vegetables. June 19, 1915."

Samuel Blum, Marion Co., Indiana, writes March 29th: "Please send me 1 lb. White Box Radish Seed. The seed you sent me last year was good and the radishes were the best I have ever grown."

J. L. Marsh, Palm Beach Co., Fla., writes Nov. 9, 1915: "Please ship seed at once and also mail me your catalogue. You failed to send me one this year and had to borrow one from a neighbor. Can't farm without Livingston's Catalogue."

If seeds are wanted in larger quantities, ask for Special Wholesale Prices.

Scarlet Globe Radishes

Non Plus Ultra, or Fireball

Radish---Round or Olive-Shaped Sorts---Continued

Model White Box

Short top, of rapid growth; perfect turnip shape; extra fine quality, remaining solid and juicy for a long time; is especially suitable for growing under glass in frames. Pkt., 5c.; oz., 10c.; ¼ lb., 25c.; lb., 75c.

French Breakfast

Of quick growth; very mild and tender; of an oval form, scarlet, tipped with white. One of the best for greenhouse or home garden. Popular with many growers. Pkt., 5c.; oz., 10c.; ¼ lb., 25c.; lb., 75c.

Early Golden Yellow Oval

A very fine olive shaped variety. Flesh is white and tender. Fine for forcing or out-door culture. Pkt 5c.; oz., 10c.; ¼ lb., 25c·lb., 85c.

Early Snowball

One of the quickest growing, besides being one of the prettiest round varieties in the whole list; white as snow, smooth as glass, very crisp and extremely tender. Pkt.; 5c.; oz., 10c.; ¼ lb., 25c.; lb., 75c.

Mr. John A. Moore, Polk Co., Fla., writes: "Wired you for 20 pounds Cincinnati Market Radish. It is the finest variety I ever saw."

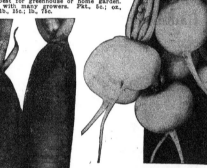

Early Snowball Radish

Early Long Radishes

Cincinnati Market

This superb Radish originated in the vicinity of Cincinnati, Ohio, with the "Glass Gardeners" there, and has been continually used by them for more than twenty years. **We introduced it to our trade in the Spring of 1895, and it at once became so deservedly popular that we have had to grow it ever since by the thousands of pounds** to supply the demand. The tops are so small that the Radishes may stand touching each other in the rows. The Cincinnati Market Radish grows perfectly straight and smooth, 6 to 7 inches in length. (See illustration.) Skin scarlet colored, very thin, the flesh crisp, brittle and of delightful flavor. Pkt., 5c.; oz., 10c.; ¼ lb., 20c.; lb., 65c.

Livingston's Pearl

A beautiful pearly-white, half stump-rooted variety of exceptional merit. It is very firm and solid and after having reached its best condition, it remains in good shape for some two weeks before becoming woody or showing any signs of going to seed. It is a Radish we can heartily recommend and a variety which for all purposes is first-class. Every one who likes a long Radish should plant Livingston's Pearl. Pkt., 5c.; oz., 10c.; ¼ lb., 25c.; lb., 75c.

Mr. R. A. Critchfield, Somerset Co., Pa., writes: "I must send a word of praise for the seed we have been getting from you. They are the best we ever have had. Last Summer we pulled Radishes eleven inches long three weeks from day we planted seed. They were the Cincinnati Market. The only trouble is, I always get your seeds planted too thick, because they all come up. We have used seed from the stores, but only about half would come up. You surely have the right name.—TRUE BLUE"

Long White Icicle

Grows about 4 inches long; slightly stump-rooted, and of transparent whiteness; short leaves, matures quickly; most excellent flavor; equally desirable for home or market gardeners. Pkt., 5c.; oz., 10c.; ¼ lb., 25c.; lb., 75c.

Half-Long Deep Scarlet

Color deep, rich red. Shade, half-long, tapering. Flesh pure white, crisp, tender, brittle, not becoming pithy until very long overgrown. Pkt., 5c.; oz., 10c.; ¼ lb., 20c.; lb., 60c.

Cincinnati Market

Early Long Radishes (Continued)

Wood's Early Frame

Five days earlier than the Early Long Scarlet Short-Top, which it resembles; excellent for forcing and for first sowing outside, being very hardy; half long. Pkt., 5c.; oz., 10c.; ¼ lb., 20c.; lb., 60c.

Early Long Scarlet Short-Top

Admirable for forcing; the leading outdoor quick-growing variety, both for private and market gardens; the average length is 6 to 8 inches; grows about half out of the ground, straight, uniform; tops small; bright scarlet in color, brittle and crisp. Pkt., 5c.; oz., 16c.; ¼ lb., 20c.; lb., 60c.

Brightest Long Scarlet

(**Cardinal White-Tipped**)—Resembles Early Long Scarlet Short-Top in shape and size; extra-early; bright scarlet; white-tipped; a rapid seller. Pkt., 5c.; oz., 10c.; ¼ lb., 20c.; lb., 60c.

Summer Radishes

Improved Chartier

A distinct and exceedingly attractive sort; a clear rose colored long Radish, shading into pure waxy white at the tips. Attains very large size. Perhaps one of the best all-seasons Radishes for the open ground. Grows very fast; ready for use or market nearly as early as Early Long Scarlet Short Top; keeps crisp a long time. Pkt., 5c.; oz., 10c.; ¼ lb., 20c.; lb., 60c.

Lady Finger
Or Long White Vienna

Beautiful in shape; skin and flesh are pure white, very crisp and brittle; a most rapid grower and long standing. A fine variety. Pkt., 5c.; oz., 10c.; ¼ lb., 25c.; lb., 85c.

Chartier or Shepherd

Giant White Stuttgart

Of large size; in shape like a top; flesh and skin white; fine quality; firm and never pithy; can be stored for Winter use. Pkt., 5c.; oz., 10c.; ¼ lb., 25c.; lb., 85c.

Large White Summer Turnip

A favorite with market gardeners. Round, smooth; very white; crisp and tender. Pkt., 5c.; oz., 10c.; ¼ lb., 20c.; lb., 60c.

Gray Summer Turnip

Crisp and tender; one of the most brittle Summer Radishes. A very choice variety. Pkt., 5c.; oz., 10c.; ¼ lb., 20c.; lb., 60c.

Golden Globe

Most perfect globe shape; golden colored skin; very quick grower; white flesh, tender, brittle; long standing. Pkt., 5c.; oz., 10c.; ¼ lb., 30c.; lb., $1.00.

Lady Finger

New Summer Radish From Germany

White Delicious
(See Illustration)

This elegant new sort has proven a decided acquisition. Roots are of distinct half long form, tapering to a point. They grow to good size, are of handsome appearance, and the pure white flesh is of elegant, mild flavor until the radishes become unfit for use. Compared with other white Summer sorts, White Delicious averages thicker, is more solid and of milder flavor. It does not grow as quickly as White Vienna, but is in good condition much longer. Pkt., 5c.; oz., 10c.; ¼ lb., 25c.; lb., 75c.

White Delicious Radish

Chinese Rose Winter Radish

Summer Radish--Con'd

White Strasburg

Handsome, oblong, tapering shape; both skin and flesh pure white; flesh firm, brittle, tender, and possessing the most desirable character of retaining its crispness, even when the roots are quite large. Excellent for summer use, as it withstands severe heat and grows very quickly. Pkt., 5c.; oz., 10c.; ¼ lb., 30c.; lb., $1.00.

> **Our Big Dollar Collection**
> of vegetables offered on page 16 is sure to please you.

Rabanos Winter Radishes Rettige

Sown in Summer and used in the Fall, or put away as you do Turnips for Winter use.

Chinese Rose Winter

A very handsome and distinct variety; color the brightest rose; crisp and tender; cylindrical in shape, very smooth; very desirable sort; keeps splendidly through Autumn and Winter. Pkt., 5c.; oz., 10c.; ¼ lb., 25c.; lb., 75c.

Long Black Spanish

Grows 5 to 8 inches long; 1 to 1½ inches through at top; skin black, flesh white and firm. One of the oldest, but nevertheless one of the best Winter sorts. Pkt., 5c.; oz., 10c.; ¼ lb., 20c.; lb., 60c.

White Chinese

(New Celestial)—(See illustration alongside.)—A large stump-rooted Radish with white skin and flesh. Can be sown from July 1 to August 15, and will keep in prime condition a long time; mild in flavor, brittle and never woody. Fine for market gardeners. Pkt., 5c.; oz., 10c.; ¼ lb., 20c.; lb., 65c.

California Mammoth White

Is grown extensively in California; 8 to 12 inches long, 2 to 3 inches in diameter; white, solid and of good quality. Pkt., 5c.; oz., 10c.; ¼ lb., 20c.; lb., 65c.

Long White Spanish

Differs from Long Black Spanish in color only. Pkt., 5c.; oz., 10c.; ¼ lb., 20c.; lb., 60c.

Round Black Spanish

Similar to Black Spanish except in shape; fine for Winter. Pkt., 5c.; oz., 10c.; ¼ lb., 20c.; lb., 60c.

Scarlet Pamir

Fine, deep red, turnip-shaped sort of crisp, mild flavor; one of the best. Pkt., 5c.; oz., 10c.; ¼ lb., 30c.; lb., $1.00.

G. Peterson, Kings County, N. Y., writes February 12, 1915: "I received your dollar collection of True Blue Vegetable Seed, which I consider a good investment. In fact I am so well pleased that I am enclosing a Postal money order for another collection which I wish you to send to my place in Florida."

White Chinese Winter

White Strasburg

Special Prices on Large Quantities of Radish Seed

Livingston's All-Seasons Radish Mixture

Livingston's All-Seasons Mixture of Radish Seed contains all shades and shapes—red, white, pink and variegated; round, half-long and long, in great variety. It is all the go for small gardens, where space is limited, and you want to make a garden and be done with it. One sowing does for the whole season, as they become ready for your table early, medium and late. You always have some that are just right—sweet, juicy, delicious, crisp. You will be surprised and delighted with our popular Radish Mixture. Your garden will not be complete without a bed of these Radishes. Large packet, 10c.; oz., 15c.; 2 oz., 25c.; ¼ lb., 35c.

Remember We pay the postage on all seeds by the packet, ounce, quarter-pound, pound, two pound, unless noted otherwise. For complete information about "Seeds by Mail," see page 3.

Remember One Sowing will supply your table with crisp delicious Radishes Spring and Summer. Large pkt., 10c.

Cidracayota **Squashes** Speise-Kürbisse

Plant after weather has become firmly settled and the ground is warm and dry in hills 5 to 6 feet apart for bush varieties, and 6 to 8 feet apart for running varieties. Hills should be thoroughly manured. Slightly elevate the hills and place 7 or 8 seeds in each, finally leaving but three plants. Press the seeds down firmly before covering, and cover early planted ones, 1 inch deep, and late ones 1½ inches. **One ounce of the Bush varieties for 40 hills, or of the large-seeded winter kinds for 15 hills; 2 to 3 pounds of the Bush sorts, or 4 to 5 pounds of the large-seeded winter kinds are needed for one acre.**

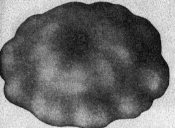

Mammoth Yellow Bush Scallop, or Golden Custard

Mammoth Yellow Bush Scallop (Golden Custard)—Decidedly the best strain of Yellow Scalloped Summer Squash. Double the size of the old sort, retaining all its good points. Pkt., 5c.; oz., 10c.; ¼ lb., 20c.; lb., 65c.

Fordhook Squash

Fordhook—Convenient size for family use. Flesh dry and sweet, and seems incapable of rotting; if placed in a cool, dry room, keeps in a perfect condition throughout the Winter and Spring, until late in June. The thin, hard stem and roots, furnish absolutely no food for the squash borer. Maturing early, it is a sure cropper and immensely productive. Skin thin and meat thick; seed cavity small. May be used at any stage of growth. Pkt., 5c.; oz., 10c.; ¼ lb., 30c.; lb., $1.00.

Livingston's Improved Cushaw

Mammoth White Bush Scallop

Excellent large strain. Nearly as early as the common sort; creamy white; splendid for market or home garden; good shipper. Pkt., 5c.; oz., 10c.; ¼ lb., 25c.; lb., 75c.

Early White Bush, or Patty Pan—Bears fruits ready for use very early in the Summer. Of true bush habit and very productive. Pkt., 5c.; oz., 10c.; ¼ lb., 20c.; lb., 65c.

Giant Golden Summer Crookneck

The largest and best of all Summer Crookneck Squashes. Of a dwarf, bushy habit and very productive; bears early and all Summer; true Crookneck type; rich golden yellow color; thickly warted. Its cooking qualities are unexcelled. One of the best varieties for the market or table use. Pkt., 5c.; oz., 10c.; ¼ lb., 30c.; lb., $1.00.

Livingston's Pie Squash

Rich, Sweet Flavor. Makes Good Pies Without Eggs. The color of the skin is similar to that of the Golden Russet Apple. Flesh yellow and very thick. Quite early, surprisingly productive and a rapid and hardy grower. The very finest for pies, making good ones even when eggs are not used. Size 8 to 10 inches in diameter. Large pkt., 5c.; oz., 15c.; ¼ lb., 35c.; lb., $1.25.

Gregory's Delicious

The result of years of selection and crossing, the Hubbard having been prominently used in its make-up. Green when matured. Flesh thick, dark orange in color; dry, sweet and of rich flavor. Is best as Fall and Winter variety, improving with age. Pkt., 5c.; oz., 10c.; ¼ lb., 30c.; lb., $1.00.

Livingston's Improved Cushaw Squash

The genuine Cushaw of "ye olden times," and a great favorite. Very beautiful in appearance, being a distinct mottled green and white striped. Flesh yellow, solid, fine grained, very sweet, and excellent for pies; also good for baking. They average about 15 pounds, but on good rich soil 30 pound specimens are common, and even 35 to 40 pounders are found. They are hardy, and bugs seldom eat them, especially when other varieties are near. Can be grown among corn, same as pumpkins; and yield a good crop, but the better way is to grow them separately on good, rich soil, in hills 10 to 15 feet apart each way. Sells well on market, and should be in the hands of every grower. Pkt., 5c.; oz., 15c.; ¼ lb., 50c.; lb., $1.75.

Hubbard Squash

Hubbard—The Standard Winter Squash—It is of good size, often weighing 9 to 15 pounds. Color bluish green. Flesh fine grained, sweet and of excellent flavor. Has a very hard shell and will keep until Spring. Pkt., 5c.; oz., 10c.; ¼ lb., 25c.; lb., 90c.

Golden Hubbard—Color bright, rich, orange-red; showy and attractive. Shell hard and warty. Flesh deep golden yellow, fine grained and of splendid flavor; cooks dry. Pkt., 5c.; oz., 10c.; ¼ lb., 30c.; lb., $1.00.

Warted Hubbard Squashes

Chicago Warted Hubbard—Large size, dark green color, distinguished by a dense covering of knots (warts), a sure indication of splendid quality; thick flesh. Pkt., 5c.; oz., 10c.; ¼ lb., 30c.; lb., $1.00.

Dunlap's Prolific, or Orange Marrow—The earliest of the Fall varieties, and much sooner ripe than any other Marrow Squash. Very prolific, a bright orange red; it is a general favorite; its quality is the best. Pkt., 5c.; oz., 10c.; ¼ lb., 25c.; lb., 75c.

Mammoth Chili—Oblong, productive; profitable for stock. Pkt., 5c.; oz., 10c.; ¼ lb., 30c.; lb., $1.00.

Mammoth Whale—Often grows 3 feet long; sometimes weighs 100 pounds or over. Slate color; prolific; flesh solid, orange color; quality good; keeps well; suitable for stock. Pkt., 5c.; oz., 15c.; ¼ lb., 30c.; lb., $1.00.

Boston Marrow—Of oval form and thin skin. Color a rich orange; of good size, excellent flavor and keeps well. Pkt., 5c.; oz., 10c.; ¼ lb., 25c.; lb., 75c.

Essex Hybrid—Hard shell; solid, thick-fleshed, fine grained, rich flavored; prolific and of the best quality. Flesh rich orange color. Turban shape. Pkt., 5c.; oz., 10c.; ¼ lb., 25c.; lb., 75c.

Livingston's Squash Mixture

One sowing will produce Squashes for the season. This mixture contains a great variety of Summer and Winter sorts, just suited for growing for exhibition or table use. Large pkt.; oz., 15c.; ¼ lb. 35c.

Special prices on Squash Seed in larger quantities.

Salsi Salsify or Oyster Plant Haferwurzel

When properly cooked it is a good substitute for oysters in taste and flavor, and is very nutritious. A most palatable vegetable; the cultivation is precisely the same as directed for Parsnips and Carrots. Salsify will keep finely through the Winter, in the ground where sown, in exactly the same manner as Parsnips. The roots are perfectly hardy; in fact they are best after the frost has touched them.

When cooking, boil the roots (a small piece of codfish, which should be discarded when the salsify is done, boiled with them strengthens the oyster flavor); when cold, mash, and fry as patties or fritters. This vegetable is also good stewed, plain boiled, and also as a salad, sliced raw in vinegar with pepper and salt. Succeeds best, perhaps in light, well-enriched soil. If it is necessary to use manure it should be very fine and well-rotted. Sow early in drills 18 inches apart and cover firmly one inch deep; thin to three inches apart in the drills. One ounce of seed will sow fifty feet of drill; eight pounds is sufficient to plant an acre.

Mammoth Sandwich Island

This splendid variety will average nearly twice the size of the White French Salsify. Grows very uniform. Mild and delicious in flavor. A popular sort with all growers. (See illustration.) Pkt., 5c.; oz., 20c.; ¼ lb., 60c.; lb., $2.00.

Mammoth Sandwich Island Salsify

Espinaca Spinach Spinat

Spinach will succeed finely in any ordinary soil, and its cultivation is a very simple matter. It is grown both as a Spring and Summer crop. To winter over for spring use, plant the seed in August or September, in drills 12 to 14 inches apart. At approach of cold weather, cover lightly with straw or any handy litter. Uncover the plants when they begin to make a new growth in the Spring. For Summer use sow early in Spring. Thin to 3 or 4 inches. One ounce of seed for 50 feet of drill; 12 to 16 pounds for an acre.

Improved Thick Leaf (Viroflay)

The market gardener's favorite for Fall or Spring sowing. A great favorite in all parts of the country as it furnishes an abundance of heavy, broad, dark green leaves of finest quality and appearance. The leaves are attractively curled, and on account of their firmness and substance they remain in prime, salable condition for a long time. Also excellent for home use. (See illustration below.) Pkt., 5c.; oz., 10c.; ¼ lb., 15c.; lb., 35c.

New Zealand—A distinct type of Spinach. The plants grow in branching form with thick, succulent leaves. The leaves and stems can be gathered at any time after they are well grown and the plants will start out into new growth. Thrives during hot weather and in any soil. Pkt., 5c.; oz., 10c.; ¼ lb., 25c.; lb., 85c.

Victoria—An excellent sort, whether grown for home use or market. It may be sown with equally good results either in the Spring or during late Summer and Fall. The plants are fit for use early and remain in good marketable condition much longer than most other kinds. The leaves are very thick and juicy and, when prepared properly, develop a delightfully distinct, mild flavor. Pkt., 5c.; oz., 10c.; ¼ lb., 15c.; lb., 35c.

Bloomsdale Savoy—Large wrinkled leaves, upright growth; fine quality. Earliest variety, but will not stand long. Pkt., 5c.; oz., 10c.; ¼ lb., 15c.; lb., 35c.

Improved Thick Leaf Spinach

Prickly Seeded Winter—A fine variety with triangular, oblong or narrow-shaped leaves. Hardiest of all, therefore best for Fall sowing where Winters are severe. Pkt., 5c.; oz., 10c.; ¼ lb., 16c.; lb., 35c.

"Long Season"—Of flat spreading, but compact growth, this sort is especially noticeable for its short-stemmed, dark-green leaves, which are heavily crumpled and savoyed. For marketing during the warm Summer months, it is unsurpassed. Stands longer before going to seed than any other sort on our list. Pkt., 5c.; oz., 10c.; ¼ lb., 15c.; lb., 35c.

Munsterland—For use in Northern latitudes where sorts with heavy, juicy foliage are injured by frost, we consider this sort a decided acquisition. Stands a long time without going to seed. Plants grow to be a foot in diameter if properly thinned. Quality excellent. Pkt., 5c.; oz., 10c.; ¼ lb., 15c.; lb., 35c.

Jos. McAllister, Palm Beach Co., Fla., writes Oct. 11, 1915: "I have had excellent success with your seed and consider them the best seeds on the market anywhere. Thanking you for promptness in filling my order, I am."

W. H. C. Lee, Harris Co., Texas, writes Oct. 12, 1915: "I have failed to secure seeds of merit by monkeying with local seed houses. Seed generally no good. I have always had success in getting good stands when I bought seeds from you."

E. W. Pickering, Palm Beach Co., Fla., writes Oct. 9, 1915: "Your seeds ordered last month by me are already starting up fine and I tell you it takes No. 1 quality seeds to come up in the early fall here where the sun is yet so warm."

Nabos Turnips Ruben

First-early varieties of Turnips should be planted just as early in the Spring as the ground is dry and warm. Sow them in drills, beds, or later broadcast, or among corn. The Ruta-Baga varieties, and also the early sorts, will do better if planted in drills; make the drills at least 18 inches apart, and thin-out the plants when well-up to six inches apart. Cultivate often and thoroughly. We call especial attention to the fact that the Ruta-Baga varieties should be planted as soon as possible after the middle of June, as they need a longer season than the earlier sorts of Turnips. **One ounce of seed sows 100 feet of drill; one pound an acre.**

Purple-Top Strap-Leaved Turnips. Pkt., 5c.

Extra-Early Purple-Top Milan

The earliest of the flat Turnips, with a beautiful purple top. They are mild and sweet. Pkt., 5c.; oz., 15c.; ¼ lb., 35c.; lb., $1.25.

Extra-Early White Milan

Similar to Purple-Top Milan, except it has pure white skin and flesh. Pkt., 5c.; oz., 10c.; ¼ lb., 30c.; lb., $1.00.

Early Snowball

Medium-sized round Turnip; pure white, very fine flavor. Pkt., 5c.; oz., 10c.; ¼ lb., 25c.; lb., 75c.

Early White Egg

An early variety. Flesh white, firm, fine grained, mild and sweet. A fine Turnip for Winter use. Pkt., 5c.; oz., 10c.; ¼ lb., 30c.; lb., $1.00.

Early Flat Dutch, or White Strap-Leaved

A standard flat variety; good size; pure white; small top, few leaves; good early or late. Pkt., 5c.; oz., 10c.; ¼ lb., 20c.; lb., 60c.

Long White, or Cow Horn

Long; grows rapidly, partly above ground; slightly crooked; productive; white, fine grained, very sweet. Used for plowing under to improve the soil. Pkt., 5c.; oz., 10c.; ¼ lb., 20c.; lb., 50c.

Purple-Top White Globe

A variety of decided merit. Globular shape, and of superior quality, either for the table or stock; heavy yielder. Pkt., 5c.; oz., 10c.; ¼ lb., 20c.; lb., 60c.

Purple-Top Strap Leaf

A popular variety for family or market use; white, purple above ground; flesh fine grained; good for Winter use or late planting. Pkt., 5c.; oz., 10c.; ¼ lb., 20c.; lb., 60c.

Large White Globe

Similar to Purple-Top White Globe, except in color, which is pure white; firm, sweet flesh. Pkt., 5c.; oz., 10c.; ¼ lb., 20c.; lb., 50c.

Yellow Globe, or Amber

Sweet; large, fine for table or stock. Pkt., 5c.; oz., 10c.; ¼ lb., 20c.; lb., 50c.

Golden Ball, or Orange Jelly

Rapid grower; globe shaped; is bright yellow. The best of the yellow sorts for table use. Keeps well. Pkt., 5c.; oz., 10c.; ¼ lb., 20c.; lb., 50c.

Seven Top

Cultivated extensively for the tops which are used as greens. Pkt., 5c.; oz., 10c.; ¼ lb., 20c.; lb., 50c.

Ruta - Bagas

(Swedish or Russian Turnips)

Ruta-Bagas are more especially adapted to sections north of Ohio. They require a longer season for maturing, hence should be sown earlier than Turnips, or about July 15.

Improved American (Purple-Top)—Very hardy and productive; flesh yellow, sweet and solid; good for stock or table use. Pkt., 5c.; oz., 10c.; ¼ lb, 20c.; lb., 50c.

White Russian, or Large White—Grows very large; excellent for table or stock; flesh is firm, white and solid; the best keeper of any white variety. Pkt., 5c.; oz., 10c.; ¼ lb., 20c.; lb., 50c.

Mrs. D. N. Coberly, Clark Co., Ohio, writes us as follows: "I have ordered garden seeds from Livingston's the past three years, and always find them reliable and true to name. I have come to look upon Livingston's Garden Seeds as standard."

Purple Top White Globe Turnips

Livingston's Famous Tomatoes
New Varieties and the Growing of Large Quantities of Seed Our Specialty
We Grow More High Grade Tomato Seed Than Any Other Establishment in the World

If it were possible for every one who reads these lines to go with us to our seed farms and trial grounds northwest of the city or to our Kirkersville farms, nearby, some idea could be gained of the extent to which Tomato growing for seed is carried on by us. As is well known, we are situated in the best Tomato growing section of the world, but all Tomatoes we grow are for seed purposes only and no portion of the crop is ever marketed. When it is considered that each year our Tomato seed crop is measured in tons and that it requires tons of seed to fill orders from growers (not other seedsmen) some idea of the magnitude of the industry can be formed. What has created this industry?

Back in the fifties the founder of our business, the late Mr. A. W. Livingston, began making a special study of the Tomato. His efforts were crowned with great success and has been kept up by our Company until to-day we have to our credit a fine series of really new, distinct and decidedly meritorious varieties. As our varieties have been introduced from time to time, they have been recognized, at once even by the most ordinary grower, as having a distinctiveness all their own and are not, as is too often the case, an old sort under a new name or so near like sorts already on the market as not to be recognized by the naked eye.

In 1870, the "Paragon" Tomato was offered for sale and to-day you can purchase Paragon Tomatoes of practically the same form and size as when introduced over forty years ago. The type was fixed and has remained so all these years. In rapid succession followed the introduction of Livingston's "Acme," "Perfection," "Favorite," "Beauty," "Stone," "Globe," etc., etc., each having some particular merit as to size, color, season of ripening, etc., and in all, some twenty-six varieties have been introduced.

Livingston's Tomatoes are known all over the world. They are the standard by which other varieties are judged. It has required years of careful study and a vast amount of labor to develop the various types and the work goes on in constant effort to maintain the high standard to which Livingston's Tomato seeds have attained.

It is needless to assure our friends that we are constantly keeping at it, improving and reselecting all the sorts introduced by us. The standard of quality of our Tomatoes is higher to-day than it has been at any previous time, and it will be kept up as long as Livingston's have anything to do with it. We take great pride in giving herewith a list of varieties introduced by us and the years in which they were first sent out. No doubt you'll find some old, familiar sorts that have "made good" with you among these varieties.

Livingston's Paragon	in 1870
Livingston's Acme	in 1875
Livingston's Perfection	in 1880
Livingston's Golden Queen	in 1882
Livingston's Favorite	in 1883
Livingston's Beauty	in 1886
Livingston's Potato Leaf	in 1887
Livingston's Stone	in 1889
Livingston's Royal Red	in 1892
Livingston's Gold Ball	in 1892
Livingston's Buckeye State	in 1893
Livingston's Aristocrat	in 1893
Livingston's Large Rose Peach	in 1893
Livingston's Honor Bright	in 1897
Livingston's Dwarf Yellow Prince	in 1900
Livingston's Magnus	in 1900
Livingston's Aristobright	in 1901
Livingston's Royal Colors	in 1901
Livingston's Dandy Dwarf	in 1901
Livingston's Multicolor	in 1901
Livingston's Princess	in 1901
Livingston's Grandus	in 1901
Livingston's Dwarf Stone	in 1902
Livingston's Purple Dwarf	in 1903
Livingston's Globe	in 1905
Livingston's Hummer	in 1907
Livingston's New Coreless	in 1908

LIVINGSTON'S
STONE TOMATOES GROWN ON STAKES
KIRKERSVILLE FARMS

Livingston's Coreless

Originated by Us and Introduced in 1908

A Perfect Shaped Canning Variety of Large Size, Globe Shaped, Full at Stem End. Bright Red, a Strong Grower and a Big Cropper.

All markets requiring a bright-red sort will be pleased with Livingston's Coreless. In shape it is almost round, being of about the same diameter each way. The depression at the stem end has been almost eliminated, making a most profitable variety for canning owing to a very small amount of loss in material and labor. Is immensely productive, clusters of 4 to 7 fruits are produced at six to eight inches apart along the stem. All of the fruits are of marketable size, and many of them are quite large, twelve to fifteen ounces. A grand, good slicing variety, the seed cells being surrounded by bright-red, heavy, meaty and delicious flesh. Its color is that bright, rich red so important to all packers of high-grade goods. Pkts., 5c. and 10c.; ½ oz., 15c.; oz., 25c.; ¼ lb., 80c.; lb., $2.75.

Livingston's Globe Tomato

The Greatest Shipping Tomato for the South and Green-house growing, and a Prime Favorite for All Classes of Growers North and South, whether for Home Use or for Market.

It is an early purple Tomato of very distinct shape, firm fleshed and almost blight proof. It is an extra good all-round sort, of a distinct globe shape, with quite a large percentage of elongated fruits. Livingston's Globe is, without doubt the best Tomato ever offered for the South. Get our seeds and make sure of originator's stock. See second page of cover for full description; also outside cover page illustrated in color. Pkts., 5c. and 10c.; ½ oz., 15c.; oz., 30c.; ¼ lb., 90c.; lb., $3.25.

W. H. Farnham, Walworth Co., Wis., writes: "I have raised your Globe and Stone Tomatoes for some years now and like them fine; have tried several other varieties, but the two named do the best with me."

Gallup Bros., Ashtabula Co., O., write May 11, 1915: "Please ship us by Parcel Post 2½ lbs. Globe Tomato Seed and 2 lbs Grand Rapids Lettuce Seed, your best. Your tomato seed is always good."

Livingston's Coreless

Livingston's Stone

The Greatest Canning Tomato in the World

(Introduced by Us in 1889.) The largest, bright red, perfectly smooth, highest yielding, best keeping, finest flavored main-crop variety in existence.

Dealers and planters everywhere recognize the merit of the Stone It is now twenty-five years since we first introduced it and it still grows in favor. More Stone Tomatoes are grown every year than any other half dozen varieties taken together. We alone supply enough seed to the leading Tomato growers every year to produce 80 million plants. Seed of Livingston's Stone, as grown by us, can only be bought from Livingston's. See second page of cover for full description. Pkts., 5c. and 10c.; ½ oz., 15c.; oz., 30c.; ¼ lb. 85c.; lb., $3.00.

Livingston's Hummer

Originated by Us and Introduced in 1907

Livingston's Hummer is round as a ball, smooth as an apple, a good variety for forcing, very prolific, and has very little indenture about the stem end. The color of the fruit is very attractive bright-scarlet. The flesh is a rich crimson-scarlet, and of the very best quality. In size, not so large as Livingston's Stone, but nevertheless a most excellent variety for canner's use, as a large percentage of the fruits can be put into the can whole; quite early is especially desirable also for canners' use in those latitudes where the crop must be produced in a short time.

It is hard to beat for market and home-garden, especially when grown on stakes or trellises of some kind. It is a healthy, vigorous grower of medium-sized vines. The fruit itself is firm and solid. If picked when "just turning", to ripen, it will carry to a distant market in excellent shape color up nicely and meet with ready sales. Pkts., 5c. and 10c.; ½ oz., 15c.; oz., 25c.; ¼ lb., 80c.; lb., $2.75.

Livingston's Hummer

Alfred A. Stevens, Dade Co., Fla., writes as follows: "I received the pound of Livingston's Globe Tomato seed in due time and am very much pleased with it. Wish I was where I could show you a sample of the fruit. Sent 17 field crates of them to packing house Friday, Packed 25 crates—22 Fancies and 3 Choice. Pretty good for first picking."

Livingston's Acme

(Introduced by Us in 1875)—One of the best, earliest purple-fruited Tomatoes. As a shipping sort for growing in Southern States, it is unsurpassed. This was the first perfectly smooth, large purple Tomato introduced by the founder of our firm. Today, after thirty-five years, it is still the leading sort with extensive growers in the South, particularly in Texas. We consider it the smoothest and most uniform, medium-sized, early, purple-fruited sort. It is a very prolific sort. Fruits are produced in clusters of four or five, are large, and free from cracks. They are solid and stand long distance shipment to perfection. The quality is fine. Pkts., 5c. and 10c.; oz., 20c.; ¼ lb., 70c.; lb., $2.25.

Livingston's Perfection

(Introduced by Us in 1880)—The demand for a first-class shipping Tomato brought about the introduction of Livingston's Perfection, which may fittingly be described as an improved Acme with red skin. This skin is sufficiently tough and the fruits are so remarkably solid that they may be shipped long distances and are sure to arrive in good condition. It is a medium-sized, smooth, bright red sort of excellent quality. It ripens about ten days before Livingston's Stone, keeps its good size to the end of the season and is excellent for either market or home use. Many canners, especially those who put up the Tomatoes whole, prefer Perfection to all others. Pkts., 5c. and 10c.; oz., 20c.; ¼ lb., 70c.; lb., $2.25.

Livingston's Honor Bright

(Introduced by Us in 1897)—The distinctive features of this sort are its solidity, long-keeping qualities after being picked and the remarkable changes of color the fruit undergoes during growth and ripening. First, it is light green, then an attractive waxy-white, then lemon-yellow, finally changing to a rich red. When in the white stage they make beautifully transparent and delicious preserves. On account of its solidity and long-keeping qualities, it is especially recommended for shipping long distances. It can be shipped in crates like apples, if picked when in the yellow stage of ripening. Clusters bear 3 to 5 perfect fruits, which ripen very evenly. Flesh is tender and melting. Pkts., 5c. and 10c.; ½ oz., 15c.; oz., 30c.; ¼ lb., 85c.; lb., $3.00.

Livingston's Favorite

(Introduced by Us in 1883)—Livingston's Favorite will always be that which its name implies—a favorite with canners and in the home garden. Favorite is one of the best shaped, largest, bright red Tomatoes in existence. The fruit ripens evenly, is always smooth, free from cracks, and holds its size to the end of the season. Flesh is of good flavor, very solid. Pkts., 5c. and 10c.; ½ oz., 15c.; oz., 30c.; ¼ lb., 85c.; lb., $3.00.

Livingston's Paragon

Livingston's Paragon

(Introduced by Us in 1870)—This was the first perfectly smooth, deep red Tomato ever offered to the American people. We have endeavored to keep it up to the original high standard, and there are many gardeners and catsup-makers who today, after 40 years, would not have any other kind for a main cropper. It is an immense yielder. In time of ripening a medium early. The fruits are of large size and remain so throughout the season. Flesh is solid, of superior quality and of appetizing appearance. Pkts., 5c. and 10c.; ½ oz., 15c.; oz., 30c.; ¼ lb., 85c.; lb., $3.00.

Livingston's Buckeye State

(Introduced by Us in 1893)—The largest Tomato bearing our name. Extra large fruits are borne in clusters of three to six. Buckeye State has a smooth skin of dark purple color. The fruit is very meaty, solid, and the flesh is of most desirable quality. The principal objection to "mammoth" sorts has been their rough and uneven skin. In Livingston's Buckeye State we have been successful in eliminating these weak points, and planters everywhere will appreciate the beautiful large fruits, which are exceedingly showy and find a ready sale. Pkts., 5c. and 10c.; ½ oz., 20c.; oz., 35c.; ¼ lb., $1.15; lb., $4.00.

Warning

We do not sell Tomato Seeds to dealers in bulk. All our Tomato Seed is put up in packages bearing our registered "True Blue" Seal. When you walk into a store and see Livingston's Stone, Livingston's G l o b e , Livingston's Beauty, etc., displayed on the counter in a bag without our blue seal, that packet does **not contain Livingston's** Tomato Seed. Every year we receive complaints that seeds bought at stores do not turn out as well as what we supplied.

The reason: **Livingston's Tomato Seeds** can only be bought from Livingston's or from a few reliable dealers who handle our **seeds in original bags** with the "True Blue" Seal.

Our "True Blue" Seal

Tomato Facts

Is the title of a unique booklet published by us. It tells all about Livingston's Famous Tomatoes and is illustrated with many half-tone reproductions from photographs. It tells how we produced many of the leading standard Tomatoes by years of patient selection and cultivation. Contains many helpful hints on plant production, culture, etc., (price 10 cents) free to customers who ask for it.

Livingston's Perfection

Livingston's Improved Dwarf Champion

Bears fruit fully one-third larger than the original Dwarf Champion in all kinds of soils. Fruit is produced in clusters of three to five. Of a beautiful glossy purple; firm, solid, thick flesh, with large meaty center. Pkts., 5c. and 10c.; ½ oz., 15c.; oz., 30c.; ¼ lb., 85c.; lb., $3.00.

Livingston's Dwarf Stone

(Introduced by Us in 1902)

The advent of Dwarf Stone marked a new epoch in Dwarf Tomatoes. The fruits are larger than those of Dwarf Champion and nearly as large as those of our original Stone.

It is very prolific. Fruit smooth; ripens evenly. The color is bright red. You may set the plants of Livingston's Dwarf Stone as close as 18x14 inches and still produce an abundant crop. We regret our crop is so short that we can only offer Dwarf Stone in a very small way this season. Pkts., 5c. and 10c.; ½ oz., 20c.

Livingston's Dwarf Purple

Introduced by Us in 1903. Large fruited Dwarf-growing purple Tomato. Smooth and not liable to crack. Flesh solid and thick, with few seeds. Pkts., 5c. and 10c.; ½ oz., 15c.; oz., 30c.; ¼ lb., 85c.; lb., $3.00.

Livingston's Dwarf Aristocrat

(Introduced by Us in 1893)

This Tomato in habit of growth and foliage resembles the Dwarf Champion, except in color; a beautiful, rich, glossy red. The size, solidity, productiveness, smoothness, flavor of its fruit are all that are to be desired. Pkts., 5c. and 10c.; oz., 25c.; ¼ lb., 80c.; lb., $2.75.

Livingston's Dwarf Yellow Prince

Introduced by Us in 1898. A very choice dwarf-growing Tomato. Very early. Flesh is solid and the flavor is desirable. Of large size and beautiful shape. When sliced with red or purple sorts, it is highly ornamental. Pkts., 5c. and 10c.; ½ oz., 20c.; oz., 30c.; ¼ lb., 85c.; lb., $3.00.

Livingston's Royal Red

Introduced by Us in 1892. A first-class variety; red and handsome. Desirable for canning and catsup making. Pkts., 5c. and 10c.; ½ oz., 15c.; oz., 25c.; ¼ lb., 80c.; lb., $2.75.

Livingston's Magnus

Livingston's Magnus

One of the Finest for Growing on Stakes

Introduced by Us in 1900. This distinct variety, of the color of Livingston's Beauty, is one of the most valuable additions to the Tomato family. It is large, early, thick, heavy and solid, and one of the most handsome varieties in cultivation. Livingston's Magnus is unsurpassed in quality and in the production of fine, large fruits. While well adapted to main-crop planting, it also takes first rank for early market purposes. The form is perfect, uniform, large, and attractive (see illustration). The flesh is very firm. A robust grower, with short joints, setting its clusters closer together than most varieties, and in a very heavy cropper. It has the broad potato foliage which prevents sunburn in hot sections. The fruits are usually very deep from stem to blossom end, some of them being almost globe shaped. Ripens evenly, does not crack about the stem. Livingston's Magnus Tomato for staking up in the open field, as well as for forcing in greenhouses, is fully equal to any for such purposes. Pkts., 5c. and 10c.; ½ oz., 10c.; oz., 25c.; ¼ lb., 80c.; lb., $2.75.

Livingston's Gold Queen

(Introduced by Us in 1882)

"Queen of all the Yellows." Its superior flavor has brought it into general favor as a table fruit. It is solid, always smooth, entirely free from ridges, large in size, ripens early. Pkts., 5c. and 10c.; ½ oz., 15c.; oz., 30c.; ¼ lb., 85c.; lb., $3.00.

Livingston's Golden Ball

Introduced by Us in 1892. Beautiful canary-yellow; flesh thick, fine quality; handsome color; grows in clusters and produces enormous crops. Pkts., 5c. and 10c.; ½ oz., 15c.; oz., 25c.; ¼ lb., 80c.; lb., $2.75.

Livingston's Beauty

(Introduced by Us in 1886)

Although introduced by us so many years ago, this is still one of the greatest of all purple colored market Tomatoes. Hosts of "new" sorts have been brought before the public since, but not one has in any sense become a real rival of Livingston's Beauty, although our "Globe" is rapidly gaining in favor among the Southern growers. The plants make a strong growth, are hardy and bear plentifully. The fruit is produced in clusters of four to six, is large, of perfect shape, and retains its size until late in the season. It ripens early, has firm flesh of excellent quality, and the seed cells are very small. For shipping and early market it is excellent. May be picked quite green; will ripen up nicely, look well and keep in perfect condition for a week after becoming fully ripe. See illustration in color on cover page. Pkts., 5c. and 10c.; ½ oz., 15c.; oz., 25c.; ¼ lb., 80c.; lb., $2.75.

Livingston's Beauty

PACKET PRICES OF LIVINGSTON'S TOMATOES—Regular Size, 10 cents each; 3 for 25 cents; one or more kinds. Smaller Sizes, 5 cents each; 6 for 25 cents, one or more kinds

LIVINGSTON'S FAMOUS TOMATOES
FOR THE GREENHOUSE

Livingston's Globe Tomato
(Originated by Us and Introduced in 1905)
The Greatest Shipping and Greenhouse Sort

An early purple Tomato of very distinct globe shape, firm fleshed, ripens evenly and is of the right size to fit the baskets used as a shipping package. This variety originated with us and we are sure you will be taking the least possible risk in using our seed stock. Pkts., 5c. and 10c.; ½ oz., 15c.; oz., 30c.; ¼ lb., 90c.; lb., $3.25.

Bonny Best
Finest Bright Red Sort for Greenhouse Growing

Of medium size, bright scarlet color, always smooth and of remarkably uniform size and shape. An elegant sort for market and shipping on account of its even size and color, as some markets demand a bright red. Pkt., 5c.; oz., 25c.; ¼ lb., 80c.; lb., $2.75.

Comet Forcing
Superior red variety for forcing. Rich scarlet-red; fruits are solid, round, smooth; exceedingly heavy cropper; medium-sized fruits. Pkt., 5c.; ½ oz., 15c.; oz., 25c.; ¼ lb., 80c.; lb., $2.75.

Livingston's Hummer
Originated by Us and Introduced in 1907

Livingston's Hummer is round as a ball, smooth as an apple, a good variety for forcing, very prolific, and has very little indenture about the stem end. Color of fruit very attractive bright-scarlet. Flesh rich crimson-scarlet, and of the very best quality. Medium in size, not so large as Livingston's Stone.
It is hard to beat for market and home-garden, especially when grown on stakes or trellises of some kind. A healthy, vigorous grower of medium-sized vines. The fruit itself is firm and solid. Can be picked when quite firm and will ripen very evenly. Pkts., 5c. and 10c.; ½ oz., 15c.; oz., 25c.; ¼ lb., 80c.; lb., $2.75.

Livingston's Magnus
One of the Finest Purple Sorts for Growing in the Greenhouse or on Stakes

Introduced by us in 1900. A distinct variety; early, thick, heavy and solid, and one of the most handsome varieties. Livingston's Magnus is unsurpassed in quality and in the production of fine, large fruits. The form is perfect, uniform, large and attractive. The flesh is very firm. A robust grower, with short joints, setting its clusters closer together than most varieties, and is a very heavy cropper. It has the broad potato foliage which prevents sunburn. Ripens evenly; does not crack about the stem, and the flavor is all that can be desired. Pkts., 5c. and 10c.; ½ oz., 15c.; oz., 25c.; ¼ lb., 80c.; lb., $2.75.

Our Mr. Harry Baltz, who calls on the Market Garden trade, in the interest of our house, writes us from Cleveland, Ohio, under date of June 15, 1915:

"Today, at the Rocky River Greenhouse Co. near this city I saw the greatest crop of Livingston's Globe Tomatoes that I ever saw. There have been growers from all over the state to see this crop, also a lot of people from the city have gone out to see it. The crop was at its best two weeks ago and now looks better than any crop I have ever seen. They have 8000 plants and have sold already over 3000 baskets. Picked 600 baskets today and expect to pick about 800 Monday (June 21). Some of the clusters had to be tied up to keep them from breaking off the vine and the largest cluster in the house had 32 tomatoes on. Any number of them have ten and twelve on now.

"P. S. Eugene and August Cook have fine Livingston's Magnus also."

Livingston's Globe Tomato is grown at the Institution for Feeble Minded at Columbus. Sixteen feet from bench to ridge of house and plants hung down four feet.

Other Selected Varieties of Standard Tomatoes

For years we have aimed to give all the new varieties of Tomatoes offered a thorough test for quality and comparative points in our True Blue Trial Grounds, near this city, which are under the personal supervision of a most efficient manager, who devotes his best energies to the testing of all the seeds we sell; both for purity of stocks, and also to determine that all seeds sent out by us shall be absolutely of the highest percentage of germination. By this plan we not only keep abreast of the times on the Tomato question, but posted on all varieties of both Flower and Vegetable Seeds, especially all novelties, and are therefore placed in a position to offer those deserving of introduction as fast as brought out by any grower or dealer in the horticultural world. Our limited space in this department of our catalogue will not admit of very full or extended descriptions of the fine Tomatoes offered below. The seed stock we offer we can recommend to be as fine as any offered by our competitors or the original introducers.

Earliana—Livingston's Selection

June Pink
A Pink Earliana

Ripens as early as Earliana. It is an enormous bearer, clusters of six to eight fruits being borne frequently. The fruit is of medium size, uniform, smooth and attractively shaped. Excellent for shipping. In color it is a bright, pleasing pink, and in markets where a pink Tomato is desired, it is a great seller. Pkt., 15c.; ½ oz., 15c.; oz., 30c.; ¼ lb., 85c.; lb., $3.00.

Early Hustler

This new sort we recommend as one of the earliest, smoothest bright-red market Tomatoes. Claimed to be earlier than Earliana. Try a small amount. Pkt., 5c.; ½ oz., 15c.; oz., 25c.; ¼ lb., 75c.; lb., $2.50.

Earliana
Livingston's Selection

The earliest smooth, bright-red Tomato of good size. It has been developed in the light, warm soil of Southern New Jersey, where effort is made to market Tomatoes at the earliest possible date. It is so far superior in hardiness, sure-setting of fruits, size and smooth uniform shape, that it is now planted exclusively in this section, which now practically controls the markets of our Eastern cities during the last week of June and the month of July. The plants are compact in growth, with short, close-jointed branches, setting fruits very freely. With the Livingston strain the Tomatoes are quite uniform in size and of smooth, regular form, averaging three inches in diameter and from two to two and a half inches in depth; they are fleshy, solid, and excellent for shipping purposes.

When this variety was first introduced it was inclined to be quite rough. Seeing its many good features and realizing that there was a place for such a variety we immediately started to work out these good points and eliminate the bad ones, foremost of which was its roughness. After several years' careful growing and selecting this roughness has almost entirely disappeared, and we now have a strain that one would scarcely recognize as the old original Earliana. In our trial ground tests we find this strain to be equal to any and surpassing most of the so-called "Extra Selections," usually sold at high prices. Our stock has become quite popular with many of the largest market gardeners in the country. Pkt., 5c.; ½ oz., 15c.; oz., 25c.; ¼ lb., 80c.; lb., $2.75.

Comet Forcing

Superior red variety for forcing under glass. Rich scarlet-red; fruits are solid, round, smooth; strong grower; exceedingly heavy cropper; medium-sized fruits; flavor excellent. Pkt., 5c.; ½ oz., 15c.; oz., 25c.; ¼ lb., 80c.; lb., $2.75.

Chalk's Early Jewel

A little later than Earliana—a heavier cropper, larger size, fine flavor. Brightest scarlet; ripens up to stem without green core. Flesh thick, bright scarlet, solid, sweet flavor. One of the largest cropping medium early varieties we grow. Comes in ahead of Livingston's Stone, almost as large. Pkt., 5c.; ½ oz., 15c.; oz., 25c.; ¼ lb., 80c.; lb., $2.75.

L. Mitchell, Jr., Oswego Co., N. Y., writes us as follows: "I purchased Tomato seed of you last season and they certainly made good."

Chalk's Early Jewel

Matchless

A fine, smooth main crop Tomato, of rich cardinal red color, with solid flesh of finest quality. Grows to good size which it maintains throughout the season. Very similar to Livingston's Stone. Pkt., 5c.; ½ oz., 15c.; oz., 30c.; ¼ lb., 85c.; lb., $3.00.

Trucker's Favorite

A purple fruited sort of excellent quality, highly esteemed in many Eastern and Southern markets. Grows to uniformly large size which is maintained until late Fall. Fruits are invariably smooth, solid and the flesh is of finest color throughout. Unexcelled for slicing or cooking. Plants are very thrifty, free from rust or blight and bear continually until killed by frost. Pkt., 5c.; ½ oz., 15c.; oz., 25c.; ¼ lb., 80c.; lb., $2.75.

Dwarf Giant

A new dwarf sort of good size and various other unique characteristics. It is very prolific, producing fruits in clusters around the base of the plant. Tomatoes are smooth and of regular size and shape. Of the same color as Ponderosa—the originator calls it a "Dwarf Ponderosa." Pkt., 10c.; ½ oz., 20c.; oz., 35c.; ¼ lb., $1.00; lb., $3.75.

Early Detroit

A very productive, early purple sort, uniform in size of fruit, free from cracks, and does not blight easily. Fruit large and smooth. Vines vigorous and quite productive. Quality excellent. Pkt., 5c.; ½ oz., 20c.; oz., 30c.; ¼ lb., 85c.; lb., $3.00.

Success

Resembles our Livingston's Stone Tomato very much, but of smaller size. A good red, smooth, solid and productive sort. Pkt., 5c.; ½ oz., 15c.; oz., 30c.; ¼ lb., 85c.; lb., $3.00.

Ponderosa

(See illustration)—The fruit ripens early and bears well until very late; very solid, almost seedless, of good sub-acid flavor and of immense size, frequently weighing considerably more than 2 pounds. Somewhat scattered on the vine, and a small percentage are rather rough. Our strain, however, is now producing a much smoother fruit than when first introduced. Good Tomato for home use; splendid slicer. Pkt., 5c. and 10c.; ½ oz., 20c.; oz., 35c.; ¼ lb., $1.10; lb., $4.00.

Bonny Best

Bonny Best

One of the finest bright red sorts for growing in greenhouses and a good one to follow Earliana in the open field. It has been highly recommended by U. S. Dept. of Agriculture as well as big growers and shippers throughout the country.

Bonny Best is a favorite Tomato of medium size. They are of bright scarlet color, always smooth and of remarkably uniform size and shape. An elegant sort for market and shipping. Pkt., 5c.; ½ oz., 15c.; oz., 25c.; ¼ lb., 80c.; lb., $2.75.

Small Fruited Tomatoes

Excellent for Preserves, Pickles and Pies

Red Currant—Pkt., 5c.   Red Cherry—Pkt., 5c.
Red Pear-Shape—Pkt., 5c.   Yellow Plum—Pkt., 5c.
Yellow Cherry—Pkt., 5c.   Yellow Pear-Shape—Pkt., 5c.

Prices of above Small-Fruited Tomatoes—½ oz., 20c.; oz., 35c.; ¼ lb., $1.00.

Mixed Small Tomatoes—Above 6 sorts. Pkt., 10c.

Odd Tomatoes

Purple Peach—This variety resembles some peaches so closely in size, shape and general appearance that at a short distance away it is frequently taken for a peach. Color purple, blended with orange-amber; very productive. Pkt., 5c.; ½ oz., 15c.; oz., 25c.; ¼ lb., 80c.

Yellow Peach—Differs from the Purple Peach in color only, being a rich golden yellow. Pkt., 5c.; ½ oz., 15c.; oz., 25c.; ¼ lb., 80c.

Strawberry (Winter Cherry, or Husk Tomato)—This delicate husk-enveloped Tomato is unequaled for making preserves and pies. Have a strawberry flavor and are very productive. We offer the following two sorts:

Golden Husk—Fruit a handsome golden color, the size of large cherries. Pkt., 5c.; ½ oz., 20c.; oz., 35c.; ¼ lb., $1.00.

Purple-Husk—This beautiful sort produces abundantly; 1 to 2 inches in diameter. Pkt., 5c.; ½ oz., 20c.; oz., 35c.

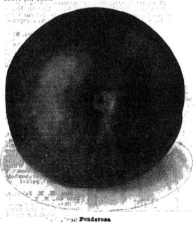

Ponderosa

Vegetable Plants

Asparagus Roots

Piantas o raices de Esperragos   Spargelwurzeln

We have for many years been making a great specialty of Asparagus Roots at our True Blue Seed Farms. Our splendid soil, together with the finest strains of seed obtainable, of the various standard varieties, places us in a position to produce enormous quantities of Asparagus Roots of the very best quality. You will find listed below the most approved sorts in cultivation. Kindly note our especially favorable prices.

500 Asparagus Roots at 1,000 rates. Special prices quoted by letter on larger quantities.

	By Mail Doz.	By Express not Prepaid 100	1000
Carolina Queen	35c	$0 75	$6 00
Conover's Colossal	30c	65	5 00
Columbian Mammoth White	35c	75	5 50
Early Argenteuil	35c	75	6 00
Palmetto	35c	75	5 50

Garlic Sets

Garlic Sets or Bulbs are planted in early Spring in rows 12 inches apart, placing the sets 4 inches apart in the rows, 2 inches deep, or in the same manner as Multiplier Onions. Garlic is used for flavoring purposes.

Bulbs, postpaid, oz., 5c.; ¼ lb., 15c.

Horse Radish Sets

Nuremberg

From Bavaria comes a variety of Horse Radish which has a great many points of superiority. By selection and most careful cultivation only, the Nuremberg Horse Radish has reached a point where individual roots 18 inches long by 2½ to 3 inches at the thickest part are produced from the growth of one year. In fact, its shape is like a parsnip. The quality is splendid; crisp, and of very fine flavor. The color is a beautiful pearl-white.

Roots ready for planting—By mail, postpaid, 6 for 15c.; dbz., 25c.; By express, 100 for $1.00; 500 for $4.00; 1000 for $7.50.

Common Horse Radish

Roots ready for planting—By mail, postpaid, 6 for 15c.; doz., 25c. By express, not paid, 100 for 75c.; 300 for $1.80; 500 for $2.50; 1000 for $4.50. Prices on large lots on application.

Rhubarb Roots

We offer strong seedling roots, which are much more easily transplanted, do better and the transportation charges are less than with old clumps. Never have we had a better lot of roots, or had them in greater quantities. Should you need a large quantity of roots, write us, please, before placing your order elsewhere.

By mail, postpaid, each, 20c. By express, not paid, each, 10c.; 10 for 65c.; 50 for $2.50; 100 for $4.00; 1000 for $30.00.

Two-year-old roots, each, 15c.; 12 for $1.50; 100 for $8.00; 1000 for $75.00. By express or freight at buyer's expense.

RHUBARB ROOTS

NOTE: With us quality is first consideration. Cheap lawn grass cannot be of "True Blue" quality.

Livingston's Capitol Lawn Grass Seed

Contains only the highest grade of grasses suitable for the purpose of making a beautiful, durable, lasting lawn. Our Capitol Lawn Grass Seed germinates quickly, roots deeply. This enables it to readily withstand the intense heat of Summer and the hard cold of Winter, showing a beautiful, rich green from snow to snow. It contains no annual grasses for making a quick show, to the detriment of a permanent lawn, but has only those which are lasting and hardy. When a lawn is once established from our seed, it lasts for years. We have made the formation of lawns a careful study, and many of the finest lawns and grass plots all over the United States were made from Livingston's Capitol Lawn Grass Seed. For a perfect and enduring lawn of closely interwoven, firm, elastic turf, which will flourish under varied conditions of soil and climate and show a luxuriant, rich green growth throughout the year, plant Livingston's Capitol Lawn Grass Seed.

Quantities to Use—One lb. for 400 sq. ft.; 5 lbs. for 2000 sq. ft.; 10 lbs. for 4000 sq. ft.; 25 lbs. for 10,890 sq. ft. (¼ acre); 34 lbs. for 14,550 sq. ft. (1-3 acre); 50 lbs. for 21,780 sq. ft. (½ acre); 100 lbs. for 43,560 sq. ft. (1 acre).

For Renewing Old Lawns—Use about one-half the quantity given in above directions.

Capitol Lawn Grass Seed is the cheapest as well as the best lawn grass seed offered. While 14 lbs. of lawn grass seed is usually considered a bushel, this will weigh 20 lbs. to the bushel. We sell by the pound instead of quart. This method of selling is very much to the advantage of the purchaser, as a pound of grass seed measures over 1½ quarts.

PRICE—First Quality, per lb., 35c.; 2 lb., 65c.; 1 bu., $5; | **PRICE**—Second Quality, per lb., 30c.; 2 lb., 55c.; 1 bu., $4.75; 5 bu., $23.75. | 5 bu., $22.50.

These prices do not include postage. See Page 2.

How to Make a Lawn.—The preparation of the soil is very important in making a good lawn. As early as possible in the Spring it should be thoroughly dug or ploughed to the depth of 10 or 12 inches and properly graded to the desired level. Remove all stones, sticks, sods, etc., harrow or rake it fine and roll it firm. It is impossible to get the soil too fine to receive the seed. After rolling the soil will be ready for the seed. If the soil is poor, wood ashes, bone meal or pulverized sheep manure should be added after digging it up. Well-rotted stable manure is also good, but it often contains weed seeds. **Sow the best seed obtainable;** it is always cheapest in the end; use quantity as indicated by table on this page. It is best to sow seed liberally, not only so as to produce a lawn quickly, but because the best lawn seed produces fine-leaved grasses which should take entire possession of the ground at once, thus choking out and preventing the development of any weed seeds, which are apt to be in all soils. Sow seed by hand, distributing it evenly, going both ways across the plot. After sowing, cover the seed by raking lightly; then roll. When the grass has become well rooted, use lawn mower. Keep the mower sharp, as if dull it will pull and injure the grass, besides causing the lawn to have an uneven appearance. Never allow the grass to become so high that the mower will take off the first joint, as this is an injury. Mow as often as necessary; in growing weather at least once a week. Let the short clippings remain on the lawn, as they wither and dry and form a protection to the roots. When the clippings are long, they should be raked off, for, besides being unsightly, they are also injurious. When dry and hot, avoid cutting too close.

To Grass a Terrace.—Take for each square rod a pound of lawn grass seed, and mix it with about six cubic feet of good dry garden loam. Place it in a tub and add liquid manure, diluted with about two-thirds water until the mixture has the consistency of mortar. Make the slope even and smooth, water it well, then apply a thin, even coat of mixture.

Shady Place Mixture

On nearly all lawns there are shaded, bare and unsightly spots on which the owners have difficulty in getting a stand of grass. For such places this mixture is adapted. It is composed of grasses which naturally grow in shaded places. They are the finest and most costly of all grasses. If the soil is covered with moss or seems "sour" and out of condition, rake off the surface and apply slaked lime at the rate of one bushel to 1000 square feet. This will sweeten the soil. Then dig and prepare the lawn as directed above. Prices: Lb., 45c.; 3 lb., $1.20; bu., $7.00.

Special Quotations.—We are always pleased to quote special prices to Parks, Institutions, Golf Clubs and others who require Lawn Grass Seeds in large quantities.

Golf Links Mixture

We make a mixture of grasses suitable to the purposes of the golf links, so it will stand rough usage. We can also prescribe for links located on poor or rich, dry or wet soils, telling which grass will best suit each location. Write us, stating your requirements.

Tennis Court Mixture

A mixture composed of low-growing hardy grasses suitable for ground of this character. Price: Lb., 45c.; 3 lb., $1.20; lb., $7.00. These prices do not include postage. See Page 2.

Kentucky Blue Grass is offered on page 69.

Prices of all Grass and Clover Seeds are subject to market changes.

Livingston's Re-Cleaned Grass and Clover Seeds

Our Grass and Clover Seeds are selected with special reference to their quality. Purchasers may rely upon our best exertions to furnish them with these vitally important qualities—fresh, pure and free from noxious weeds and foreign seeds.

Prices on Grass and Clover Seeds are changing almost daily, **AND WE CAN ONLY GIVE PRICES SUBJECT TO FLUCTUATIONS.** No charge for bags at prices quoted below; do not forget this important item when comparing our prices with others. **These prices do not include postage. See page 3 for Parcel Post Rates.** Owing to the European war, prices on imported seeds are more unsettled than usual. If interested in imported Grass Seeds or for larger quantities, write for special rates.

Best Grasses

Awnless Brome Grass (Bromus inermis)—Will stand long droughts and still produce heavy crops in dry sections where other grasses would surely perish. Has also proven itself one of the hardiest grasses. Especially desirable for permanent pastures. Succeeds in a wider range of temperature than any other grass. Sow from 25 to 30 lbs. per acre. (Bu., 14 lbs.) Lb., 20c.; 10 lbs., $1.80; 100 lbs., $16.00.

Creeping Bent Grass (Agrostis stolonifera)—Excellent for pasture when mixed with other grasses. Succeeds well in most sections and thrives in moist land. Sow 40 lbs. per acre. (Bu., 14 lbs.) Lb., 55c.; 10 lbs., $5.00; 100 lbs., $48.00.

Crested Dog's Tail (Cynosurus cristatus)—May be sown on lawns; forms a close turf, remaining green a long time; valuable for sheep pasture; succeeds on dry, hard, and gravelly soil. Height 1 to 1½ feet. Sow 25 lbs. per acre. (Bu., 21 lbs.) Lb., 45c.; 10 lbs., $4.00; 100 lbs., $38.00.

Hard Fescue (Festuca duriuscula)—Not very productive, but is of very fine quality; thrives in dry situations where many other grasses would fail, thus making it desirable for pasture. Sow 30 lbs. per acre. (Bu., about 12 lbs.) Lb., 40c.; 10 lbs., $3.50; 100 lbs., $33.00.

Blue Grass.

Meadow Fescue (Festuca pratensis)—Thrives in all soils; excellent for permanent pastures; starts early; productive. Sow 25 to 35 lbs. per acre. (Bu., 24 lbs.) Lb., 20c.; 10 lbs., $1.75; 100 lbs., $16.00.

Orchard Grass (Dactylis glomerata)—Extremely hardy and widely known. One of the earliest to start in the Spring; grows rapidly; furnishes an abundance of pasture the entire season. Sow 20 to 30 lbs. per acre. (Bu., 14 lbs.) Lb., 30c.; 10 lbs., $2.50; 100 lbs., $22.00.

Kentucky Blue Grass, June Grass (Poa pratensis)—Universally known; desirable for pastures and lawns. Sow in Fall or Spring at rate of 30 to 40 lbs. per acre. (Bu., 14 lbs.) Export Fancy Clean Seed—Lb., 20c.; 10 lbs., $1.75; 100 lbs., $14.00.

Perennial Rye Grass (Lolium perenne)—Very nutritious; valuable for meadows or permanent pastures; rapid grower. Sow 25 to 35 lbs. per acre. (Bu., 24 lbs.) Lb., 15c.; 10 lbs., $1.35; 100 lbs., $11.00.

Red Top Grass (Agrostis vulgaris)—Thrives well in any soil, but best on low land; produces a firm sod. Sow 15 to 20 lbs. per acre. (Bu., 14 lbs.) Fancy Clean—Lb., 20c.; 10 lbs., $1.80; 100 lbs., $16.00.

Rhode Island Bent Grass (Agrostis canina)—Valuable for lawns. Sow 35 to 50 lbs. per acre for lawns, 20 to 30 lbs. for pasture. (Bu., 12 lbs.) Lb., 45c.; 10 lbs., $4.00; 100 lbs., $39.00.

Sheep's Fescue (Festuca ovina)—Grows naturally on light, dry, sandy soils and mountain pastures; considered valuable mixed with other grasses for permanent early Spring pasture. Sow 15 lbs. per acre. (Bu., about 12 lbs.) Lb., 40c.; 10 lbs., $3.50; 100 lbs., $22.00.

Tall Meadow Oat Grass (Avena elatior)—Used for soiling. Succeeds well in sandy lands, and owing to its long fibrous roots, stands cold and drought well. Sow 25 to 30 lbs. per acre. (Bu., 10 lbs.) Lb., 30c.; 10 lbs., $2.50; 100 lbs., $22.00.

Timothy (Phleum pratense)—A well-known variety. When ready to buy, write us for latest prices, whether you want a bag or a carload. Sow 8 lbs. per acre. (Bu., 45 lbs.)

Prime Seed....Lb., 15c.; 10 lbs., $1.10; 100 lbs., $9.20
Choice Seed...Lb., 15c.; 10 lbs., $1.20; 100 lbs., $9.60

Wood Meadow Grass (Poa nemoralis)—Adapted for pasture or pleasure grounds; of early growth; thrives under trees. Sow 25 to 30 lbs. per acre. (Bu., 14 lbs.) Lb., 60c.; 10 lbs., $6.50; 100 lbs., $55.00.

Mixed Grasses

For Meadows and Permanent Pastures—We are prepared to furnish seeds adapted to all soils, all situations and all purposes—for light, medium, and heavy soils. By light soils we mean that which is more or less of a sandy or gravelly nature; the heavy, clay and heavy loams, while the medium is an intermediate between these two. A light, wet soil, with respect to grasses suited to it, may be considered same as too heavy soils; a dry, heavy soil more as the light soils. Write us what you want, giving nature of soil, number of acres, etc., and we will, with pleasure, give you estimate and terms.

NOTE—Owing to the war in Europe we are forced to name prices higher than usual because of the unstable conditions. When ready to buy write for price. We will take pleasure in naming lowest price possible at any time.

Red Top Grass (Agrostis vulgaris)

Timothy

Sudan Grass (Andropogon Sorghum)

A New Forage Crop of Immense Value to the South and Middle West

Sudan Grass was introduced into the United States in 1909 from Sudan under the name of Garawi. The result of this test by the Government proved so promising that it at once sprang into favor in the dry Middle West and South, and recommended for the Central States as a substitute for Millet in its use as a catch crop.

The dry region has no other satisfactory hay crop and Sudan Grass will be of great value there, as it has all the good qualities of Johnson Grass, but does not have the creeping root-stalks which are so objectionable that it becomes a dangerous pest.

Sudan Grass is strictly an annual and dies each year like Millet. This makes it fit into any system of rotation.

Sudan Grass grows from 5 to 9 feet tall. The stems are very small, rarely thicker than a lead pencil.

The plant stools freely when given plenty of room and often produces 100 stems from one crown. The tendency to stool is greater after the first cutting and the hay is finer from the second cutting.

Sudan Grass is not very particular as to soil, but does best on rich loam fairly well drained.

In seeding Sudan Grass, a firm seed bed is best and should be made quite fine. Seed should not be sown until the soil is well warmed up. The best tool for seeding is the common grain drill and seed should be covered from half inch to one inch. When drilled in rows 18 to 24 inches apart, 4 to 6 pounds are required. When sown broadcast, 16 to 24 pounds per acre should be used.

Sudan Grass grows strictly erect and stiff enough to be valuable to sow with Cow Peas and Soy Beans as a support.

Sudan Grass cures readily and can be cut in the morning and raked in the afternoon. The blades are retained well and if properly handled make a bright, leafy hay of best quality. From Central United States Southward it is possible to have from 2 to 3 cuttings. From seeding to cutting 75 to 80 days are required. The second cutting comes on in about 45 days. The yields vary from 1 to 8 tons cured hay per acre.

Price—Large pkt., 10c.; 1 lb., 35c., postpaid. 10 lbs., $2.50; 25 lbs., $5.25; 100 lbs., $18.00.

Single Plant Sudan Grass

Millet (German or Golden)

True Southern grown-cultivated Tennessee grown stock is far superior to Western grown stock; will grow in any climate or soil and where conditions are favorable its yield is very heavy; often from two to seven tons per acre of most nutritious feed. It is of special importance, however, to secure the true Southern grown stock.

If the seed used is common Millet or mixed, the yield is very greatly reduced and quality of hay not so good. Common or mixed millets are not so leafy and straw more woody.

True Southern grown produces a heavy and luxuriant growth, has very large heads which ripen evenly, and if cut while in bloom or before seed ripens it is a quickly produced, cheap and valuable food, that is eaten readily by all our farm animals.

Have the land well plowed and thoroughly pulverized before sowing. Sow for hay not less than 50 lbs. per acre at any time between May 1st and July 1st. If sown broadcast cover with single stroke of harrow or light board drag, or it may be sown with a grain drill set to sow one bushel per acre having the hoes hooked up so as not to cover seed over one inch deep. We prefer putting seed in with a drill. (Bu., 50 lbs.)

Head Golden Millet   Price—Lb., 10c.; 10 lbs., 60c.; 100 lbs., $4.00. —

Hungarian Millet. (Grass)

For good low ground or rich high land, Hungarian becomes even more valuable than German Millet. It is one of the earliest annual hay crops and can be sown later than any of the millets. Is often sown as a catch crop after early Potatoes, or other early maturing crops, thus giving two crops a year on the same land.

Hungarian is not so large and coarse as German Millet; it is very leafy and much finer in the straw, and if cut for hay before seed is ripe enough to grow or just as it goes out of bloom it is considered nearly equal to Timothy and under favorable conditions should yield from two to four tons per acre of good nutritious hay that is relished by dairy, cows, young cattle or horses.

Hungarian grass is generally looked upon as being much better feed for horses than Millet.

Sow from May 15th to July 15th on well prepared soil at the rate of three pecks to 1 bushel per acre. (Bu., 50 lbs.)

Price—10c. per lb.; 10 lbs., 50c.; 100 lbs., $3.50.

Write for prices of Ohio and Western grown German Millet.

All prices subject to market change.

All Prices of Grass, Clover and
Field Seeds are Subject to
Market Changes

Livingston's Re-Cleaned Clover Seeds

Parties wishing large quantities will do well to get samples and prices before placing their orders. We handle it on a close margin and supply the finest grades. It is impossible to tell how low our prices are without seeing samples, which will be sent free on application. A bushel of Clover Seed is 60 pounds. These prices do not include postage. For Parcel Post rate see Page 3.

Alfalfa or Lucerne

Sweet Clover, or Bokhara

Melilotus Alba (White), Melilotus Officianlia (Yellow) are Biennial; Melilotus Indica (Yellow), Annual.

Are the varieties in general use. The white-flowered variety (Melilotus Alba) is the one we handle unless otrwise mentioned. It is the strongest grower and by far the best.

When young it resembles Alfalfa, but when mature it often stands 5 to 8 feet high and blooms from June to October. The roots of all varieties are large and much branched and penetrate the ground several feet, being a Biennial all top and roots die at the end of the second year if the plant ripens seed.

If cut before seed is ripe or if pastured so that seed is not matured, the plant lasts over several seasons.

Is found growing under very varied conditions of both soil and climate. It, however, prefers a limestone soil and has been largely used to reclaim old, worn-out, abandoned lands. It is of great value for this purpose.

Apart from its value as a nitrogen gatherer and humus producer, Sweet Clover is rapidly coming to the front as a hay and pasture crop. Its feed value is nearly equal that of Alfalfa and in a short time stock eat it as readily as they do red clover and seem to thrive on it equally well. For hay cut just before it comes into bloom, and is handled as you would Alfalfa. It is also used extensively as a Bee pasture, the small white blooms yield much fine honey.

Sow clean hulled seed at the rate of 15 to 20 lbs. per acre from April to Sept. 15th with or without a nurse crop.

Price: Lb., 35c.; 10 lbs., $3.00; 100 lbs., $28.00.

Mammoth Clover—Valuable with other grasses, for mixed hay. Ripens about with Timothy. Being a rank grower, it is used largely for plowing under. Sow 10 lbs. per acre. Lb., 40c.; 10 lbs., $3.50; 100 lbs., $30.00.

Medium, or Common Red—The most important and valuable of the Clover family. Makes the best of hay. Sow 10 lbs. per acre. Lb., 35c.; 10 lbs., $3.25; 100 lbs., $27.00.

Crimson Clover—Should be sown in July, August and September of each year. Can be sown with corn, or any cultivated crop. Sow 10 to 15 lbs. per acre. Cover lightly. Use only American grown seed. The Spring following it can be cut for soiling May 1st; for ensilage, May 1 to 15; for seed about third week in June. Lb., 30c.; 10 lbs., $2.00; 100 lbs., $15.00.

White Dutch Clover—Good in permanent pastures, especially for cattle; valuable for bees, and the best variety for lawns. Sow in Spring at the rate of 5 lbs. per acre when sown alone; ½ the quantity when sown with other grasses. Lb., 60c.; 10 lbs., $5.50; 100 lbs., $50.00.

Alfalfa, or Lucerne (Medicago sativa)

The Greatest Feed on Earth

Alfalfa is being more generally grown as experience is teaching our farmers the proper methods to follow. Different soils do not now seem so difficult to overcome, especially where they can be properly drained, pulverized, sweetened and inoculated.

Alfalfa does not thrive on acid or sour land, nor will it do its best without inoculation on any kind of soil.

Treat your land to a liberal dressing of fine ground lime or more liberally to fine ground limestone well worked into the soil some three months to a year before seeding to Alfalfa.

Sow from 10 to 15 lbs. well inoculated seed per acre, using Nitragin. From April 1st to June 15th for the early Spring sowing, either drilled or sown broadcast. If broadcast cover lightly with a light drag or with single stroke of a barrow.

Much seeding is now done later and many prefer sowing from July 15th to September 15th, when seeded late it gives the grower an opportunity to have his land clean and free from weeds.

Alfalfa naturally prefers a deep, sandy or gravelly sub-soil. Roots from 3 to 15 feet deep and a good stand on properly selected land should yield from 3 to 5 cuttings a year. We make a specialty of extra high grade seed that tests 99 per cent. pure or better. Get our samples and prices before ordering. Prices: Lb., 35c.; 10 lbs., $3.25; 100 lbs., $27.00.

Alsike, or Hybrid (Swedish)—Hardiest of all clovers. On rich, moist soil, yields large quantities of hay or pasturage. Will thrive in soils which are so wet that the common Red Clover would not live. Unlike some of the other clovers, which have tap roots, Alsike has many fibrous roots, hence is not injured by freezing and thawing of the ground. Esteemed highly by beekeepers. Sow 5 lbs. per acre. Lb., 40c.; 10 lbs., $3.50; 100 lbs., $27.00.

NITRAGIN SOIL INOCULATOR

Get a perfect "catch," a bigger yield, of better feeding value. For Alfalfa, Clover, Vetch, Cow Peas, Soy Beans and all other legumes.

For full description and price see page 75.

Alsike or Swedish

Livingston's the Place to Buy Seeds

To our old friends, and to those looking for a reliable place to buy their supply of seeds, and who are not acquainted with us, our methods, advantages or our location.

We would call attention to a few points that we consider should be of interest to you, namely—

In place of being mere seed merchants, we are seedsmen, and have been for three generations. Established in 1850 we have been in a manner born and reared on the garden and farm. We were there taught method of preparing, fertilizing, cultivation and curing. Still more important, acquired a keen sense of discrimination, a keen eye for selection, and plant variation, so valuable in judging and determining varieties of merit to both farmer and gardener.

Situated as we are in almost the exact center of the state, and nearly the center of that portion of the United States between the sea board on the East and the Mississippi River on the West, and in the heart of the great grain-producing valleys of the Ohio and Mississippi River basins where all our cultivated crops are unsurpassed and where entire failure has never been known.

We have sixteen steam railroads and eleven electric railways operating out of Columbus, radiating from the center like the spokes of a wheel. These, in turn, make direct connection in such manner that in 18 hours' by rail or within a radius of 500 miles we are in touch with 65,000,000 people or over half the population of the United States.

In addition to our splendid railroad facilities we have all the large express companies, all the regular telegraph companies, and occupy a strategic position as to telephones.

These great trunk lines of commerce and quick means of communication, along with the Parcel Post service, places us in position to get in touch with more people and place goods in their hands in a shorter length of time than any city we know of.

With our experience, training and knowledge of the business, our acquaintance with sources of supply, for such seed as we do not grow, our unsurpassed shipping facilities by freight, express or Parcel Post, our location, and backed by the best soil in the world, and this all backed by a disposition to serve you to the best that can be had in the shortest possible length of time, we feel we occupy a position that should have your careful and thoughtful consideration.

We, in turn, assure you our best efforts to serve you honestly and faithfully.

THE LIVINGSTON SEED CO.

Livingston's Finest Grain Seeds

Selected Seed Oats

We have always realized the importance of supplying growers with the best selected Seed Oats, and we can truly say that our efforts in this direction have resulted in our customers obtaining increased yields by sowing our superior stocks.

Owing to the extreme wet season Oats of good quality are scarce and we offer seed while stocks last at the following prices:

Prices subject to market fluctuations.

Items on this page are shipped at buyer's expense except as noted.

Regenerated Selected Swedish Oats

(See illustration)—Originated and introduced by Garton Seed Co., of England, are now well acclimated and have given excellent satisfaction. Weighs from 32 to 40 lbs. per measured bushel. The straw is heavy and strong and not liable to lodge. Heads are large, upright and bushy. Grains are white, large, thick and plump with thin hull, making a very fine appearance and very desirable for feeding. Their strong root development enables them to withstand drought better than many varieties; are quite early and less liable to damage by rust than many sorts. Price—Lb., 10c.; pk., 35c.; bu. (32 lbs.), $1.10; 2 bu., $2.10; 5 bu., $5.00; 10 bu., $9.50.

Silver Mine Oats

This Oat has a reputation of long standing and is noted for its heavy and reliable yielding properties. It is very hardy and produces beautiful white kernels very desirable for the manufacture of rolled oats. The heads are large and sprangled and borne low down on the stalk, which is stiff, bright and clean and seems to prevent lodging. We have handled this very reliable Oat for a number of years. Many farmers will sow no other sort as they offer all the desirable points, namely: Large, plump white grain, good straw, medium early and good yielder. Price—Lb., 10c.; pk., 35c.; bu. (32 lbs.), $1.10; 2 bu., $2.10; 5 bu., $5.00; 10 bu., $9.50. Bags free.

New Victory Oats

Of new blood, lately from the North, the land of heavy Oats, strong and vigorous in habit of growth, large, white, plump grains and stiff straw. Very desirable. Introduced last season, but owing to the wet weather this season's crop is a failure. Stock we offer is crop of 1914 and very limited. Price—Lb., 10c.; ¼ bu., 45c.; ½ bu., 75c.; bu. (32 lbs.), $1.35; 2 bu., $2.50; 5 bu., $6.00.

Spring Wheat (60 Lbs. to Bushel)

Marquis (New)—Is similar to Red Fife; quite early; beardless; yellow chaff, very plump flinty kernel; said to be one of the best. Lb., 10c.; by express or freight, pk., 70c.; bu., $2.40.

Blue Stem—A very popular variety in the Northwest. Heads are large and well-filled; stools freely; kernels very hard. Lb., 10c.; by express or freight, pk., 60c.; bu., $2.25.

Barley (48 Lbs. to Bushel)

Beardless—Barley needs a rich land, more sandy and lighter than that adapted to Wheat. It is sown in the Spring and can be grown farther North than any other grain. It should be cut before fully ripe (unless intended for seed), as it is then of better quality and less liable to shell. Use about 2 bushels per acre. Lb., 15c.; pk., 45c.; bu., $1.50; 10 bu., $14.50.

Speltz or Emmer (40 Lbs. to Bushel)

A valuable grain recently introduced from Russia. It is adapted to dry sections and poor soils, often yielding 50 bushels or more of grain per acre. The straw and grain of Speltz have feeding value equal to barley and are relished by all kinds of stock. Sow in the Spring, 50 lbs. per acre. Large pkt., 10c.; lb., 15c., postpaid; 10 lbs., 60c.; 25 lbs., $1.00; 50 lbs., $1.75; 100 lbs., $3.00.

All prices subject to market change.

Beardless Barley

Livingston's Thoroughbred Field Corn Seed

Prices of all Farm Seeds quoted in this Catalogue are subject to market changes. The prices given are those ruling at the time this Catalogue is published, January 1st. But we reserve the right to change prices without notice.

One bushel of Field Corn Seed will plant from five and one-half to seven acres, according to variety and whether the hill or drill method of planting is followed. Livingston's Thoroughbred Field Corn Seed only costs you 30 to 40 cents for sufficient seed to plant an acre. We earnestly urge you to plant the best Field Corn Seed that our many years of experience has been able to produce. Our strains are pure and each a distinct type—no two resembles one another, and all grown in Central Ohio.

Situated, as we are, in the very best territory in this country as regards both soil and climate, for growing and perfecting Field Corn, we would impress upon you the fact that our facilities and opportunities for securing and supplying the most thoroughbred strains of Field Corn are not exceeded by any seed firm.

All our Field Corn Seed is well matured, thoroughly cured, and shelled with the greatest care. We test all varieties before sending the seed to our customers, that there may be no doubt as to the vitality. **To avoid delay** when ordering late in the season, it would be well for you to **mention your second choice,** or state whether we shall send you a sort adapted to your locality, or refund the money, provided we are sold out of your **first choice** when your order arrives. **Field Corn Seed on the ear can only be supplied while our present stock lasts.**

Our Grand New Field Corn

Kilbury's Yellow Hybrid

Introduced by us in 1908

A NEW AND VERY DESIRABLE VARIETY. EARLIEST LARGE-EARED CORN IN CULTIVATION. HANDSOME, UNIFORM EAR. DEEP GRAINS.

This splendid Corn is one of the most valuable new varieties which has come under our notice this long time. (See illustration.) The following is originator's description: "Kilbury's Yellow Hybrid Corn is deep in color, with red cob, which tapers uniformly from butt to tip, with deep grains well compacted on cob. Ears large, from 9 to 12 inches in length. Fodder large; ears 3½ to 5 feet from ground, husks easy, does not fall off in handling. The earliest large Corn on the market. Plant any time in May; it has matured planted as late as June 15th. This Corn has been successfully grown for nineteen years on black loam and clay soils, and is well adapted to both."

"After careful examination of this Corn, both growing in fields and after being harvested, we believe it to be all that Mr. Kilbury claims. It is the result of careful selection from hybrids of Leaming and Clarage, but is much larger than either of the parents. It is a large, medium early Corn; safe to plant in localities no colder than Ohio." If you want the **earliest big-eared** Corn grown, with large, heavy, deep grains and small cob, a yellow corn, plant **Kilbury's Yellow Hybrid.** For prices see below.

Neller's Cattle Corn

This very desirable strain of Corn was brought into Licking County, Ohio, from an adjoining county some thirty or more years ago by a local cattle breeder. And as it was especially well adapted to cattle feeding became very popular wherever tried not only for cattle feeding, but for general feeding as well.

Our attention was directed to this Corn some time since and four years ago when good seed Corn was so hard to procure, we introduced it to our trade through our retail store. Three years ago we catalogued this variety and reports from all directions to this date (October, 1915) are especially satisfactory and we look upon it as one of our very best strains for general growing; quite uniform in shape and style of ear and a sure cropper.

The Corn is a good strong yellow in color, has deep well-formed kernels, well-dented but not chaffy, set on a small dark red cob. Ears have 12 to 16 rows and often 12 inches long and well-grained over the ends, fodder an average in size and leafage. In this locality will ripen in 90 to 100 days.

Prices for either of the above—Shelled, large pkt., 19c.; pint, 25c.; quart, 40c.; postpaid. By Parcel Post, Express or Freight, purchaser paying the transportation charges, ¼ bu., 85c.; ½ bu., $1.50; bu. (56 lbs.), $2.75; 5 bu., $13.00; 6 select ears, 60c.; bu. (68 lbs.) of ears, $3.25.

Kilbury's Yellow Hybrid

Neller's Cattle Corn

Livingston's Golden Surprise Field Corn

The Large Amount of Corn Produced on Such Small Cobs Surprises Everyone. Entirely Distinct. Stalks Short and Strong. Ripens in 90 to 100 Days. Ears Medium Size. Deep Grained. Small Cob. A Great Feeding Corn.

A variety of great merit offered and named by us in 1898, and, as anticipated, it has met with great favor wherever it has been thoroughly tested. Our description of Golden Surprise Field Corn consists of plain statements and simple facts.

Our illustration is from a photograph and will give you a very accurate idea of the ears. The **cob is small.** The Corn, as a whole, is indicative of its name, and is indeed a **genuine surprise** to all who grow it. Beautiful in its rich golden color and even size from butt to tip of the ear. **Profitable** in its depth of grain and small per cent. of waste in cob. **Convenient** in its short fodder growth and easy break of ear from the stalk. **Certain** in its early maturity, and, all points considered, the **best early Corn up to date.**

Golden Surprise was not offered to the general public until, after ten years and more of the closest and most critical observation, careful breeding and selection to its present perfect type. Tested for years in various localities in comparison with well-known sorts, we find it fully equal in average bulk to any on the market, but in depth of grain and weight of shelled Corn per bushel, it has no competitor. Its habit of growth is a very vigorous, medium sized, strong stalk, with broad, closely set leaves, which makes it a valuable fodder Corn. For prices, see below.

Johnson County White Dent

This variety is a cross between Boone Co. White and Forsythe Favorite and developed and introduced by L. B. Clore and has had 21 years of careful painstaking and intelligent selection and breeding. For the corn-growing belt, we are quite sure there is no White Corn grown to-day of equal merit. The Corn has become famous for yield and quality, and especially valuable, where one wishes to grow show stock.

The shape of the ear is cylindrical to within about 2 inches of the tip, then slightly tapering. Tips fill well over the end and a large per cent. of the ears are entirely covered with grains; the butts are well rounded out with a medium-sized shank, kernels very uniform wedge shaped, pure white and white cob; ears average about 10 inches in length with the circumference about three-fourths of the length.

Of strong and vigorous habit of growth and well covered with broad blades, very valuable for ensilage. The length of season is about 120 days. This corn has been successfully grown as far north as Ft. Wayne, Ind., or Marion, Ohio. We especially recommend it for the great corn-growing valleys in latitudes of Columbus and south.

Prices—Shelled, large pkt., 10c.; pint, 25c.; quart, 40c.; postpaid. By Parcel Post, Express or Freight, purchaser paying the transportation charges; ¼ bu., 85c.; ½ bu., $1.50; bu. (56 lbs.), $2.75; 5 bu., $13.00; 5 select ears, 60c.; bu. (68 lbs.) of ears, $3.25.

As corn prices are made before corn conditions are fully known, those wanting larger quantities will please write for special quotations.

Golden Surprise

Johnson County White Dent

The splendid varieties of Corn described and priced in this catalogue have all been grown especially for seed, and will be found well cured and true to name—in fact, first-class in every respect. We would ask our customers to place their orders as early as possible while our stocks remain unbroken. **Prices of Field Corn by Packet include postage. On larger quantities, by Parcel Post, express or freight, purchasers must pay the transportation charges.** See page 2 for Parcel Post rates.

True Yellow Leaming

The Standard Variety for Quality.

An extensively grown, large, Yellow Dent variety, which we have grown and sold with the greatest satisfaction for years. **Our improved strain we do not believe is excelled, if equaled, by any other now offered.** It has pure, glossy yellow ears, growing low, on very strong, heavy stalks; grains square and deep; ripens quite early—frequently in 100 days from planting. Yields from 75 to 100 bushels per acre. Adapted to rich soils. (See illustration.)

For prices, see below.

True Yellow Clarage

Best Second Early. Sure to Ripen

This variety has been grown extensively in this locality for over 50 years, and is one of the surest cropping varieties ever grown here. Ripens between Pride of the North and True Yellow Leaming. Ear medium in size, very uniform its entire length and well filled out at both ends. Husks very easily; of rich golden yellow color and very productive. In favorable seasons will ripen planted as late as the first of July. **Highly recommended as one of the best in points of early maturity, productiveness and very rich in feeding qualities.** (See illustration.)

For prices, see below.

White Cap Yellow Dent

An old popular variety. This old favorite has been known for many years as a good yielder on all kinds of land. A very strong and hardy strain and recommended for thin soils. The ears are large and well covered, cob is both red and white. The grain has white cap, is well dented and of good depth with lemon colored body. Can be planted safely in any part of Ohio and similar latitudes. **For price, see below.**

Pride of the North

A very early Yellow Dent Field Corn, and can be successfully grown farther North than can any other Dent variety. It ripens very readily, even in New England. It also matures perfectly in 90 days and is very frequently safe from frost in 75 days. Very hardy, ears of uniform size; too small for a main crop, but right size for stock feeding; cob small, kernels set closely on cob and are long and compact. This variety is planted quite largely for early crop to feed stock while yet green; and is also planted late when larger varieties could not possibly mature before the frosts.

UNIFORM PRICES FOR ALL VARIETIES LISTED ABOVE:
Shelled large pkt., 10c.; pint, 25c.; quart, 40c., postpaid. By Parcel Post, Express or Freight, purchaser paying the transportation charges, ¼ bu., 85c.; ½ bu., $1.50; bu. (56 lbs.), $2.75; 5 bu., $13.00. Select ears, 60c.; bu. (68 lbs.) of ears, $3.25.

True Yellow Leaming Field Corn.

True Yellow Clarage Field Corn.

Livingston's Mammoth White Dent Field Corn

Has Been Grown Continuously on One Farm for Over Fifty Years

A very large White Dent Field Corn. Has a broad, very deep, pure white kernel and cob. Grades strictly white in any market. It is very desirable for white cornmeal, and those desiring a large white corn cannot fail to be pleased with this splendid variety. As a grain crop or for ensilage we consider it the equal of any variety we have ever seen tried, and have sold it in large quantities to nearly all the dairymen around this city and many others throughout the country. We have sold this excellent Corn for many years past, and we can honestly pronounce it one of the best large White Dent sorts. Matures as early as any of the yellow varieties of the same large-sized ear. (See illustration to right from our own photograph.) For prices see below.

Reid's Thoroughbred Yellow Dent

(See illustration to the left, from our own photo.)

If any seed grain can truly be called pedigreed, the Reid's Yellow Dent Field Corn is certainly entitled to be known as such, as its history dates many years back. It has been bred up and selected with painstaking care to what is at the present time one of the best varieties of yellow Corn grown. Ear medium in size, remarkably uniform, and of a bright yellow color, with solid, deep grain and small red cob. Has from 18 to 24 rows of kernels on the cob, 50 to 60 grains in the row and is well filled over the ends, and especially the butt, leaving a small shank, which makes it a great favorite with huskers. Best shredding sort, as it shatters the least of any by actual test.

In some of the principal Corn growing states of the West, it has no equal, and reports from many other states are very flattering. The Iowa Experiment Station report of 1901 gave the Reid's Yellow Dent an average of 100 bushels per acre, while the Agricultural Students' Union of Ohio in 1903 gave it a yield of 14 per cent. above all other varieties. As a winner of prizes from the World's Fair at Chicago in 1893, and at Western Corn carnivals and shows down to the present time, it stands at the head. For prices, see below.

Prices: Shelled, large pkt., 10c.; pint, 25c.; quart, 40c., postpaid. By Parcel Post, Express or Freight, purchaser paying the transportation charges: ¼ bu., 85c.; ½ bu., $1.50; bu. (56 lbs.), $2.75; 5 bu., $13.00; 6 select ears, 60c.; bu. (68 lbs.) of ears, $3.75.

Chas. E. Ball, Erie Co., Pa., writes as follows: "Our field of Kilbury Yellow Hybrid Corn will average 7 feet high and just tasseling out. Neighbors say it is the finest field of corn they ever saw. Three ears formed on some stalks."
J. M. Hatheway, Kendall Co., Ill, writes as follows: "Your corn and garden seeds are at hand, and will say this for your house, I never saw such fine seeds before and they were sent so nice. I thank you for them."
J. E. Shawyer, Clark Co., Ohio, writes as follows: "The seeds which I ordered from you have arrived in good condition and I am well pleased with them. I wish to say that the Alfalfa seed is the prettiest, clean seed I have ever seen; in fact, all the seeds look fine. Thanking you for your promptness, I remain."
Mary A. Love, Buchanan Co., Iowa, writes as follows: "I have used your seeds for the last 36 years. I am well pleased with them. They are just fine and the best there is. Your tomatoes are better than any other. I had three tomatoes; after they were cooked good they more than filled a one-quart can. Lots of them measured 13½ and 14 inches. Who wants them any larger?"

Reid's Yellow Dent   Mammoth White Dent

Fodder and Ensilage Corn Varieties

Red-Cob Ensilage Corn
A Southern type of large, white corn, with strong, leafy stalks and short joints. Farmers growing the Red-Cob Ensilage for the first time tell us they hardly know what to do with the enormous yield of fodder. Pk., 50c.; bu., $1.50; 2 bu., $2.80; 5 bu., $6.75; 10 bu., $12.50.

Sweet Corn for Green Fodder
There is nothing better or more greedily eaten by stock of all kinds. Can be planted the same as other corn, or sown thickly in drills or broadcast. Pk., 65c.; bu., $2.50.

True Yellow Leaming Corn
Highly recommended by the best ensilage authorities for Northern states, as True Yellow Leaming produces large quantities of leaves. Bu., $2.75; 5 bu., $13.00.

Mammoth White Dent Corn
Yields immense crops of excellent fodder, which makes fine feed for stock of all kinds, either as ensilage or fodder corn. Bu., $2.75; 5 bu., $13.00. For fuller description of this variety see page 80.

Popping Corn
Selected White Rice
Our stock of this variety is choice, having been selected very carefully for many years. **This variety is the best for popping; grains pointed; pops full and white;** ears large sized, very handsome; productive; excellent quality; very crisp and delicious. By mail, postpaid—Nice Sample Ear, 10c.; pkt., 5c.; ¼ lb., 10c. By express or Parcel Post, not prepaid: 5 lbs., 75c.; 10 lbs., $1.20; 25 lbs., $2.50.

Miscellaneous Farm Seeds

Our grades of Farm Seeds are away above the average in quality, and this makes a big difference in the value—the low, trashy grades being costly at any price—and yet our prices will be found very little, if any, above those quoted by others. The man in charge of this department, having been with us more than thirty years, is thoroughly posted and will take pleasure in giving customers any information desired. The prices quoted below are **Net Cash, free** on cars, this city, purchaser paying all transportation charges, except when quoted postpaid. At the prices given here we make no charges for bags or cartage. The prices quoted are subject to market fluctuations. Should any article seem high, or when customers are in need of large quantities, we will be pleased to submit samples and quote, **on application, the lowest prices that the market will justify at the time. Please state quantities when writing for prices. Prices on Farm Seeds are subject to important market changes. Ask for Samples and Prices before placing your order.**

Artichoke Roots
The Jerusalem Artichoke can be grown only from the tubers. It is especially valuable as a cheap and healthful hog food, and the hogs do the harvesting. Tubers—4 ozs., 10c. postpaid. By express or freight: Pk., 60c.; ½ bu., $1.00; bu. (50 lbs.), $1.75; bbl. of 3 bu., $4.50. 3 to 5 bushels of tubers for an acre.

Soy Beans
The Soy Beans have attracted much attention in recent years on account of their great value as a feed, being much richer in protein than flaxseed, oilmeal, bran or oats, and can be used to balance a feed ration to good advantage; are used extensively in silage with corn, cane, etc. May be used for cover crop or feed in matured state. (60 lbs. per bushel.)

Soy Bean

Medium Green or Guelph—Plant erect, foliage coarse and abundant. Stems medium stout, well branched, height 25 to 36 inches, ripens in about 125 days. Pk., 85c.; bu., $3.00.

Ito San—Plant erect, branches are slender and fine. Height 25 to 30 inches. Matures in about 100 days. Fine for the North. Pk., 85c.; bu., $3.00.

Ebony—Plant slender, much branched, leafy, height 30 to 40 inches, ripe about Sept. 15th. A good hay bean. Pk., 85c.; bu., $3.00.

Mammoth Yellow—The latest maturing variety. Plants rather coarse, height 3 to 5 ft., ripens in 130 to 150 days. Good yielder, excellent to plow under as green manure. Pk., 75c.; bu., $2.75.

Ohio Grown Stock—To be sown north of the Ohio River. **Price same as Early Green.** (60 lbs. per bushel.)

Prices are based on present market rates and are subject to market changes. Lowest market prices on large or small quantities will be given on application as long as stocks last.

All prices subject to market change.

Buckwheat
Should be sown about the middle of June, using from 1 to 3 pecks of seed per acre. (50 lbs. to bushel.)

New Japanese—This new sort has proven to be much earlier and more productive than any other variety. Grains very large and of rich brown color. It excels all in yield and earliness. By express, not prepaid: Pk., 50c.; bu., $1.80.

Silver Hull—A very good and popular variety. The grain is of light gray color, rounder than the common variety; has a much thinner hull. By express, not prepaid, pk., 60c.; bu., $1.85.

Cow, or Southern Peas
There is no surer or cheaper means of improving and increasing the productiveness of soils than by sowing Cow Peas. They put plenty of nitrogenous vegetable matter into the soil at a small cost. For hay they are most valuable. For ensilage they are unsurpassed. When it is desired to turn the entire crop under as a soil improver, it is better to do so after the vines are partly dead. A good picking of the dried peas can be made before plowing under. Cow Peas can be sowed in May or June, after the ground is warm, or about the close of the corn planting, at the rate of one-half to one bushel per acre. (60 lbs. to bushel.)

Black—Is quick to mature. Well adapted for Northern sections. A vigorous grower and a great yielder. Pk., 85c.; bu., $3.00.

Whip-Poor-Will
(See illustration)—An early bunch-growing variety; a great favorite in the North and West; is quite prolific. Pk., 85c.; bu., $3.00.

Black-Eye—A prolific vine-growing variety of merit; seed often sold for table use. Pk., $1.00; bu., $3.50.

Market Price on Cow Peas changes often. Write for prices on larger quantities when ready to buy.

Whip-Poor-Will Cow Peas

For NITRAGIN INOCULATOR, see page 75.

Various Types of Sorghum (The Great Dry Land Forage Plants)

Feterita

White Kaffir Corn

Sorghum, or Sugar Cane

(50 lbs. to bushel)

For Fodder—Sow 1st to 15th of June, 100 lbs. seed per acre, and harrow to cover 1 to 2 inches. Harvest after first frost. Cut with self-binder or mower, and after three days of sun put up in large cocks and feed from field, or store in long, 8-foot-wide ricks near feed lot. Yield 8 to 10 tons per acre. Cows and all stock do as well when fed on it as on grass. They will eat it up "slick and clean." Our sales grew from a few hundred pounds to many tons as soon as we found out and recommended this way of growing it. **For Syrup,** plant in hills and cultivate same as corn.

Early Amber Cane—The earliest and makes the finest quality of forage or syrup. Oz., 5c.; ¼ lb., 15c., postpaid; 10 lbs., 50c.; 50 lbs., $2; 100 lbs., $3.75.

Early Orange Cane—A strong grower; stalks heavier and a little later than Amber. Oz., 5c.; ¼ lb., 15c., postpaid; 10 lbs., 50c.; 50 lbs., $2.00; 100 lbs., $3.75.

Write for Prices on larger quantities, stating amount you can use. Will send samples gladly if you so desire.

Kaffir Corn

A Great Fodder Crop. The Finest Grain for Poultry and Pigeons.

(50 lbs. to bushel.) Eaten by all domestic animals, whether fed in the grain or ground and cooked. For grain, sow at rate of 5 to 7 lbs. per acre and cultivate same as corn. Average yield 50 bushels per acre. For hay, sow in drills or broadcast at rate of 50 to 75 lbs. per acre, an cut when seed is coming to the dough stage. Makes valuable hay, yielding from 5 to 10 tons per acre. Oz., 5c.; ¼ lb., 10c.; postpaid; 10 lbs., 50c.; 50 lbs., $1.75; 100 lbs., $3.25.

Feterita

An Extra-Early Strain of White Kaffir Corn.

A New Non-Saccharine Cane.

Introduced 1912, has again proved its worth planted on both muck and upland on our own farms and has verified the claim we made for it last year. In fact, we thought so well of it that we give it a place on Catalogue Cover 1915, and recommend it will full confidence to all Poultry men, and for use wherever Kaffir Corn can be used. It is twenty to thirty days earlier than Kaffir Corn and more productive, heads equally as large, withstands drought as well or better and branches from the root. One seed produces anywhere from 3 to 10 stalks usually 6 to 8 each bearing a full-sized head, all filled with fine white plump grains, a little larger than Kaffir Corn. The stalks are well covered with large blades from the ground up, and after the heads are removed there is from two-thirds to three-fourths as much stover left as would be furnished by any average crop of corn. Seed planted after April 16th ripe and harvested on our lands Sept. 21st. Plant a few acres to feed your hens and fill your egg basket. It is one of the surest croppers and one of the best feed for poultry and pigeons. Owing to its earliness the best of its class for latitudes south of Chicago. Prices: Pkt., 5c.; ¼ lb., 10c., postpaid; 10 lbs., 60c.; 50 lbs., $2.25; 100 lbs., $4.00.

All Prices Subject to Market Changes

Head of Sorghum

Peanuts

Improved Large Virginia

A very profitable variety to grow, and is easily cultivated, very erect; the largest pods and kernels with fewer imperfect pods than any variety. The vines make valuable forage for stock. (Bu., 22 lbs.) By mail, large pkt., 10c.; ¼ lb., 15c., postpaid; 5 lbs., 90c.; 10 lbs., $1.50.

Sweet Spanish Peanut

The earliest variety grown. Pods are small, remarkably solid, well filled, and of an extra fine quality. Yield per acre very large. Large pkt., 10c.; ¼ lb., 15c., postpaid; 5 lbs., 90c.; 10 lbs., $1.50.

Canada Field Peas

Every year there is more inquiry for Field Peas. They stand in the front rank as a fodder, especially for hogs. They can be fed green or dry. They will grow on land that will not produce clover. Sow 1½ to 2 bushels to the acre, or, if with oats, sow 1 bushel of each. Sow the peas first and plow under, 4 to 5 inches; then oats on top and harrow in. Pk., $1; bu. (60 lbs.), $3.50. For large quantities, write for prices, stating quantity you can use.

All Prices Subject to Market Changes

Dwarf Essex Rape

Best Quick Growing Pasture for Sheep and Hogs.
There is but one variety of Rape that has proven profitable in the United States and that is the Dwarf Essex Rape. No other plant known that will give so much pasture in so short a time at so little cost. Under favorable conditions it is ready for pasture in six weeks from time of sowing and can be sown any time from April to September at the rate of 3 to 5 lbs. per acre. Land should be prepared same as for Turnips. It is grown for pasture and green manuring and is especially valuable for these purposes. Rape fed lambs should have free access to salt. One acre of good Rape will furnish feed for a flock of twelve sheep for 45 to 60 days. Our stock is the True Dwarf Essex and not the worthless annual. Weight per bushel, 50 lbs. Price: Packet, 5c.; ¼ lb., 10c.; postpaid. Lb., 20c.; 10 lbs., $1.50; 50 lbs., $6.50; 100 lbs. $12.00. **Write for prices on larger lots.**

Broom Corn

Improved Evergreen—The best variety for general cultivation on account of the color and quality of brush. Ripens early; grows about 8 to 10 feet high; brush of good length, fine and straight, and always of green appearance when ripe. Our stock is select, having been saved by professional growers for their own planting. (46 lbs. to bushel.) ¼ lb., 10c.; lb., 15c., postpaid. By express: 10 lbs., $1.00; 25 lbs., $2.25; 100 lbs., $7.50.

Sunflower

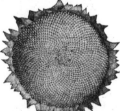

Mammoth Russian Sunflower

Mammoth Russian — Immense yielder — 125 bushels of seed to the acre has been grown at less expense than corn. Very highly recommended for poultry. Best egg-producing food known. Good feed for horses as well. (See illustration.)

Choice Stock—Oz., 5c.; ¼ lb., 10c., postpaid; 10 lbs., $1.00; 25 lbs., $2.25; 100 lbs., $8.00.

Tree and Hedge Plant Seeds

Osage Orange—The best of all hedge plants. Oz., 10c.; ¼ lb., 25c., postpaid; 10 lbs., $6.00; 25 lbs., $13.75.

Catalpa (Speciosa)
A rapid grower and makes the best timber trees. Pkt., 5c.; oz., 20c.; ¼ lb., 50c., postpaid.

Russian Mulberry
Easy grown; hardy; fine for hedges; makes fence posts in five years; fruit good. Pkt., 10c.; oz., 20c.; ¼ lb., 85c., postpaid.

Black Locust
A very rapid grower, as fence posts or ties may be cut in 10 years from planting seed, and will last a lifetime. Oz., 10c.; ¼ lb., 25c., postpaid; 10 lbs., $7.00; 25 lbs., $16.00; 50 lbs., $30.00.

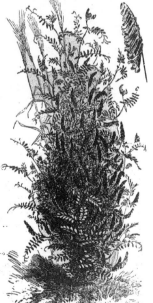

Sand or Hairy Vetch

One of the Newer Leguminous Plants of Value

(Vicia Villosa)—Since its introduction into this country this plant has made a splendid reputation for itself, especially as a crop to turn under. It succeeds on almost all soils, even poor sand soils produce quite good crops, though it is much more vigorous on good land. It is very hardy and remains green all Winter; it should be sown during August and September, and we advise that it be sown with rye—the rye helps to hold it up. It is much hardier than scarlet Clover and is giving excellent returns in the Northern and Northwestern states where the Winters are very severe and where many forage plants Winter kill. It is equally valuable in the South for a hay crop. Every gardener, dairyman and farmer should use this wonderful soiling plant.

Where conditions of soil, time of sowing, and rainfall have been favorable, it will make from 10 to 15 tons of green top turn under by the 1st to the 15th of May.

The root system is quite heavy and like all leguminous plants bear to a greater or less extent nitrogen gauls or nodules according to season, land and inoculation.

If the crop is to be used for hay, it will be well to sow 45 to 60 lbs. of Vetch, and with it ½ bu. Rye per acre. Write for circular giving fuller culture directions.

If you want any considerable quantity, write for special quotations.

Vetch is largely grown in Europe and on account of the war seed is scarce.

Prices: Oz., 5c.; 4 ozs., 15c.; lb., 40c., postpaid. By express or freight not paid: 10 lbs., $2.75; 25 lbs., $6.25; 50 lbs., $11.00; 100 lbs., $20.00.

Spring Vetches

A good forage plant; also used for plowing under. Sow 50 to 75 lbs. to the acre broadcast, like wheat or barley.

Prices: Oz., 5c.; 4 ozs., 15c.; lb., 25c., postpaid. By Express or Freight not paid: 10 lbs., $1.30; 25 lbs., $2.75; 50 lbs., $5.50; 100 lbs., $10.00.

For NITRAGIN INOCULATOR, See Page 75

Prices on Farm Seeds do not include shipping charges except as noted.

Patatas Livingston's Superior Seed Potatoes Kartoffeln

The necessity for changing seed often is universally admitted by all well-posted growers, especially when the best seed can be had at so little additional outlay. Owing to the perishable nature of seed potatoes and the unsettled condition of all markets, prices are made subject to market change and confirmation of order on receipt of same.

Special Instructions

Owing to the perishable nature of seed potatoes and the unsettled condition of markets, all prices are made subject to market change and confirmation of order on receipt of same, and will fill all orders just as soon as the weather, in our judgment, will permit. However, we cannot become responsible for changes in the weather by which the potatoes might be damaged while en route. We will ship at any date our customers may designate, when requested to do so, regardless of the weather, if customers wish to take their own risk. When ordering late, please state whether we shall return the money or send some other kind of equal value, provided we cannot supply the sort ordered. Please give plain and explicit shipping directions.
Order Seed Potatoes Early. We would most earnestly request our customers to send in their orders early. We then book and fill them in the order received. By so doing you take very little risk in getting what you want, as compared with waiting until the last moment.

Seed Potatoes by Express or Freight

At Barrel, Bushel, Peck, Half-Peck or Pound Prices, buyer pays the freight or express charges. Our barrels contain 2¾ bushels, good measure.

Seed Potatoes by Mail

Prices for small quantities of any of our Seed Potatoes, unless otherwise quoted. Lb., 15c.; 3 lbs., 35c., not postpaid.
All transportation charges must be paid by the buyer, except when offered postpaid, by mail. No potatoes sent C. O. D.

Culture

Any good soil will produce Potatoes, but a sandy loam is best. Make furrows of good depth, 3 feet apart; drop the cut-seed pieces about 8 or 10 inches apart. If grown in hills, one or two pieces of potatoes, containing one or more eyes in each piece, are placed in each hill, which are made 3 feet apart each way. Cover the seed four inches, but not so deep in wet, cold land. When the sprouts appear, cultivate and hoe to keep the soil free and clear of weeds. As the vines increase, draw earth around them, forming a slight ridge. Just as soon as the bugs appear use Paris Green. One peck will plant about 100 feet of row, or 100 hills. Ten bushels are required to plant an acre.
By planting Our Northern Grown Seed you are assured of Early Maturity, Increased Yield and a Vigorous Growth. To produce healthy stock we use first-class potato land, nothing but pure, well-matured, good-sized seed. The seed potatoes are very carefully handled when digging and barreling, that they may not be bruised or otherwise injured. Our seed potato stocks should not be compared with potatoes picked up on the market, named at a guess, and sold for seed.

Seed Potato Eyes

For those at very great distances, or where for any special reasons the express or freight charges would be exorbitant, these Seed Potato Eyes afford an inexpensive way to obtain and test any of the varieties we offer. Three dozen Eyes, any kind, 30c., postpaid.

THE RELIABLE POTATO

Extra Early Cobbler (Irish Cobbler)

One of the most reliable first-early Potatoes ever sent out. It ripens almost with the Early Ohio and is so uniform that every hill seems to ripen at one time. The yield is very large for an early variety —equal to some of the late ones. Form oval and round; skin lightly netted, creamy white and having few eyes, which are quite shallow—some even with the surface. Flesh pure white and of the finest quality—not exceeded by any early variety. Keeps perfect until Spring, when it starts late, strong and vigorous sprouts. Its strong growth, earliness, uniformity, large yield, fine quality and very handsome appearance have brought the Extra-Early Cobbler right to the front as a profitable variety for market or home use. PRICES—Choice Sorted Northern Grown Stock: ½ pk., 40c.; pk., 60c.; ½ bu., $1.00; bu., $1.75; bbl., $4.75.

Extra-Early Ohio

Extra Early Ohio Potato

Our Specialty. A Grand Potato.

Some early varieties will yield edible Potatoes about as soon as the Extra-Early Ohio, but their tops will be green for days after the Extra-Early Ohio have fully ripened. The Extra-Early Ohio is fully two weeks ahead of the Early Rose, and is a general favorite with potato growers and marketmen alike, and is the most profitable Potato they can possibly grow. The sprouts are very strong, the vines grow erect and are easy to cultivate. Maturing early, it brings the highest prices, and the land can be used for another crop after it; does well on any soil suitable for Potatoes. The tubers grow compact in the hill, are easily dug, with very few small ones—nearly every Potato is of marketable size; has few eyes, which are even with the surface. With heavy manuring, close planting and good culture, a very large and profitable crop can be expected—300 to 500 bushels per acre is not an unusual yield. We are confident that many growers do not really know a true Extra-Early Ohio, and have been growing some other sort for it. We know ours is right, because the stock is the product of original headquarters seed.

PRICES—Choice Northern Grown Seed: ½ pk., 30c.; pk., 50c.; ½ bu., 90c.; bu., $1.60; bbl., $4.25. Special prices will be quoted on larger quantities.

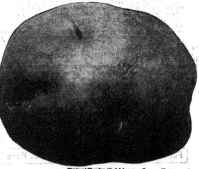

Extra-Early Cobbler

The "Livingston" Potato

It is "a White Seneca Beauty," and the Seneca Beauty is admitted by all who have ever grown it to be one of the most beautiful of the many rose-colored varieties; and those familiar with it will at once realize what a beauty it would be in a white jacket, and especially if it retained its delicate Peachblow eyes. This is exactly what we have in "The Livingston." It is a very strong grower and most productive and not subject to blight. Tubers of beautiful form, medium to large size, oblong, and of uniform thickness; slightly flattened; skin white and slightly russeted—all of which denotes the very highest quality. Cooks dry and has splendid flavor. Prices, Choice Sorted Northern Grown Stock: ¼ pk., 50c.; pk., 75c.; ½ bu., $1.10; bu., $2.00; bbl., $5.25.

The Seneca Beauty Potato

Very Smooth, Uniform Size, Almost Blight Proof, Productive, Splendid Quality, Fine Keeper

A grand good medium late Potato, and too much has not been said in its praise. Its beautiful and distinct appearance sells it in any market, and its fine table qualities please all. The tubers are large and smooth, with few eyes close to the surface, and of a beautiful pink color. Uniform in size and shape, scarcely any small ones. Vines rank and healthy, and loaded with beautiful blossoms. Good keeper and a heavy cropper. Prices, Choice Sorted Northern Grown Stock: ¼ pk., 40c.; pk., 60c.; ½ bu., $1.00; bu., $1.90; bbl., $5.00.

David Salser, Meigs Co., O., writes April 7th: "I planted 1¼ bu. of your Extra Early Ohio Potatoes April 7th and dug and marketed part of them June 8th, good size, just sixty-one days from date of planting."

M. S. Boylan, Calhoun Co., Mich., writes as follows: "Thirteen years ago I purchased from you a peck of Livingston's Seneca Beauty Potatoes and have raised them ever since and they are just as good today as ever. They are certainly a grand good Potato for home use. I also raise the Livingston Potato, securing seed of them 8 or 9 years ago and they are a fine Potato. In fact I consider your two varieties the best that I have ever grown and I have raised and tested over 300 different varieties. I would not be without them for my own use if I had to pay double the price for the seed."

Livingston Banner

Livingston's Banner Potato
The Best Main Crop Variety

The Banner is a seedling and is one of the finest main crop white Potatoes on the market. No Potato ever made so good a record in so short a time with all classes of growers and on all kinds of soils. None surpass it in uniform, handsome appearance. Its slightly rusty skin is of a light cream-white color. Its shape is a little oblong and slightly flattened (cooking through easily). The eyes are very shallow. The size is large and desirable, very few being under marketable size. Always smooth and regular in form; grows strong and vigorous from the very sprout. Is also a great drought resister. As near blight and scab proof as any variety we have ever known. The flesh is very white, and whether boiled or baked is of the same delicious tasty quality. Medium late. Choice Sorted Northern Grown Stock: ½ pk., 30c.; pk., 50c.; ½ bu., 90c.; bu., $1.50; bbl., $4.00. Write for special prices on larger quantities.

Livingston's Rusty Coat Potato

Uniformly long and slightly flattened; is entirely free from prongs, and the eyes are even with the surface. Beautiful buff skin, heavy netting, like a russet apple; flattened shape; of very highest quality, especially as a potato to bake. Its flesh is of the finest texture and very free from hard or black spots. Cooks white as flour, bursting open at any season of the year, and is of the finest flavor. It is an abundant yielder. They sell on sight in the market. This splendid Potato always brings the very highest market prices, and commission men tell us they cannot get enough of them. The seed we offer is strictly pure, hand-sorted. Price, Choice Stock Seed, Northern Grown: ½ pk., 30c.; pk., 50c.; ½ bu., 90c.; bu., $1.50; bbl., $4.00.

Rusty Coat Potato

Seed Sweet Potatoes, New Jersey Grown

Carefully dug, handled and stored over Winter for us, expressly for sprouting purposes. The seed stocks are selected from the most perfect and prolific hills at the time of digging. We have been bedding and selling this stock for more than thirty years, and find the potatoes much dryer and sweeter than those grown from Ohio or Western grown seed. We repack before shipping, but we wish is distinctly understood that customers take all risks after we deliver in good condition to express or railroad company here. We book orders at any time, but do not ship until about planting time. Our barrels contain 3 bushels, good measure. No Sweet Potatoes shipped C. O. D. Prices quoted are subject to market changes after March 1. Order early.

"Up Rivers"

Select strain of smooth, short, "chunky" Yellow Jersey Sweet Potatoes, which yield a larger per cent. of marketable stock and sell higher than most other varieties we know. Dry and sweet. A splendid Sweet Potato. This is our specialty in Seed Sweets; we recommend it as very fine. Pk., 50c.; ½ bu., 80c.; bu., $1.50; bbl. (3 bus.), $4.00, by freight or express, not prepaid.

Yellow Jersey, or Nansemond

Fine old favorite. Pk., 50c.; ½ bu., 80c.; bu., $1.50; bbl., $4.00, by express or freight, not prepaid.

We make special prices for larger quantities. If you bed out several barrels, it may pay you to write us before you buy your seed.

FLOWER SEED DEPARTMENT

O UR list of flower seeds will be found to contain all varieties of real merit. Many times varieties are listed which are of no value whatever in the garden or are so difficult to grow that unless one has every facility for propagation, disappointment is sure to follow the purchase of seed. We want our seeds to give satisfaction and prefer not to have a very extended list, rather than to cause disappointment in any of the varieties procured. Cultural directions will be found on most of our seed packets. We will also give free to customers, on application, a very instructive and helpful leaflet—**Annuals from Seeds.**

Annuals are those flowers that bloom and ripen their seed the first year, then die. Among these are Asters, Balsams, Mignonette, Sweet Peas, Nasturtiums, Morning Glories and many other very brilliant and fragrant sorts.

Biennials from seed, generally bloom the second year, then die. Some varieties, if planted early, bloom the first season; therefore there are treated as Annuals.

Perennials are those that endure our Northern Winters with little or no protection and live and bloom several years in succession. A large majority of the Perennials will bloom the first year if started early in the Spring. Hollyhocks, Columbine, Larkspurs, Foxglove, Poppies, etc, are in this popular class.

Discounts on Packet Flower Seeds. For 25 cents select 6 Five-cent, or 3 Ten-cent pkts. For 50 cents select Packets to the amount of 65 cents. For $1.00 select Packets to the amount of $1.30. For $2.00 select Packets to the amount of $2.75.

☞ Collections of seeds in Packets cannot be included when taking advantage of these discounts.

Showy Flowering Annuals for Beds and Massing

	See page		See page
Ageratum	90	Eschscholtzia	98
Alyssum	90	Gaillardia	98
Antirrhinum	91	Lobelia (Compacta)	101
Asters	87	Marigolds	102
Balsams	92	Nasturtium (Tom	
Calendula	92	Thumb)	105
Calliopsis	92	Pansy	106
Candytuft	93	Petunias	108
Carnation	93	Phlox Drummondi.	108
Celosia	93	Poppies	109
Chrysanthemum	94	Portulaca	109
Convolvulus Minor	103	Salvia Splendens.	110
Cosmos (Dwarf)	95	Stocks	111
Dahlias (Tom		Verbena	116
Thumb)	95	Vinca	116
Dianthus (An'als)	97	Zinnias	117

Large Showy Annuals for Backgrounds and Borders

Amaranthus	90	Marigolds	102
Celosia Plumosa	93	Nicotiana	104
Centaurea	94	Poppies	109
Cosmos	95	Ricinus	110
Datura	96	Salvia	110
Euphorbia	98	Sunflower	111
Hibiscus	99	Zinnias	117
Larkspur (Br'ch'g)	101		

Colored Foliage Plants for Ribbon Beds

Centaurea, White.		Pyrethrum A're'm.	107
Coleus	94		

Climbing Annuals for Arbors, Verandas, Trellises, etc.

	See page		See page
Balloon Vine	91	Moonflowers	103
Balsam Apple	91	Maurandya	101
Canary Bird Vine	92	Morning Glories.	103
Cobaea	94	Nasturtium	104
Cypress Vine	94	Sweet Peas	112
Dolichos	97	Thunbergia	116
Gourds	99	Wild Cucumber	116
Humulus (Hop)	100		

Hardy Flowering Perennials for Permanent Beds and Borders

Aquilegia	91	Hollyhock	100
Campanula	92	Lavender	101
Candytuft	93	Myosotis	104
Canterbury Bells	92	Pinks (hardy)	97
Carnation	93	Poppy (hardy)	109
Chrysanthemum	94	Primrose (Japan)	108
Coreopsis (hardy).	92	Pyrethrum (h'rdy)	107
Delphinum	96	Scabiosa	111
Dianthus (hardy)	97	Stokesia	111
Digitalis	96	Sweet William	115
Gaillardia	98	Valeriana	116
Gypsophila	99	Violet	116
Hibiscus	99	Wallflower	116

Plants Succeeding in Partial Shade

Antirrhinum	91	Matricaria, or	
Aquilegia	91	Feverfew	98
Asperula	90	Mimulus	101
Bellis (Daisies)	96	Myosotis	104
Canterbury Bells.	92	Pansy	106
Coreopsis	92	Poppies (hardy)	109
Delphinum	96	Violet	116
Digitalis	96		

Plants for Vases, Hanging Baskets, Veranda Boxes, etc.

Drooping Sorts		Upright Growing	
	See page		See page
Alyssum	90	Centaurea	94
Asparagus	90	Coleus	94
Lobelia Gracilis.	101	Fuchsia	98
Maurandya	101	Geranium	99
Nasturtium	104	Heliotrope	99
Petunia	108	Impatiens	100
Begonia Vernon.	91	Pansy	106

Long-Stemmed Flowers for Cutting

Aquilegia	91	Larkspur	101
Asters	87	Marigolds	102
Calliopsis	92	Matricaria	98
Carnations	93	Mignonette	102
Centaurea-Cyanus.	94	Poppies	109
Centaurea Sweet.	94	Salpiglossis	110
Chrysanthemum	94	Scabiosa	111
Coreopsis	92	Stokes	111
Cosmos	95	Stokesia	111
Dahlias	95	Sunflowers	111
Delphinum (hardy)	96	Sweet Peas	112
Gypsophila	99	Sweet Sultans	94
Gaillardias	98	Zinnias	117

Plants Suitable for Edgings

Ageratum	90	Marigold, Legion	
Alyssum	90	of Honor, 9 in.	102
Begonia Vernon.	91	Phlox D. Com-	
Bellis (Daisies)	96	pacta	108
Candytuft	93	Pinks (hardy)	97
Centaurea Candi-		Portulaca	109
dissima	94	Pyrethrum Aure'm.	107
Cosmos (Dwarf)	95	Verbena	116
Lobelia Compacta.	101	Zinnia, Dwarf	117

Semple's Late Branching Aster

Asters

The Aster is, perhaps, the most popular annual flower grown in this country, and justly so on account of its ease of culture, season of bloom and lasting qualities both in the garden and as a cut flower. Seed can be sown in the house in shallow boxes (cigar boxes are good), and in the hot bed in March or in cold frames the first of April and later (about May 1st) in the open ground. Transplant the smaller varieties about eight inches apart in the row and such varieties as Semple's Branching, fifteen inches apart, the rows to be twelve inches apart. The richer the ground the better your flowers will be and water is very necessary if you wish to grow fine blooms.

Semple's Giant Late Branching

Without question, the finest Aster grown. It has size, vigor, fine stems, beauty of form and varied color to recommend it and, while not so early as many of the other varieties, it stands at the head of the list both for the home garden and as a florist's flower.

1400 Semple's Giant Finest Mixed Colors—All shades and colors. Pkt., 10c.; ¼ oz., 20c.; ¼ oz., 35c.
1401 Semple's Giant Lavender. Pkt., 10c.
1402 Semple's Giant Royal Purple. Pkt., 10c.
1403 Semple's Giant Pure White. Pkt., 10c.
1404 Semple's Giant Crimson. Pkt., 10c.
1405 Semple's Giant Shell Pink. Pkt., 10c.

Collection of Semple's Giant Asters, 5 above sorts, 35c.

Mikado Pink

In type Mikado Pink belongs to the Comet class. Petals are narrow, very long and gracefully reflexed. The outer petals show to their full extent, while gradually toward the center they bend and curl across each other, forming a perfectly double flower. 1381—Pkt., 10c.

Mikado White

A magnificent new Aster, same as Mikado Pink, except in color, which is pure glistening white. 1383—Pkt., 10c.

Pink Enchantress

A new variety of upright growth. The flowers are very double and are produced on good stems. The color is of the Enchantress Carnation shade, a very delicate pink. It is a mid-season variety. 1492—Pkt., 20c.

Peerless Pink

The introducers of this variety state that it is midway between Crego and the Late Branching varieties and of a beautiful shade of pink. It blooms a little ahead of the Late Branching and produces its flowers on long stems. 1406—Per pkt., 15c.

Queen of the Market

About two or three weeks earlier than most other Asters. They bloom profusely and are of graceful habit. Their shape is very similar to Semple's Giant Branching Aster. The perfect flowers are borne on long stems and in great variety of colors, making them extremely useful for cutting. A favorite sort. Height 1½ feet.

1440 Mixed Colors—All colors in finest mixture. Pkt., 5c.; ¼ oz., 15c.; ¼ oz., 25c.

Separate Colors—1441 Scarlet, 1442 Pink, 1443 Crimson, 1444 Pure White, 1445 Dark Blue, and 1446 Light Blue— Each color, pkt., 5c.

Collection Queen of the Market Asters, 6 separate colors, 20c.

Daybreak

Flowers are very large and double, beautiful shell-pink color. A grand Aster for cutting purposes, growing 2 feet high. 1384—Pkt., 10c.; ¼ oz., $1.00.

Snowdrift

A white Aster of Comet type and one of the earliest of all. In bloom same time as Queen of the Market. 1485— Pkt., 10c.

Invincible

A very popular Aster in many parts of the country. It is a mid-season variety, very similar in form to the late branching, but flowering a couple of weeks earlier. 1435 White, 1436 Light Rose, 1437 Lavender, 1438 Purple, 1439 Crimson—Each 10c. per pkt.; set of five varieties, 40c.

Crego Pink

A large variety of a most beautiful shade of pink unlike any other Aster. It comes into bloom just ahead of the late branching Asters and being of Comet type affords variety in the garden. 1409—Pkt., 10c.

1408 Crego White—Similar to the above, only white. Pkt., 10c.

1407 Crego Purple—A new color added to this popular type last year. Pkt., 10c.

Royal Asters

Royal Asters

Without doubt one of the best early flowering sorts. It is quite similar in type of flower, to the Late Branching, but will come into bloom only about a week later than Queen of the Market. The flower stems start from the plant close to the ground, are free from laterals and consequently give their full strength to the production of numerous large, handsomely proportioned flowers. **1486 White, 1487 Purple, 1488 Shell Pink, 1489 Lavender**—Each 10c. per pkt.

Purity

Double flowers of a glistening pure white; similar to Daybreak in form and habit. **1386**—Pkt., 10c.; ¼ oz., $1.00.

Violet King

The habit of growth of this Aster is similar to the Branching type, growing vigorously about 2½ feet high; has long, stiff stems. In form the flower is entirely new and distinct from any other variety; round, full and very large, many of the flowers measuring from 4 to 5 inches in diameter. Petals somewhat resemble the quilled varieties, but are much longer and broader. **1380**—Pkt., 10c.; ⅛ oz., 50c.; ¼ oz., 75c.

Vick's New Early Blanching Aster

The habit of growth is identical with its parent, the late Branching Asters. Plants branch freely, are vigorous in growth. They produce flowers on long, stiff stems and luxurious foliage. The shape of the flower is round, and the size extraordinary large. A very valuable flower for commercial growers and the home garden.

The new Aster comes in two dainty and desirable colors—pink and white. Our stock of seed is true and comes direct from the original introducer. **1410 White**, per pkt., 10c.; **1411 Pink**, pkt., 10c.; **1412 White and Pink Mixed**, pkt., 10c.

Truffaut's Peony-Flowered Perfection Aster

The improved strains of this grand Aster are considered the finest in cultivation. It is one of the most beautiful and extensively cultivated classes, and it deserves to be, as the large, perfectly double flowers are fine. The petals are beautifully incurved. Very profuse bloomers, producing rich and beautiful flowers. We can recommend them very strongly, as we all know they will delight you. Height 2 feet.

1390 Peony Flowered, Mixed Colors—Fine assortment. Pkt., 10c.; ¼ oz., 25c.; ½ oz., 45c.

Peony-Flowered Perfection Asters in the following separate colors: **1391 Snow White, 1392 Brilliant Rose, 1393 Rich Crimson, 1394 Sky Blue, 1395 Dark Blue, 1396 Brilliant Scarlet**, at 10 cents per packet.

The Collection of 6 separate colors, one pkt. of each as named above, 50c.

Giant Ostrich Plume Asters

A very large-flowering class, the blooms of which are of most perfect shape; splendid for cut flowers. Resemble the Giant Comet Asters, as they have the same curled and twisted petals. However, the petals are longer, and the whole flower larger. Individual blooms often measure 4 to 6 inches in diameter. Plants of luxurious branching habit, with flowers on long slender stems. Height 2 feet.

1416 Giant Ostrich Plume, Mixed Colors—Embraces all the desirable colors in splendid mixture. Pkt., 10c.; ⅛ oz., 25c.; ¼ oz., 45c.

1417 Ostrich Plume Snow White. Pkt., 10c.

1418 Ostrich Plume Rose Pink. Pkt., 10c.

1419 Ostrich Plume Light Yellow. Pkt., 10c.

1420 Ostrich Plume Azure Blue. Pkt., 10c.

1421 Ostrich Plume Lavender. Pkt., 10c.

1422 Ostrich Plume Dark Blue. Pkt., 10c.

1423 Ostrich Plume Crimson. Pkt., 10c.

Collection of Giant Ostrich Plume Asters, 7 separate colors, 55c.

Asters (Continued)

Autumn Glory

Victoria Asters

The Victoria Asters resemble Truffaut's Peony-Flowered Asters very closely, except that the petals recurve to the edge of the flower instead of incurving to the center. Superb colors, elegant sort. 2 feet.

1388 Miss Roosevelt (Victoria)—The flowers of this new Aster are of a clear primrose tint, which changes to delicate flesh color, like the popular Gloire de Dijon rose. Fine cut flower. Pkt., 10c.; ¼ oz., 50c.

1459 Pink Beauty—Of upright growth, with flowers carried on long, strong stems. Of chrysanthemum shape with incurved inner and reflexed outer petals. Of beautiful, soft blush pink color. Pkt., 15c.

1450 Victoria Asters, Mixed Colors—Very fine. Pkt., 10c.; ⅛ oz., 35c.; ¼ oz., 60c.

1460 Dwarf Victoria Asters—Perfect flowers of large size, produced profusely. 10 inches high. Effective in beds and borders. Choice Mixed. Pkt., 10c.

Livingston's Exhibition Aster Collection

This magnificent collection contains the finest and most complete assortment of mammoth-flowering Asters it is possible to offer—the newest kinds, all colors, all varieties; early and late. The symmetrical globe-shaped and the fluffy Chrysanthemum sorts.

One large packet each Semple's Giant Branching, Mixed; Giant Ostrich Plume, Mixed; Giant Comet, Mixed; Truffaut's Peony Perfection, Mixed; Livingston's Superb Mixture of Giant Asters; Vick's Early Branching Asters; Violet King.

In the bag with each collection, we will enclose our leaflet, "Aster Culture," telling how to grow big Asters successfully.

All for 50c., postpaid. At regular rates these seeds would cost 80c.

Livingston's Superb Mixture of Giant Asters

Is absolutely unexcelled. A magnificent mixture, producing beautiful flowers, gigantic in size, gorgeous in colors, perfect in form.

This mixture includes the cream of all the Asters on this and the other two pages, together with many other sorts of the most beautiful forms and brilliant colors. Our special strain has been especially selected from the finest large sized double flowering types. Height about 2 feet. 1490—Pkt., 10c.; three packets for 25c.; ¼ oz., 50c.

Vick's Autumn Glory
(See Illustration Alongside)

1494—Pure sea-shell pink. While similar in color to Semple's Pink, it has a better and more substantial flower, a deeper and longer keeping color, larger and stronger type of plant. Its most distinctive characteristic and chief claim for recognition, however, is the fact that it is later in season than any of the other varieties. Vick's Autumn Glory comes into bloom after other late Asters are past their prime, and before early Chrysanthemums are ready. It comes uniformly true to color and type. The flowers are very double and are borne on stems of unusual length. Pkt., 15c.

Giant Comet Asters

An ideal class for cut flowers, being not only most profuse bloomers, but each individual flower is borne on a stiff stem and resembles an exquisitely curled and twisted Japanese Chrysanthemum. Height 2 to 2½ feet.

1430 Giant Comet Crimson, 1431 Giant Comet Light Blue, 1432 Giant Comet Rose Pink, 1433 Giant Comet Dark Blue, 1434 Giant Comet, the Bride, 1428 Giant Comet, Mixed Colors, 1429 Giant Comet Snow White.

Collection Giant Comet Asters, 5 separate colors, 40c.

Rose Flowered

This is a very pretty type, somewhat resembling Queen of the Market, but larger, and has a greater range of colors. 1463 Mixed Colors—Pkt., 10c.

Mrs. Mary A. Love, Buchanan Co., Iowa, writes, April 7, 1915: "I have planted your seed ever since 1875. They are so reliable, I am afraid to use others. You sent me two catalogues. I gave them to my neighbors. I know they will send to you for seeds."

Vick's Lavender Rochester
(See Illustration Below)

1495—The magnificent flowers are more double and more Chrysanthemum-like than those of the original Lavender Pink Rochester. The long, narrow petals fall over one another in a charming cascade of color, forming a wonderful shaggy mass that cannot be equaled for richness of effect. In addition to their great diameter they have a most remarkable thickness, making them truly massive. Vick's Lavender Rochester is an exquisite shade of clear light lavender. Pkt., 10c.

Lavender Rochester.

Alyssum
Little Gem
Pkt., 5c.

SWEET ALYSSUM

Abronia

Pretty trailing plants with verbena-like fragrant flowers. In bloom a long time. Adapted to beds, rock-work and hanging baskets. Annuals; good mixture; many varieties. 1300—Pkt., 5c.

Abutilon

(Flowering Maple, or Chinese Bell-Flower)—Universally admired for garden or house culture; flower the first season if seed is sown early; rapid growth; bear elegant bell-shaped flowers. Half hardy shrubs. 1302 Mixed—Pkt., 10c.

Arabis Alpina

1306—Dwarf perennial plant; covered with pretty white flowers in May. Thrives well in dry, sandy places. Pkt., 10c.

Acroclinium

1308 Rose and White, Mixed—An Everlasting. Yields a great number of flowers, which should be gathered the first day they open and dried in the shade for winter bouquets. Annuals; one foot. Pkt., 5c.; ½ oz., 15c.

Adlumia Cirrhosa

1310 Mountain Fringe, or Allegheny Vine—A beautiful, hardy climber, flowering the first season. Clusters of small rosy-lilac flowers and pale green feathery foliage. Pkt., 5c.

Amaranthus

1333 Fine Mixed—Foliage brilliantly ornamental, producing a striking effect in the border as a background, or as a center of beds. Of the easiest culture. Annuals; 3 feet. Pkt., 5c.; ¼ oz., 15c.; oz., 25c.

Sweet Alyssum

One of the sweet-scented flowers that should always be in every garden. An easily grown annual; fine for beds, edgings or for cutting. In bloom all Summer and through the greater part of Fall.

1325 Sweet Alyssum (Maritimum)—One of most popular of our hardy annuals, both for cutting and for edging. The pure white flowers are noted for their exquisite fragrance. Blooms continually from earliest Summer until hard frosts. Pkt., 5c.; ½ oz., 15c.; oz., 25c.

1327 Little Gem, or "Carpet of Snow"—A dwarf, very compact-growing variety, that, while only 6 inches in height, each plant will carpet a circle from 20 to 30 inches in diameter. From early Summer until very late Autumn the plants are a solid mass of snow-white flowers of delicious fragrance. Pkt., 5c.; ¼ oz., 15c.; ½ oz., 25c.; oz., 40c.

1329 Saxatile Compactum (Golden Saxatile, or "Basket of Gold")—A hardy perennial variety; its flowers are a most brilliant golden-yellow. Fine for rock-work. Nine inches high. Pkt., 5c.; ¼ oz., 20c.; ½ oz., 35c.

Ageratum (Floss Flower)

Very showy plants; bloom profusely the whole Summer; fine as cut flowers. Splendid for borders, ribbon beds, etc. Half hardy annuals. (See illustration.)

1312 Perfection Blue—Splendid large heads of deep amethyst blue. Compact growth, 9 inches high. Deepest colored of all Ageratums. Fine bedder. Pkt., 10c.; ¼ oz., 25c.

1314 Princess Victoria Louise—A very pretty dwarf sort. Bushes 5 to 6 inches high; splendid combination with Sweet Alyssum. The color is a bright blue, with white center. Pkt., 10c.; 2 pkts., 15c.; ¼ oz., 25c.

1316 Little Blue Star—Exceedingly dwarf, bushy growth, not over 4 or 5 inches high. Densely covered with clusters of bright blue flowers. Very fine for edging. Pkt., 10c.

1318 Imperial Dwarf Blue—8 inches. Pkt., 5c.
1319 Imperial Dwarf White—8 inches. Pkt., 5c.
1320 Mexicanum—Lavender-blue. 1½ feet. Pkt., 5c.
1321 Finest Mixed—Splendid. Pkt., 5c.; ¼ oz., 15c.

Asparagus

1372 Plumosus Nanus (Climbing Lace Fern)—One of the prettiest house plants. Its feathery foliage is indispensable for bouquets and lasts a long time after cutting. Half hardy perennials. Pkt. (10 seeds), 15c.; 25 seeds, 30c.; 100 seeds, $1.00.

1374 Sprengeri (Emerald Feather, or Abyssinian Parlor Fern)—This is one of the most beautiful plants for either pot culture or hanging baskets. Useful for bouquets. Grows freely all the year; a popular house plant. Pkt. (15 seeds), 10c.

Asperula

1377 Sweet Woodruff—This charming plant delights in moist, shady situations. Its fragrant leaves and flowers when dried impart an agreeable perfume. Perennials; one foot. Pkt., 5c.

AGERATUM

Aquilegia or Columbine

Exceedingly showy, early blooming hardy plants; always favorites, and of the easiest culture. The graceful, long-spurred flowers are very brilliant. They delight in the moister portions of the garden. The new varieties are greatly enlarged, and the range of colors and shades has been largely increased. Hardy perennial. 1½ to 3 feet.

1365 Chrysantha—This beautiful variety is a clear yellow, being an unusual color in Columbines, and of the long-spurred type. It also has the characteristic of flowering nearly all Summer. One of the best and very hardy. Pkt., 10c.

1368 Coerulea—The true Rocky Mountain variety, a beautiful blue and free-flowering. The State flower of Colorado. A splendid plant for the hardy border. Pkt., 10c.

1355 Haylodgensis—Hybrids of Coerulea. Long-spurred varieties in many colors. Pkt., 10c.

1354 New Double Hybrids—Large-flowering, long-spurred. Very beautiful, with several rows of cornucopia-like petals. Includes various charming shades of blue, yellow, lavender and white. Pkt., 10c.

1356 New Long-Spurred "Rose Queen"—A beautiful novelty, producing in great profusion very graceful, large-flowered, long-spurred flowers, shading from light pink to dark rose, with white center and yellow anthers. Very delicate and beautiful. Pkt., 15c.

1360 Double Varieties Mixed—A very choice assortment. Pkt., 5c.

1362 Single Varieties Mixed—All the best sorts and colors. Pkt., 5c.

Balsam Apple and Pear

1518 Mormordica, Mixed—Very curious vine with ornamental foliage. Its large, golden-yellow fruit opens when ripe and shows its brilliant blood-red inside. Hardy annuals. 10 feet. Balsam Apple and Pear Mixed. Pkt., 5c.; ¼ oz., 10c.

Begonias

1523 Finest Mixed—Our strain contains a great variety of colors, both in flowers and foliage. A superior assortment. Pkt., 10c.

1524 Vernon—An elegant variety, with bright orange-carmine flowers and very dark leaves. Start the seed early in the house or greenhouse. Pkt., 10c.

1520 Tuberous Rooted, Best Double Mixed—Prize strain. Pkt., 25c.

1521 Tuberous Rooted, Best Single Mixed—Prize strain. Pkt., 25c.

1522 Begonia Rex (Ornamental-Leaved Varieties)—A collection of house plants without some of these elegant pot plants seems incomplete. The leathery leaves are bronze, red, silver and gold. Finest sorts. Pkt., 25.

Balloon Vine --- "Love in a Puff"

1498—Rapid growing, pretty annual climber; delights in a light soil and warm situation; produces white flowers, followed by seed vessels that look like small balloons; makes a fine porch screen. 10 feet. Pkt., 5c.; oz., 20c.

Bachelors Button—See Centauria, page 94.

Giant - Flowered Antirrhinum

(Snap Dragon)

This old favorite is one of the most beautiful and useful border plants of our gardens. Its very graceful flowers are borne on long spikes and in the greatest diversity of colors. The spikes of flowers are most brilliant and showy. Two feet.

1340 Giant White—Pure snow-white. Pkt., 10c.

1341 Giant Rose—Delicate rose-pink. Pkt., 10c.

1342 Giant Scarlet—Brilliant scarlet. Pkt., 10c.

1343 Giant Yellow—Pure soft yellow. Pkt., 10c.

1344 Giant Queen Victoria—Extra large, superb; pure white. Pkt., 10c.

Antirrhinum

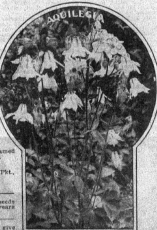

AQUILEGIA

1346 Giant-Flowering Finest Mixed Colors—An elegant assortment of innumerable rich colors and shades, including all the named varieties offered by us. Pkt., 10c.; 3 pkts., 25c.; ¼ oz., 30c.; oz., $1.00.

Collection Giant Antirrhinums, 5 separate colors, 35c.

1347 Dwarf Mixture—Contains the very choicest colors. 12 inches. Pkt., 5c.; ¼ oz., 20c.

1348 Tall Mixture—The best colors; 2 feet. Pkt., 5c.; ¼ oz., 15c.

Mrs. T. J. Gammon, Kennebec Co., Me., writes March 15th: "Your seeds are the finest I have ever bought. I have bought of you for several years and they always come true."

John Wiemann & Sons, Des Moines Co., Iowa, says: "Your seeds give perfect satisfaction." June 12, 1915."

Double Balsams

1500 Livingston's Premium Balsams, Finest Mixed—Our strain is unsurpassed. The large double flowers are as fine as the most elegant Camellia. The size, fine form, varied and brilliant colors of our Premium Balsams are greatly admired. Pkt., 10c.; ¼ oz., 40c.

1502 Camellia-Flowered White—A superb variety. The flowers are extremely large, full centered, with reflex petals, pure snow-white. The most elegant of all Balsams. Pkt., 5c.; ¼ oz., 25c.; oz., 75c.

1504 Double Camellia-Flowered Finest Mixed—A very choice assortment of all the best varieties and colors in these favorite Balsams. Pkt., 5c.; ¼ oz., 20c.; ½ oz., 35c.

1507 Double Lavender; 1509 Double Bright Scarlet; 1511 Double Dark Blood Red; 1513 Double Peach Blossom; 1514 Double Red Spotted White. Each of above separate colors, pkt., 5c.; oz., 60c. Collection Double Balsams, 6 separate colors, 25c. **1515 Double Mixed Balsams,** pkt., 5c.; ½ oz., 30c.; oz., 50c.

Canterbury Bells. Pkt., 5c.

Double Balsams

Campanula
(Canterbury Bells)

This old-fashioned flower is a favorite with all. Stately and showy and of the easiest growth. Hardy biennials.

1560 Livingston's Prize Mixture—An elegant mixture of all the finest classes and colors of single and double and "Cup and Saucer" varieties. Pkt., 10c.; 2 pkts., 15c.

1561 Calycanthema "Cup and Saucer"—Our mixture includes all the best colors and varieties. Pkt., 5c.

1563 Finest Double Mixed. Pkt., 5c. **1564 Finest Single Mixed.** Pkt., 5c.

1566 Pyramidalis—The Chimney Bell-flower; a hardy perennial flowering in late Summer. Finest mixed. Height, 3½ feet. Pkt., 10c. **1568 Carpatica**—Beautiful free-flowering, hardy perennial; fine for groups and edgings. Blue and White, mixed. 9 inches. Pkt., 10c.

Calliopsis, or Coreopsis

One of the easiest grown annual flowers; can be used with fine effect anywhere—in beds, borders or masses. Blooms all the time. Sow the seed thinly when weather becomes warm and soil dry. 1 to 2 feet.

1530 Hybrida Superba—Very showy new hybrids in great variety of color, varying from pale yellow to rich orange and velvety brown. 1 foot high. Pkt., 10c.; ¼ oz., 25c.

1532 Golden Wave (Drummondii)—Bushy, compact plants covered with very large bright golden-yellow flowers with brown centers. Pkt., 5c.; ¼ oz., 10c.

1534 Coronata—Showy, large, pure yellow flowers. Pkt., 5c.; ½ oz., 15c.

1536 Mixed Tall Sorts—All choice sorts. Pkt., 5c.; oz., 20c.

1537 Mixed Dwarf Sorts—For bedding. Pkt., 5c.; oz., 25c.

1539 California Sunbeams (Grandiflora)—An improved large-flowering strain. Fine light-yellow and brown blooms. Pkt., 5c.

1540 Lanceolata Grandiflora (Harvest Moon)—One of the grandest perennial plants. Fine in masses, or as cut flowers. The individual blooms are very large and of the richest golden yellow. Pkt., 10c.; ¼ oz., 20c.; oz., 60c.

Canary Bird Vine

1543—Easy-growing, free-blooming annual climber for house or garden. Bright yellow flowers resembling a canary bird with extended wings. 10 feet. Pkt., 5c.; ½ oz., 15c.

Calendula (Pot Marigold)

One of the easiest grown, most showy and free flowering, hardy annuals, producing a fine effect in beds of mixed borders; blooms all the time; fine for cut flowers. 1½ feet.

1529 Fine Double Mixed—Contains the choicest sorts. Pkt., 5c.; oz., 20c.

Cannas

Cannas seem to be especially adapted to the American climate, as they do well everywhere. They grow nicely from seed, and will bloom the first Summer if started early. It is hard to describe the elegance of a fine bed of Cannas. Soak the seeds in warm water until they begin to swell; then sow them in a box in a sunny window or in the greenhouse. When up to the second leaf, transplant singly into pots and set out in the garden when the weather has become warm and settled.

1580 Large-Flowering French Hybrid Cannas, Mixed—Early flowering, and remarkable for large size and beauty of flower and foliage. This collection contains all that is best in Cannas. Pkt., 5c.; oz., 25c.

1582 Dark Leaved Cannas—This mixture contains the very choicest varieties we grow in the dark-leaved Cannas. Pkt., 5c.; oz., 20c.

Canna Plants—See page 118.

Candytuft (Iberis)

Candytuft is among the most highly prized of Summer flowers, and no garden is complete without a large quantity of it. Grows easily and blooms all the time until frost. Splendid for cut-flowers. Hardy annuals. 1 foot.

1547 Rose Cardinal—Very large umbel of bright rose-cardinal flowers, so prolific that a bed presents an unbroken sheet of bloom. Height 8 inches. Pkt., 10c.; ½ oz., 40c.

1550 Empress, or Giant Hyacinth-Flowered—An improved strain, producing immense trusses of pure white bloom, frequently measuring 4 inches in length by 2 inches through. Fine for bedding and cutting. Height 1 foot. Pkt., 10c.; ¼ oz., 15c.; ½ oz., 25c.; oz., 40c.

1545 Large-Flowering Dwarf, Mixed—Pkt., 10c.; ½ oz., 35c.

1546 Large-Flowering Dwarf, White—Pkt., 10c.; ¼ oz., 35c.

1551 White Rocket—Compact spikes. Pkt., 5c.; oz., 15c.

1553 Odorata—Pure white; most fragrant. Pkt., 5c.; oz., 20c.

1554 Candytuft, Mixed Annual Sorts—Our mixture contains all the best varieties and colors. Pkt., 5c.; oz., 15c.

1556 Gibraltarica—A dwarf evergreen plant flowering in early Spring and Summer. Much used for rockeries, edging or in the foreground of perennial borders. A fine little plant worthy of more general cultivation. Lilac, shading to white. Pkt., 10c.

1557 Sempervirens—Similar to the above except pure white. Pkt., 10c.; ¼ oz., 25c.

Candytuft

Celosia, or Cockscomb

Very attractive annuals. The crested heads of flowers resemble a cock's comb. The plumed heads are like great feathers. Sow the seed directly in the garden or start early and transplant. Make fine pot plants.

Ostrich Plume Sorts

Very graceful. Handsome, pyramidal plants 3 feet high. Each branch gracefully tipped with brilliantly colored plume resembling an ostrich feather. (See illustration.)

1600 Thompsoni Magnifica—Mammoth blossoms of vivid scarlet; purple, blood-red, golden yellow, salmon, etc., 2 feet. Mixed colors. Pkt., 10c.; ¼ oz., 25c.

1602 Gold Plume—Golden yellow. Pkt., 5c.

1604 Fire Plume—Fiery scarlet. Pkt., 5c.

Collection, the 3 new Ostrich Plume Celosias, listed above, 15c.

Comb Varieties

1608 Queen of the Dwarfs—Grows only about 8 inches high. Immense combs of perfect form; brilliant dark rose. Pkt., 10c.

1609 Glasgow Prize—Large and very showy dark crimson combs. 9 inches. Pkt., 10c.; ½ oz., 30c.

1610 Empress—Combs of colossal proportions; rich crimson. Pkt., 10c.; ¼ oz., 50c.

1611 Finest Dwarf Mixed—A choice mixture of all sorts and colors. Pkt., 5c.; ¼ oz., 25c.

Celosia, New Ostrich Plume

Choice Carnations

Seeds may be sown under glass in the Spring, or in open ground, but must be protected in the Winter. Half hardy.

1596 Giant Marguerite—The flowers enormous; the colors most varied and brilliant, and they come into full bloom in four months from sowing, and continue until hard frosts. Our strains are semi-dwarf and strong growers. 1 foot high. Our mixture is splendid. Pkt., 10c.

Giant Marguerite Carnations. Pkt., 10c.

1587 Marguerite Double White—Pure white, large flowers; stiff stalks. Pkt., 10c.

1588 Marguerite Double Yellow—Pkt., 15c.

1589 Marguerite New Half Dwarf Mixed—A grand new sort. Flowers are very large, double and fragrant. Pkt., 10c.; ¼ oz., 40c.

1585 Livingston's "Peerless" Carnation Mixture—All bloom the first Summer. A very choice mixture including all superb sorts. Pkt. (about 75 seeds), 10c.

1590 Chabaud's New Giant Perpetual—Comes into bloom in a little over 4 months from seed; extra large size; fine range of colors; is very sweet-scented. Mixed colors. Pkt., 10c.

1591 Carnation, Giant of Nice—Blooms in four to five months from date of sowing the seed. The flowers are very large; colors varied; very free flowering. Pkt., 20c.

1592 Fine Double Mixed. Pkt., 10c.

1594 Red Grenadin—For yielding a quantity of double red flowers, no outdoor Carnation can equal it. Pkt., 10c.

Catchfly
(Silene)

1599 Mixed sorts and colors—A very showy, free-blooming annual. 6 inches. Pkt., 5c.

Centaureas

The various varieties of this popular annual include such favorites as the Bachelor's Buttons or Corn-Flowers, and Sweet Sultans, Old-fashioned flowers of easiest culture. 2 feet.

1616 Bachelor's Buttons (Centaurea Cyanus)—Our strain is especially fine. The true old-fashioned Bachelor's Buttons of your grandmother's garden. Also called Blue Bottle, Ragged Sailor, Korn Blume, etc. Mixed colors. Pkt., 5c.; ½ oz., 10c.; oz., 15c.

1617 Emperor William—Rich, deep blue Bachelor's Button. Pkt., 5c.; ½ oz., 10c.

1618 Double Varieties—A comparatively new strain; about three-quarters of the flowers come double; many choice colors. Pkt., 5c.; ½ oz., 15c.

GIANT-FLOWERING SWEET SULTANS (Centaurea Imperialis)

The blooms are borne on long stems. Of the easiest growth; very showy in the garden all Summer long. (See illustration.)

1620 Giant Mixed Colors—An elegant assortment of colors. Pkt., 5c.; ¼ oz., 25c.; oz., 75c.

1621 Giant White—Splendid for bouquets. Pkt., 5c.; ¼ oz., 25c.

1622 Giant Odorata—Light blue; very large. Pkt., 5c.

1623 Giant Suaveolens—The popular yellow. Pkt., 5c.

1627 Livingston's Choice Mixed Centaureas—A grand mixture of all the above Bachelor Buttons and Giant Sweet Sultans. Pkt., 5c.; ¼ oz., 25c.; oz., 75c.

WHITE-LEAVED CENTAUREAS (Dusty Millers)

Silver-foliaged plants; extensively used for edgings, hanging baskets, etc.

1629 Candidissima—Very thick, broadly cut, slippery white leaves. 1 foot high. Pkt., 10c.

1628 Gymnocarpa—Leaves fern-like; silvery gray color. Fine for borders. 1½ feet. Pkt., 5c.

Chrysanthemums

The annual sorts bloom throughout the Summer, while the perennial varieties are gorgeous in the garden every Fall. The plants grow from 1 to 3 feet in height.

SEEDS OF ANNUAL VARIETIES

1632 Double White—Pkt., 5c.　**1633 Double Golden Yellow**—Pkt., 5c.

1634 Double Sorts Mixed—All the most desirable colors. Pkt., 5c.; ¼ oz., 15c.

1635 Livingston's Choice Mixed Chrysanthemums, Single and Double Sorts —Very desirable for the Summer garden; showy; free-flowering. Pkt., 5c.; ¼ oz., 15c.; ½ oz., 25c.

1654 Tricolor "Northern Star"—Fine hardy annual, with large daisy-like flowers produced freely on long stems. Pkt., 10c.

SEEDS OF PERENNIAL VARIETIES

1641 Japanese Hybrids—The best double-flowering varieties. Pkt., 15c.

1642 Frutescens (Marguerite, or Paris Daisy)—Large, single white flowers. Pkt., 5c.

1643 Maximum (Triumph Daisy)—Large, single, pure white, yellow center. Pkt., 10c.

2433 Shasta Daisy—Pkt., 10c. For description, see page 111.

1644 Chrysanthemum Inodorum (Bridal Robe)—New; pure white; extra fine. Pkt., 10c.

Centaurea Imperialis—Giant-Flowering Sweet Sultan

Cineraria

A favorite free-flowering greenhouse plant, with flowers of great richness and diversity of colors. Cinerarias bloom during the Winter and Spring months and can be planted out in Summer. The plants thrive best in a mixture of loam, leaf-mould and sand.

1648 Livingston's Prize Mixture—Contains only the richest and most beautiful colors; large. Pkt., 25c.

1650 Cineraria Maritima (Dusty Miller)—Silvery white foliage; for edgings, ribbon beds, hanging baskets, etc. 1 foot. Perennial, but usually grown as an annual. Pkt., 5c.; oz., 40c.

Cobaea Scandens

A fine annual climber, often growing 15 to 25 feet in a season. Has handsome foliage and large bell-shaped flowers of a beautiful deep violet-blue. 1658—Pkt., 5c.

Cyclamen

These elegant greenhouse plants have the most beautiful foliage and the richest colored flowers. Seed may be sown in the Spring and autumn. For large size blooms, substance and brilliant colors, our strains are unsurpassed.

1683 Livingston's Superb Mixture —Is our best strain; obtained by a continued selection of the choicest varieties of Cyclamen Persicum. The individual flowers are enormous in size; plants are profuse bloomers. The colors are rich and varied. (See illustration.) Pkt., 25c.

1684 Cyclamen Persicum, Finest Mixed—A choice assortment of varieties and colors. Pkt., 10c.

Coleus

Beautiful foliage plants, both for greenhouses and bedding out in the garden. The striking colors and brilliant variegated leaves are much admired.

1662 Extra Fine Mixed Hybrids —A mixture made up of the finest and showiest varieties possible to obtain from specialists. Pkt., 15c.

1663 Fine Mixed Hybrids—Mixed seed from a very fine collection. Pkt., 10c.

1664 New Large-Leaved "Fringed" Coleus—The leaves are large, superbly variegated, deeply cut, laciniated, fringed. Colors and markings new and striking. Pkt., 20c.

Cypress Vine

Ipomoea Quamoclit—This is a beautiful, rapidly growing annual climber, with delicate dark green finely cut fern-like foliage and masses of the most brilliant and graceful star-shaped flowers. The two shades, white and scarlet, are very striking. Planted by the side of a veranda, tree or stake, and trained properly, nothing is prettier.

1686 Pure White—Pkt., 5c.　**1687 Bright Scarlet**—Pkt., 5c.　**1689 Finest Mixed**—A mixture of Pure White and Bright Scarlet. Pkt., 5c.; ½ oz., 15c.

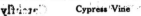

Livingston's Giant Cyclamen. Pkt., 25c.

Livingston's Mammoth Cosmos

Early
Flowering
Cosmos.
Pkt., 5c.

None of our autumn flowers are more prized than the Cosmos. The thrifty plants produce thousands of the most elegant blooms, in pure white, pink and crimson shades. As a decorative garden plant its value is inestimable, while as cut flowers for home decoration nothing is finer, especially as Cosmos are in bloom when other outdoor flowers are getting scarce. Plant the seed directly in the garden as soon as the settled Spring weather comes, or you may start the plants early in a box in the house and transplant them. In the garden set the plants 1 foot to 18 inches apart. One of our most desirable and easy-growing annuals. 5 to 6 feet.

Early Summer-Flowering Cosmos

1668 Dwarf Early-Flowering "Dawn"—Coming into flower in July, continuing until frost. Can be grown in the North where the seasons are too short for other strains. Dwarf, compact growth—4 feet. Flower beautiful and large; petals broad, pure white, flushed with a delicate tinge of rose; profuse bloomer. Pkt., 5c.; ¼ oz., 15c.; ½ oz., 25c.

Dwarf Early-Flowering Mixed

1669 Mixed—Identical with above, but contains all elegant colors known in Cosmos. Pkt., 5c.; ¼ oz., 15c.; ½ oz., 25c.

Mammoth Perfection Cosmos

Giants of California—A magnificent strain. The individual flowers are of enormous size and the most perfect form, while the colors are richly brilliant. These represent the highest developed types in Cosmos. Will keep a week in water after being cut.

1672 Mammoth Perfection, Mixed—A superb mixture of every color and shade in these splendid Cosmos. Pkt., 5c.; ¼ oz., 10c.; oz., 30c.

1673 Mammoth Perfection, Pure White—A splendid large flower. Pkt., 5c.; ¼ oz., 15c.

1674 Mammoth Perfection, Light Pink—Blooms are truly superb. Pkt., 5c.; ¼ oz., 15c.

1675 Mammoth Perfection, Crimson—A rich and brilliant shade. Pkt., 5c.; ¼ oz., 15c.

Coix Lachrymae

(Job's Tears)—Very ornamental plant, producing hard, shining seeds. Much used for bead curtains, raffia work, etc. 1660—Pkt., 5c.; oz., 10c.; ¼ lb., 25c.; lb., 75c.

New Gigantic Orchid-Flowered Cosmos

1680 Lady Lenox

This gigantic Cosmos is the forerunner of an entirely new race of Cosmos. It is of extraordinary size and beauty. Visitors to the floral exhibitions last Autumn were enraptured with its size and magnificent color. Flower 4 to 5 inches in diameter. Color a delightful shell pink, lighting up beautifully at night. 6 to 7 feet high. Splendid variety. Pkt., 10c.; 3 for 25c.; ¼ oz., 40c.

Dahlias from Seed

Dahlias are easily grown from seed and bloom the first season. The earlier they are started the better, which can be done nicely in a box in a sunny window or the greenhouse. Some specimens grown from seed are fully equal to many of the named sorts, and there is always the chance of getting some entirely new varieties. The Single Dahlias are being planted more extensively every year; they are quick and profuse bloomers, and their colors are especially rich and brilliant.

Dahlia Bulbs. See page 120.

Seeds from Single Dahlias

1693 Twentieth Century or Orchid-Flowered—A truly exquisite single Dahlia. Has created a sensation everywhere. Individual flowers are 5 to 8 inches across. Innumerable colors, that have the sheen of velvet. We cannot describe their elegance. Pkt., 10c.

1694—Striped and Spotted Varieties—A very beautiful class, with finely cut foliage and large single flowers of perfect form in many brilliant colors. Pkt., 5c.

1695 Large-Flowering Single Mixed—Splendid assortment of single-flowering varieties. Pkt., 5c.

Seeds of Double Dahlias

1698 Large-Flowering Choicest Double Mixed—This elegant assortment of seed is saved from round, double flowers; many beautiful colors. Pkt., 10c.

1700 Pompon Varieties, Fine Mixed—These have small, round, perfectly double flowers; many beautiful colors. Pkt., 5c.

1701—Double Tom Thumb, Superb Mixture—A splendid strain, growing about 18 inches high; very double; fine for beds. Pkt., 10c.

1702 Cactus Varieties, Choicest Mixed—Most popular at the present time; distinct and elegant; petals pointed; blooms perfectly double. Pkt., 10c.

1705—Livingston's Superb Dahlia Mixture—This splendid assortment embraces every variety of Dahlias, both single and double, described on this page, as well as many other fine sorts. Will make an elegant bed at small cost. Pkt., 15c.

Double Dahlia

Giant Double Daisies (Bellis Perennis)

A charming little plant for pots, edgings and borders. (See illustration.) Sow the seeds very early and plants will bloom the first season and continue to bloom each season if given some protection during winter. They do best in a rich soil and quite cool situation. Especially desirable for cemetery decoration. Perennial. Height about 6 inches.

1710 Giant Longfellow—A very desirable double sort; dark pink; flowers very large. Pkt., 10c.

1711 Giant Snowball — A large and very double pure white variety. The flowers make fine cut flowers, as the stems are long. Pkt., 10c.

1712 Giant Mixed Daisies —This assortment includes the Giant Longfellow, Giant Snowball and Giant Red, as well as many other finest sorts. Pkt., 10c.

1713 Double White—A very fine white variety. Pkt., 5c.

1714 Double Rose— Clear rose-pink. Pkt., 5c.

1715 Fine Double Mixed— A very choice mixture. Pkt., 5c.

Giant Double Daisies

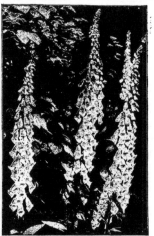

Foxglove (Digitalis)

Delphinium

Hardy Perennial Larkspurs—One of our most brilliant and effective hardy garden plants. Of late years the size and colors of the flowers have been wonderfully improved. Persistent bloomers, even in the dryest seasons, 2 to 4 feet.

1726 New Giant-Flowering Hybrids — These magnificent hybrids, the grandest of Delphiniums in existence, produce splendid spikes of immense flowers, semi-double and double. Flower spikes are from 2 to 5 feet in length. The colors are very beautiful, ranging from pure white through all the shades of lavender and blue. Mixed colors. Pkt., 25c.

1730 Elatum Hybridum — Finest mixed. Pkt., 10c.

1732 Formosum — Elegant spikes of the richest dark-blue flowers, with a white center; especially fine for cut-flowers. 4 feet. Pkt., 5c.

1733 Formosum Coelestinum —Light sky-blue flowers, with darker centers; a very fine variety. 4 feet. Pkt., 10c.

1735 Zalil — The splendid spikes of bloom are a lovely shade of sulphur-yellow. 4 feet. Pkt., 10c.

1737 Mixed Chinese Varieties — This elegant mixture contains a great variety of shades, from pure white to gentian-blue. The plants are brilliantly showy. Pkt., 5c.

Annual Delphiniums. See Larkspur, page 96.

Mrs. Mary A. Love, Buchanan Co., Iowa, writes April 7, 1915: "I have planted your seed ever since 1875. They are so reliable, I am afraid to use others. You sent me two catalogues. I gave them to my neighbors. I know they will send to you for seeds."

Delphinium

Digitalis (Foxglove, or Witches Fingers)

The Foxglove, in common with all the hardy perennials, is being planted more extensively each season. The large tube-like flowers, which are produced so freely in beautiful spikes, add much to our hardy beds and borders. Being of the easiest growth, and doing finely in partially shaded situations, they fill in many gaps most advantageously. 3 feet.

1782 Gloxiniaeflora — A beautiful class, with spotted flowers. We offer a mixture of the finest varieties. Pkt., 5c.; ¼ oz., 20c.

1784 Grandiflora—A variety that grows about 2 feet in height. A very fine yellow in color. Pkt., 5c.; ¼ oz., 20c.

1786 Monstrosa (Mammoth Foxglove)—A grand strain. The top flowers of the spikes are of enormous size. Our assortment of colors is very fine. Splendid mixed. Pkt., 5c.; ¼ oz., 30c.

1788 Purpurea, Finest Mixed —This is the common Foxgloves so generally known. Contains many fine varieties. Pkt., 5c.; ¼ oz., 15c.

Datura (Trumpet Flower)

Very attractive, bushy plants of easy growth, that during the whole season are covered with elegant, fragrant, trumpet-shaped flowers. Hardy annual. 3 feet.

1720 Cornucopia (Horn of Plenty)—A magnificent variety. The blooms average 8 inches long by 5 inches across; the color is white inside, while the outside is most beautifully marbled with royal purple. Pkt., 5c.; ¼ oz., 20c.

1722 Finest Double Mixed —A very choice assortment of all the best colors and varieties of this effective annual. Pkt., 5c.

Grass Pinks.

Dianthus or Pinks
(New and Choice Varieties)

This elegant family contains many of the most valuable and popular flowers in cultivation. All the sorts classed as annuals may be sown directly in the garden as soon as danger from frost is past, and will in a short time become a mass of bloom, and so remain all Summer. Elegant as cut flowers for bouquets, as the stems are good. Grow about 1 foot high, and are of easiest culture.

Hardy Garden or Clove Pinks

This splendid class of hardy perennial Pinks should be in all gardens. They have the delightful clove fragrance.

1778 New Double Large-Flowering Grass, or Spice Pinks (Plumarius semperflorens, Fl. Pl.)—One foot high. The flowers, which are beautifully fringed, are much larger and more double than the old varieties, while the colors are far richer, including a large variety of colors and markings not known to the old-fashioned Pinks. Many are exquisitely spotted and splashed. They emit a delightful, sweet-scented spicy odor. Perfectly hardy, requiring only the ordinary culture of Pinks. They increase in size and beauty every year. Bloom profusely during the Spring and early Summer. Pkt., 25c.

1772 New Single Large-Flowering Grass, or Spice Pink, Mixed—Same as above, only single. Pkt., 5c.

1773 Plumarius (Pheasant's Eye Pink)—A single hardy Pink; fringed edge, white flowers with dark centers. Pkt., 5c.

1774 Double Clove Pink (Plumarius flore pleno)—Double and semi-double varieties. Many colors; of strong clove fragrance. Pkt., 10c.

1776 Cyclops Hybrids—Superb, double-flowering red and scarlet varieties; very fragrant. Pkt., 5c.

1777 Livingston's Mixture of Hardy Garden Pinks—A magnificent strain of hardy garden pinks containing all the sorts described on this page and many new varieties not listed by us. Choicest single and double sorts of bright and brilliant colors make this mixture one of the most desirable for the hardy garden. Pkt., 10c.; 3 pkts., 25c.; ½ oz., 50c.

Double Annual Pinks

1740 New Giant Fringed and Ruffled Pinks, Double Marvelous or Japanese Fringed Pinks (Mirabilis Fl. Pl.)—This remarkable and perfectly distinct new strain produces large, perfectly double flowers on stiff, upright stems. The petals are deeply cut into fine strips of thread-like fringes for about half their length, and are twisted in all directions, presenting a novel aspect. In color, they vary greatly, having all shades from pure white to deep purplish-red. Pkt., 15c.; 2 pkts., 25c.

1742 Double Royal Pinks (Nobilis Fl. Pl.)—A splendid new double-flowering strain of Royal Pinks. The flowers range in colors from blood-red to pure white, and are beautifully frilled and fringed. The enormous blooms are especially adapted for cutting, the stems being long. Vigorous growers and abundant bloomers. Pkt., 10c.

1744 Laciniatus (Double Fringed Pinks)—Magnificent flowers; very large; double. Mixed colors; striped and fringed edges. Pkt., 5c.; ¼ oz., 25c.

1746 Heddewigi (Double Japan Pink)—Flowers very large; perfectly double; many elegant colors and shades, from delicate rose to richest crimson. Pkt., 5c.; ¼ oz., 20c.

1752 Imperialis (Double Imperial Pink)—Charming varieties of these popular pinks. Our mixture includes a great number of colors. Pkt., 5c.

1754 Snowball—Double white, fringed flowers; fine variety. Pkt., 5c.

1756 Fireball—A brilliant dark scarlet; plants grow dwarf and bushy; is very fine for bedding or cut flowers. Pkt., 5c.; ¼ oz., 25c.

1758 Chinensis (China or India Pink)—Our mixture includes all best colors and shades. Pkt., 5c.; ¼ oz., 15c.; oz., 50c.

1760 Livingston's Mixture of Double Pinks—A splendid combination of all the best varieties. Pkt., 5c.; ¼ oz., 25c.

Dolichos
(Hyacinth Bean)

A splendid annual climber, with hyacinth-like clusters of purple and white flowers, which are followed by exceedingly ornamental seed pods. Is of most rapid growth and stands Summer heat well. Sow the seeds in the garden in May where the plants are to remain.

1796 New White Bush Dolichos—Strong, healthy plants, 18-30 inches tall according to soil, carry an abundance of elegant flower spikes 12 to 16 inches long, well above the foliage. Individual flowers measure about an inch across and resemble a pea flower. As the lowest flowers on stalks drop off, they are followed by ornamental creamy-white seed pods. Bush Dolichos succeed anywhere, are highly ornamental planted singly or in rows and bloom continuously from middle of July until frost. Pkt., 10c.

1790 "Daylight"—A splendid variety from Japan. Large snow-white Wistaria-like racemes, that are most fragrant, followed by attractive silver-white seed pods. A very showy and rapid-growing sort. Pkt., 5c.; ½ oz., 15c.

1792 Purple Soudan—A most decorative climber. The twining stems are of the most intense purple, while the beautiful spikes of bloom are of the richest shade of brilliant rose. Pkt., 5c.; ½ oz., 10c.

1794 Finest Mixed—Very choice mixture of all the best climbing varieties. Pkt., 5c.; ½ oz., 10c.; oz., 15c.; ¼ lb., 50c.

Dimorphotheca Aurentiaca

1718 Golden Orange Daisy—One of the newer annuals from South Africa. Grows 10-12 inches high, with pretty daisy-like flowers. Orange-yellow. Pkt., 10c.

African Golden-Orange Daisy

California Poppies

Eschscholtzia

(California Poppies)

Most attractive annuals of the easiest culture, their flowers being very bright and showy. They are splendid for bedding, massing or ribbon-work. The plants grow bushy and about 1 foot high. They are favorites everywhere. Bloom profusely from Spring sown seed. (See illustration.)

1804 "The Golden West"—Early and continuous bloomer. Magnificent flowers of gigantic size. Color intense shining yellow and orange. The state flower of California. Pkt., 5c.; ¼ oz., 15c.

1806 Finest Double Mixed—A splendid assortment of colors. Pkt., 5c.; ¼ oz., 15c.; oz., 50c.

1808 Finest Single Mixed—All the best varieties. Pkt., 5c.; oz., 25c.

1811 Bush Eschscholtzia (Hunnemannia)—A fine new perennial plant; forms a bushy shrub 2 feet high, producing large cup-shaped flowers on stems 12 inches long; of clear jonquil yellow and vivid bright orange stamens. Begins to bloom in July from Spring-sown seed. Pkt., 5c.

Euphorbia

Easily grown annuals with very ornamental foliage; very fine in mixed beds.

1814 Variegated (Snow on the Mountain)—Foliage is veined and margined with white. 2 feet. Pkt., 5c.

Echeveria (Hen and Chickens)

These plants easily grown from seeds. Our mixture contains a great variety, both in shapes and colorings.
1797 Mixed—Pkt., 10c.

Erigeron Speciosa

1770—Hardy perennial, bearing pretty blue flowers for a long period. Grows about two feet high. Useful in hardy border. Pkt., 10c.

Feverfew (Matricaria)

1824—Free-flowering annuals about one foot high; very compact and bushy. Splendid for beds and borders; also fine as cut flowers or for pots. The double, white blooms are very useful in bouquets. Pkt., 10c.

Fuchsias (Lady's Eardrops)

These well-known plants will flower the first season from seed, if started early. As house plants for Winter they are always general favorites. The seed we offer is saved from a fine collection of double and single sorts.

1826 Best Sorts Mixed—Pkt., 15c.

Four O'clock—Marvel of Peru, page 101.

Forget-Me-Not—See Myosotis, page 104.

Gaillardia

(Blanket Flower)

There are Annual and Perennial Gaillardias. The Annual sorts bloom all Summer and Autumn, and are noted for the profusion, size and brilliancy of their flowers; excellent for beds and borders. The Perennial varieties are grand and wonderfully effective in the hardy borders, their especial value being constant blooming from July until hard freezing weather. They require no Winter protection, although applications of manure increase their strength. If the seed is sown early they will begin flowering at mid-Summer. Both classes are splendid as cut flowers. They are of the easiest culture, doing finely anywhere. Height 2 feet.

1830 Finest Single Annual Mixed—A very fine assortment of many brilliant colors. Pkt., 5c.

1832 Finest Double Annual Mixed (Lorenziana)—All the best double-flowering varieties in richest mixture. They bloom freely all the season. Splendid for bouquets. Pkt., 5c.

1834 Grandiflora Hybrids, Finest Mixed—One of the most elegant perennials; is in continuous bloom from June until frost. The enormous flowers are a magnificent combination of red and yellow. Splendid to cut for vases. Pkt., 5c.

1836 Grandiflora Compacta—A compact-growing variety similar in bloom to the Grandiflora Hybrids, but only grows about 15 inches high. Its flowers are of the richest colors, and the stems are long. A very fine variety. Pkt., 5c.

1838 Grandiflora Semi-Double—Very large flowering; same as both the preceding, except that the greater part of the flowers are semi-double. The ray florets from the center of the blooms are in two or three rows, and often tubular or broad and lacinated. Colors range from light to deep golden yellow, often tinged with wine-red. A most effective variety. Pkt., 10c.

Gaillardia Grandiflora. Packets, 5c. and 10c.

Geraniums

These popular plants are most easily raised from seed, and if started early will product flowering plants the first Summer. Start in the house and transplant to the garden as soon as the weather is warm. You will find that the varieties we offer are of very superior quality.

1842 Finest Mixed—Pkt., 10c.

1843 Large-Flowering Double Varieties—Splendid strain; seed is saved from the finest double sorts. Pkt., 25c.

1844 Variegated-Leaved Sorts—Bronze, gold, silver and tricolored foliaged varieties. Elegant collection. Pkt., 15c.

1845 Lady Washington—These are the well-known rich-colored show Pelargoniums. Our mixture includes all the best varieties. Pkt., 20c.

1846 Apple-Scented—The old-fashioned favorite apple-scented Geranium. Pkt., 10c.

Godetia

(Satin Flower)

An attractive and very beautiful hardy annual. In full bloom all Summer, so profuse that the foliage is almost hidden by the large, wide-open flowers; of shining-satiny texture and the most delicate and brilliant colors. Our mixture contains all the best varieties. 1½ feet.

1854 Mixed—Pkt., 5c.

Ornamental Gourds

1860 Livingston's Extra Fine Gourd Mixture—A splendid mixture of Gourds, including all the ornamental kinds, both large and small, of various shapes and colors, such as Japanese Nest Egg, Mock Orange, Dish Cloth, Turk's Turban, Dipper, Serpent, Bottle, Warty Gourd, Hercules' Club, and many other curious and unique varieties. Gives unlimited pleasure to both elders and children. Many odd and fantastic shapes. Pkt., 5c.; ½ oz., 20c.; oz., 35c.

1862 Bath-Sponge, or Dish Cloth—A most admirable natural dish-cloth is furnished by the peculiar sponge-like lining of this fruit. Pkt., 5c.; ½ oz., 20c.; oz., 35c.

1865 Dipper—Used for dippers; 9 to 12 inches long; hold from 1 to 4 pints; will last for years. Pkt., 5c.; oz., 20c.

1867 Hercules' Club—Longest of all; white. Pkt., 5c.

1868 Japanese Nest Egg—Exactly like a hen's egg in shape, color and size. Pkt., 5c.; ½ oz., 15c.; oz., 25c.

1871 Snake, or Serpent—Has long fruits, sometimes 5 feet, and striped like a serpent. Pkt., 10c.; 3 pkts., 25c.

1872 Sugar Trough—Holds 4 to 10 gallons; hard; thick shells; very light, strong and durable. Pkt., 5c.; oz., 15c.

Gypsophila Paniculata (Baby's Breath)

An elegant hardy perennial plant that should be in every garden. It is not only pretty in beds, but its delicate little flowers, produced in feathery white panicles, and branching foliage lend a daintiness to bouquets that is most elegant. Its sprays are much used in making up bouquets of Sweet Peas. 1878—Pkt., 5c.

Heliotrope. Pkt., 10c.

Geraniums

Heliotrope

Easily raised from seeds. Spring planting giving fine Summer blooming plants. As a bouquet flower always a favorite.

1880 Lemoine's Giant Hybrids—Grand flowers, double the size of the older sorts. Bushes compact, about 18 inches high; heads of mammoth blossoms often measure a foot across. Deliciously fragrant. Seed sown in the Spring will produce flowering plants by July, which continue in flower until frost. Mixed, including purple, white, lavender and blue. Pkt., 10c.

1882 Dark Varieties Mixed—All best dark blue and lavender shades in mixture. Pkt., 5c.

1884 All Sorts Mixed—In best assortment; all shades, both light and dark. A very desirable strain. Pkt., 5c.

Hardy Garden Heliotrope—See Valeriana.

Helichrysum

(Straw Flower)

A hardy annual of the easiest culture; one of our best "Everlasting" flowers, the dried double blooms being very handsome in Winter bouquets. 2 feet.

1888 Mixed—Pkt., 5c.; ¼ oz., 20c.

Hibiscus

(Marshmallow)

Tall growing; especially adapted to backgrounds and shrubbery borders. Of easiest culture, and bloom the entire season. Plants grow 4 to 5 feet tall.

1890 Africanus—A very choice annual variety. Flowers yellow, with maroon center. Pkt., 5c.

1892 Crimson Eye—The beautiful white flowers, with deep crimson centers, are of immense size, often 6 to 7 inches in diameter. Perfectly hardy. Pkt., 5c.

1994 Mallow Marvels—A robust type of upright habit, producing an abundance of flowers of enormous size in all the richest shades of crimson, pink and white. Mixed colors. Pkt., 10c.

Hollyhocks

Hollyhocks require a rich soil, but it must be well drained. We give especial attention to this flower, and you will find our strains of seed of the finest quality. Once thoroughly established, they bloom stronger and more brilliantly every year. Seeds sown early, and the young plants transplanted several times, will bloom the same season, July and August sown seed, following year. 5 to 8 feet.

Livingston's Prize Hollyhocks

These are the largest flowering and most perfectly double Hollyhocks we have been able to procure after many years of selection of only the best varieties. The colors are rich and brilliant, the plants free from disease, as well as very robust and strong growers; in fact, we believe our strain to be unsurpassed in every respect. We offer several separate colors and our best mixture.

1896 Double Black. Pkt., 10c.	1900 Double Rose Pink. Pkt., 10c.
1897 Double Lemon Yellow. Pkt., 10c.	1901 Double Crimson. Pkt., 10c.
	1904 Double Scarlet. Pkt., 10c.
1898 Double White. Pkt., 10c.	1905 Double Salmon. Pkt., 10c.

Livingston's Prize Mixture

This is our best mixture. It is composed exclusively of the finest double-flowering varieties. It contains not only the above elegant colors, but also innumerable other shades. 1908—Pkt., 10c.; ¼ oz., 25c.

Mammoth Allegheny

Attractive variety. Its lovely arranged, fringed and transparent petals look as if they were made from the finest China silk. The individual flowers are enormous in size, and in color they range from the palest pink to deepest red. In form the flowers are double, semi-double and single. Plants are in full bloom from July until frost. 1910—Pkt., 10c.; ¼ oz., 30c.

Livingston's Prize Hollyhocks. Pkt., 10c.

Humulus
(Japanese Hop)

Splendid climber. Has handsome foliage, which resembles that of the Common Hop Vine. Never suffers from heat or attack of insects; easiest culture.
1920 Japonicus—Has bright green foliage. Pkt., 5c.
1922 Silver-Leaf Japanese Hop—Unusually beautiful variety of rapid-growing Summer climbing vine. Leaves deep green, beautifully striped and blotched with silvery white and gray. Will reach a height of 20 to 30 feet in three or four weeks' time. Pkt., 5c.; ½ oz., 15c.

Impatiens
(Zanzibar Balsam)

A very pretty plant, for house culture, and the garden as well. Its flowers are very rich colored. They are borne in great abundance, and the plants are continuous bloomers. Tender perennial. 2 feet. 1928—Pkt., 10c.

Holstii Hybrids

Very handsome Zanzibar Balsam discovered in Africa. It forms bushes 1½ to 2 feet high and resembles above, but surpasses it in its quicker and more vigorous growth, and its larger and brighter colored flowers. Seed sown indoors in Spring will form plants ready to set out in May. 1930—Mixed—Pkt., 15c.

Kudzu Vine

1936 Pueraria Thunbergiana—This wonderful climber is of Japanese origin and is the most luxuriant and rapid-growing vine known in horticulture. It will grow 8 to 10 feet the first year from seed, and after becoming established will produce vines 50 feet high in a season, sometimes growing 12 inches in a single day. Produces a tuberous root which is perfectly hardy everywhere. Foliage is very luxuriant, quickly forming a dense shade. Unequaled for porches, arbors, trellises, etc. Pkt., 10c.; 3 pkts., 25c.

Kochia Tricophylla

1934 Summer Cypress, or Burning Bush—This splendid annual plant grows very quickly from seed sown in the open ground as soon as the weather permits in Spring. The plants always make attractive globe-shaped bushes, as large sometimes as 3 feet high and 2 feet across in one season. Leaves slender and of a light peagreen color until September, when they turn to carmine and blood-red; at the same time the ends of the shoots are thickly set with small bright scarlet flowers, and produce a very striking effect. Pkt., 10c.; ¼ oz., 25c.

New Annual Everblooming Hollyhocks

These glorious new hybrids may be grown from seeds and will flower the same year as quickly as any garden annual. The plants can be treated as annuals. The seeds may be started in the house, or in hot-beds, frames, etc., in March or April. Plants transplanted by the beginning of May in the open ground will commence to flower about end of July, ten days after Hollyhocks that have been treated as biennials. 1913 Mixed Annual Hollyhocks—Pkt., 10c.; ½ oz., 40c.

Ice Plant
(Mesembryanthemum)

A very pretty trailing annual that has fleshy, wax-like leaves, which have the appearance of being covered with ice crystals. Splendid for rock-work, or hanging baskets. Flowers are white. Start seed in the house. 1925—Pkt., 5c.

Kenilworth Ivy

1932 Linaria Cymbalaria—A hardy perennial trailing plant suitable for vases, etc. Adapted to shady locations. Easily grown from seed. Lovely little lavender and purple flowers and an exquisite foliage. Pkt., 10c.

Kochia Tricophylla in our trial grounds. It makes a beautiful and symmetrical hedge.

Lantana

Popular, free-blooming and very rapid-growing plants with flower heads of various colors, which are continually changing; emit a powerful aromatic perfume, plants are completely loaded with blossoms, succeeded by berries, which, when ripe, turn deep blue. Used largely for bedding out in Summer and are also fine Winter-blooming plants. Start seeds in the house or hot-bed. Tender perennial. 1½ feet. **1938 Mixed**—Pkt., 5c.; ½ oz., 20c.

Lunaria Biennis

Or, as it is popularly called, "Honesty," is a plant we seldom see now, though many inquire for it and it used to be largely grown. It has pretty purple flowers, but it is most prized for its silvery, flat, moon-shaped, seed pods which succeed them. These are used largely for house decoration, the same as Everlasting flowers, as they last through the season when dried. **1918**—Pkt., 5c.

Linum

Everybody has admired the common Flax with its beautiful blue flowers, but it is of no value in the garden. In **Linum Grandiflorum** we have an annual variety of Flax with large, brilliant scarlet flowers about three times the size of the regular Flax. **Linum Perenne** is a hardy perennial, an evergreen plant with the fine soft foliage and beautiful sky blue blossoms of our common Flax. **1939 Linum Grandiflorum**—Pkt., 5c.; **1940 Linum Perenne**—Pkt., 5c.

Lantana. Pkt., 5c.

Larkspurs (Annual Delphinium)

1945 Azure Fairy—An annual variety of Larkspur and a most beautiful shade of blue. It grows about 12 inches high and is covered with flowers for a long period. It is very hardy and satisfactory in every way. Pkt., 15c.

1944 Stock - Flowered Larkspur—These tall-growing and branching Larkspurs produce the most brilliantly beautiful spikes of double flowers; continuously in bloom all Summer. All colors mixed. Pkt., 5c.

1947 Dwarf Hyacinth - Flowered—Resembles a Dutch Hyacinth in style of bloom. Our mixture includes a very fine range of colors and shades. Pkt., 5c.; ¼ oz., 10c.

1949 Giant Hyacinth - Flowered—Tall, a superb class. The splendid flowers are very large, very double and of various beautiful colors, shadings and markings; long spikes of bloom like immense Hyacinths. Pkt., 10c.; ½ oz., 25c.

1951 Double Dwarf Rocket—A most choice mixture of varieties, that grow about 1 foot in height. Pkt., 5c.; ½ oz., 15c.

1953 Double Tall Rocket—This well-known mixture embraces the very choicest colors in the taller growing sorts. Pkt., 5c.; ½ oz., 15c.

Perennial Larkspur—See Delphinium, page 92.

Lavender

(Lavendula vera, true Lavender)—Popular sweet-scented hardy perennial; fine for mixed border. 3 feet. **1957**—Pkt., 5c.; ¼ oz., 15c.

Lobelia

Exceedingly pretty, profuse blooming plants of great value both in the garden and for hanging-baskets, window boxes and vases, especially prized for edgings of beds and borders. Plants grow about 6 inches high. They are treated as annuals and are of the easiest culture.

1958 Crystal Palace Compacta—Best dark blue sort for edgings and carpet bedding. Pkt., 10c.; ⅛ oz., 50c.

1960 Emperor William—A brilliant, compact-growing light blue; a very fine variety. Pkt., 5c.

1962 Gracilis—Fine for hanging-baskets, vases and window boxes. Light blue. A trailing variety. Pkt., 5c.

1964 Mixed Compacta Sorts—A very fine mixture of all the best varieties for edgings and bedding. Pkt., 5c.

Marvel of Peru (Four O'clocks or Mirabilis)

This old-fashioned favorite is one of our easiest grown annuals. The plants are bushy, about 2 feet high, and completely covered all Summer with large, showy, very fragrant blooms.

1995 Variegated—The brilliant flowers, in many colors, contrast finely with the golden-hued foliage. Pkt., 5c.; oz., 15c.

1997 Finest Mixed—An elegant assortment of these old-fashioned favorites. Pkt., 5c.; oz., 10c.; ¼ lb., 25c.

Maurandya

Elegant twining, climbing plants, with handsome foliage and flowers. They bloom profusely all Summer in the garden, and are also particularly adapted for the house and conservatory. **1999 Blue, White and Mauve, Mixed**—Pkt., 10c.

Mimulus (Monkey Flowers)

Very showy and free-blooming plants, having brilliant and greatly varied blooms. Fine for pots, or in the garden. They do best in rather shaded, moist situations. 1 foot.

2018 Tigrinus—Striped and spotted varieties; very fine. Pkt., 10c.

2020 Moschatus (Musk Plant)—Fine for hanging baskets, etc. Small yellow flowers. The foliage has a strong odor of musk. Pkt., 5c.

Lychnis

Few plants produce as bright flowers and bloom as continuously as Lychnis. A hardy perennial, but flowers the first season from seed if same is sown early. 2 feet.

1971 Finest Mixed Hybrids—Plants are compact and bushy; colors include all the most brilliant shades, from pure white to deepest red. Pkt., 5c.

Livingston's Superb Marigolds

These old-fashioned favorites are annuals of the very easiest cultivation. Both the French and African classes are very effective; the former have the small, velvety flowers, in pretty combinations of yellow, brown, maroon and striped effects; the African sorts are the enormous flowered ones, in very showy orange and lemon shades. (See illustration.) Both kinds are most popular for beds and borders, and planted in large blocks are very attractive. They bloom profusely all Summer. Start the seed early in a box in the house, or plant directly in the garden when the weather is warm. Fine as cut-flowers. French sorts make nice pot plants.

African Marigolds

1974 Mammoth Lemon Queen—Flowers very large; rich lemon color; double. 3 feet. Pkt., 5c.; ½ oz., 25c.

1976 Mammoth Orange Prince—Enormous double blooms, of an intense, very striking orange. 3 feet. Pkt., 5c.; ½ oz., 25c.

1978 Mammoth Tall Mixed—A splendid assortment of all the best shades in African Marigolds. 3 feet. Pkt., 5c.; ½ oz., 20c.; oz., 35c.

1980 Mammoth Dwarf Mixed—The flowers are enormous in size, but the plants grow dwarfer. 1½ feet. Pkt., 5c.; ½ oz., 20c.; oz., 35c.

French Marigolds

1984 Legion of Honor (Little Brownie)—Handsome single variety, covered with a multitude of flowers. In color it is a velvety golden yellow blotched with purple. 1 foot. Pkt., 5c.; ¼ oz., 20c.

1988 Tall Double Mixed—A splendid assortment of all the best colors in striking combinations. 2½ feet. Pkt., 5c.; ½ oz., 15c.; oz., 25c.

1990 Dwarf Double Mixed—Similar mixture to No. 1980 in colors, but the plants grow much dwarfer. 1 foot. Pkt., 5c.; ½ oz., 15c.; oz., 25c.

Livingston's "True Blue" Flower Seeds

are grown for us by specialists who have had years of experience, and are situated where the climate is best suited to their perfect development. You will take little risk in using them.

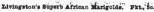

Livingston's Superb African Marigolds. Pkt., 5c.

Mignonette (Reseda)

Without Mignonette in our gardens, something indeed would be missing. Its large, deliciously fragrant spikes of bloom are everyone's admiration. Make successive sowings in the garden, from April to July, for continuous bloom until frost; and if the plants are thinned out to six inches apart, and the tops pinched off when about two inches high, stronger plants, with larger spikes of elegant bloom, will be the result. Height 1 to 2 feet, according to the variety.

2061 Mammoth Red Goliath (See illustration)—This is the ideal mignonette for garden or pot culture. Of strong stocky growth, luxuriant rich green foliage. Branching habit; dense in length and 2½ inches in diameter. Surpasses all others in brilliancy of color. Strong, delightful fragrance. Pkt., 10c.; ¼ oz., 50c.

2005 Machet—A very fine variety, especially for growing in pots; has large, fragrant spikes of reddish bloom. Pkt., 5c.; ¼ oz., 20c.; ½ oz., 35c.

2006 Golden Machet—A distinct variety of the above, having golden-yellow flower spikes. Very sweet and elegant. Pkt., 10c.; ¼ oz., 20c.

2007 Defiance—Has immense spikes of bloom. Keeps long time after being cut, and very fragrant. Pkt., 5c.; ¼ oz., 15c.

2008 Victoria Red—An elegant sort; fine flower-spikes of the most brilliant dark-red; very sweet. Pkt., 5c.; ¼ oz., 20c.; ½ oz., 35c.

2009 Golden Queen—A very compact-growing sort; flower spikes golden yellow. Fragrant and fine. Pkt., 5c.; ¼ oz., 15c.

2010 Parson's White—A robust grower, bearing large spikes of bloom; pure white and very fragrant. Pkt., 5c.; ¼ oz., 10c.

2011 Sweet Mignonette (Reseda Odorata)—The old fashioned, deliciously sweet scented variety. Pkt., 5c.; oz., 10c.; ¼ lb., 35c.

2016 Finest Mixed Varieties—An elegant mixture of above fine varieties, and many other choice sorts. Pkt., 5c.; ½ oz., 15c.; oz., 25c.

Mammoth Red Goliath Mignonette. Pkt., 10c.

Marigolds

Sprouts
us...

Moonflowers

(Ipomoea Noctiflora—See Illustration Below)

Splendid annual climbers of most rapid growth, with beautiful and varied flowers; for covering old walls, trellises, arbors, or stumps of trees, they are valuable. The seed should be lightly cut at the end and soaked over night before planting.

2038 Northern Light—The earliest blooming of all the Moonflowers. Its lovely pink flowers are produced by the thousands, all Summer and Fall. Pkt., 10c.

2040 Moonflower, White-Seeded—The variety most generally grown, being large in flower, firm in texture, and very fragrant. It bears in greatest profusion its immense lovely white flowers, 5 to 6 inches in diameter, with a 5-pointed star in the center. Pkt., 10c.

2042 Moonflower, Cross-Bred or Hybrid—A variety of great value for the North, as it in bloom a month earlier than the above. Flowers are pure white, large and fragrant. A very rapid grower; 20 to 40 feet. Pkt., 10c.

One packet of each of above three Moonflowers, 25c.

Three Other Splendid Moonflowers

2044 Ipomoea Coccinea (Star Ipomoea)—Splendid climber; bears small, starshaped, scarlet flowers, in great abundance. Pkt., 5c.

Cardinal Climber

2045 Ipomoea Bona Nox (Evening Glory)—A favorite climber; with very fragrant violet flowers, that open in the evening. Pkt., 5c.

2046 Ipomoea Rubro - Coerulea (Heavenly Blue)—The popular climber; has immense blooms of bright sky-blue. Very fine sort. Pkt., 10c.

Giant Japanese Morning Glories

New Cardinal Climber

(Ipomoea Quamoclit Hybrida)

A new annual climber of the Ipomoea or Morning Glory family. It is a wonderfully vigorous grower, climbing 20 feet in a season from seed sown in the Spring. The foliage is beautifully cut and is very graceful. The flowers are very brilliant, being a fiery scarlet, the individual blooms being about 1½ inches across and produced in clusters of 5 to 7. It flowers very profusely the entire Summer, and bids fair to take a place as one of our best annual climbers, having attracted much attention wherever grown. It should be planted in a warm sunny location in good soil and will then give a good account of itself.
1598—Pkt., 15c.

Dwarf, or Bedding Morning Glories

Beautiful and showy plants, producing an abundance of richly colored flowers, which, in fine weather, remain open all day. Hardy annual. 1 foot.

2036 Choice Mixed—A very large assortment of these richly colored favorites. Pkt., 5c.; oz., 15c.

Morning Glories

(Convolvulus)

2024 Giant Imperial Japanese—One of the most valuable and popular annual climbers introduced in years. This strain of mammothflowering Morning Glories is most justly celebrated for the beauty of both flowers and foliage. Magnificent in size of bloom—4 to 6 inches across. The great variety of rich and delicate colors, tints and markings is wonderful. Our mixture of seed of these is superb. Pkt., 10c.; ½ oz., 15c.; oz., 25c.; ¼ oz., 75c.

2026 Finest Mixed Japanese—Very choice strain; flowers large, and in greatest variety of colors and shades. Pkt., 5c.; ½ oz., 10c.; oz., 15c.

2028 Fancy Fringed Japanese—This is a splendid mixture, made up exclusively from the best fringed varieties. The range of color is very great, and the fringed-edged blooms very beautiful. Pkt., ½ oz., 25c.; oz., 35c.

2022 Morning Glories (Convolvulus Major)—These are the old-fashioned favorites that everybody loves. No climber is more useful, as they grow so quickly and cling to anything. Splendid mixed with other vines, especially Nasturtiums. Our mixture contains all the choicest and brightest colored sorts. Pkt., 5c.; oz., 10c.; ¼ lb., 25c.; lb., 75c.

2030 Brazilian Morning Glories (Ipomoea Setosa)—This desirable climber makes a thick, dense growth of great lobed leaves, and is brilliant with an endless profusion of immense clusters of rosy-colored flowers, with a satiny-pink star in the center of each. Pkt., 10c.

MOONFLOWER

Myosotis (Forget-Me-Nots)

The Forget-Me-Not is an old favorite, bearing clusters of star-shaped flowers. Succeeds best in a moist, shady situation, and blooms the first year from seed if sown early. Seed sown in Autumn flowers in early Spring. Hardy perennial. **2050 Palustris (True Forget-Me-Not)**—Beautiful blue; 6 inches. Pkt., 10c.; ¼ oz., 30c.

2051 Alpestris—Bright blue. Pkt., 5c.

2054 Semperflorens—Splendid dwarf Forget-Me-Not; will thrive in sun or shade; covered from early to late with beautiful blue flowers. Pkt., 5c.

2058 Finest Mixed Varieties—A Forget-Me-Not Mixture of all the finest sorts. Pkt., 5c.

Livingston's Giant-Flowering Tall Nasturtiums

Giant Golden Yellow

Mammoth flowers, frequently 2½ inches in diameter; borne on long, strong stems well above the foliage; exquisitely formed with overlapping crinkled petals of a rich golden yellow. Strong, vigorous grower; large, bright green leaves. A grand and distinct variety. **2066**—Pkt., 5c.; oz., 20c.

Giant Cream Pink

The extremely large flowers are of full expanded form; the daintiest of all Nasturtiums. Its superb coloring is of blush cream, flushed with rose. Nothing we can say can convey an idea of its fairy-like beauty, mammoth size and splendid substance. **2068**—Pkt., 5c.; oz., 20c.

Giant Deep Crimson

The deepest and richest of all dark-red Nasturtiums. The foliage is dark green; the mammoth flowers, which are borne in great abundance, have a soft, velvety texture; slightly crumpled petals and wonderfully rich coloring. **2070**—Pkt., 5c.; oz., 20c.

Giant Striped Hybrids

A gorgeous strain of brilliantly striped beauties of various shades and tints; gigantic in size. Its wonderful variety of colors and markings show many unique combinations **2071**—Pkt., 5c.; oz., 20c.

Giant Brilliant Scarlet

A glowing, flaming scarlet, intense and vivid; the largest of its color; of splendid substance and beautiful form. **2072**—Pkt., 5c.; oz., 20c.

Rainbow Collection of Giant-Flowering Nasturtiums

Seven Large Packets of the above New and Wonderfully Beautiful Kinds, postpaid, for 25c.

Livingston's Top-Notch Mixture

A wonderful diversity of rich colors and new and striking combinations are found in this unequaled mixture. A row in full bloom is beyond description, containing shades of yellow, rose, scarlet, orange, lemon, bronze, maroon, ruby, cream and pink, both in solid colors and mottled and striped in many showy and exquisite ways. For many years this mixture of Nasturtiums has been our special pride. Every year we have improved it, until now we unhesitatingly offer our new Giant-Flowering Nasturtiums as absolutely the finest. We strongly recommend our customers to plant liberally.

2100 Top Notch Mixture of New Giant-Flowering Nasturtiums—A large packet, 10c.; oz., 15c.; ¼ lb., 40c.

2094 Mixed Tall Nasturtiums—There is no flower of which you need seed in larger quantities for liberal planting than Tall, or Climbing Nasturtiums. For the low price, this mixture is very choice. Pkt., 5c.; oz., 10c.; ¼ lb., 20c.

Ivy-Leaved Trailing Nasturtium

This is a most distinct variety, both in flower and foliage. The plants are of very sturdy, running growth, and the leaves, which are of a deep green, veined with silvery-white and star-like, resemble the hardy English Ivy. The flowers are intense glowing scarlet and most distinct in form, the petals being finely feathered. Especially graceful in hanging baskets, window boxes and vases.

2101 Scarlet—Pkt., 10c.; ¼ oz., 20c.; oz., 30c.

Giant Lemon and Rose

Grand, extra large flowers of clean pale lemon, varying to bright yellow; beautifully blotched with bronzy crimson. **2069**—Pkt., 5c.; oz., 20c.

Giant Rose

A most desirable variety, with flowers of a soft rosy-pink color; foliage light green. The brightest rose-color Nasturtium we have ever seen. Abundant bloomer. **2067**—Pkt., 5c.; oz., 20c.

Specimen Flowers from Livingston's Top-Notch Mixture

Madame Gunther Hybrid Climbing Nasturtiums

These are of French origin, and for rich and striking colors are not surpassed by any class of climbing Nasturtiums. Very fine.

2076 Tall French Chameleon—This variety produces blooms of many distinct colorings upon the same plant. Pkt., 5c.; oz., 15c.

2077 Dark Crimson—Splendid variety; fine foliage. Pkt., 5c.; oz., 10c.

2081 Jupiter—Giant-flowered. Color a deep, very clear, golden yellow, of the strongest growth; profuse bloomer. Pkt., 5c.; oz., 20c.

2082 Tall King Theodore—Deep crimson-maroon, so velvety that it is almost black; has dark foliage. One of the best sorts. Pkt., 5c.; oz., 15c.

2096 Mixed Colors—Pkt., 5c.; oz., 15c.; ¼ lb., 50c.

Lobb's Climbing Nasturtiums

(*Tropaeolum Lobbianum*)—Both foliage and flowers of this class are somewhat smaller than the Tall varieties, but the splendid profusion of bloom and the intensely brilliant colors of the flowers render them of the greatest value. 12 to 15 feet.

2083 Tall Pearl—Nearly white; for contrast. Pkt., 5c.; oz., 10c.

2084 Regelianum—Deep purplish violet. Pkt., 5c.; oz., 10c.

2086 Scarlet—Bright; good foliage. Pkt., 5c.; oz., 10c.

2095 Lobb's Finest Mixed—This elegant assortment of Lobb's Climbing Nasturtiums is composed of the most brilliant colors in this class. Pkt., 5c.; oz., 10c.; ¼ lb., 30c.

New Fringed Nasturtiums

A decidedly novel and distinct new Nasturtium, with magnificent large flowers, deeply fringed. Climbing variety, reaching a height of 10 to 12 feet. Deep green foliage. A unique and beautiful variety.

2104 Mixed Colors—Pkt., 10c.

Marble-Leaved Queen

2110 Mixed—A beautiful variety and a new type, having leaves marbled, striped and blotched with white, yellow and green. Many colors mixed. Pkt., 5c.; oz., 25c.

Madame Gunther Hybrid Nasturtium

Dwarf Nasturtiums

2135 Golden King—A rich orange-yellow. Foliage dark. Pkt., 5c.; oz., 15c.

2136 King of Tom Thumbs—Glowing, darkest scarlet flowers. Foliage very dark green. A most rich and brilliant variety. Pkt., 5c.; oz., 15c.

2137 Dwarf King Theodore—A velvety crimson-maroon, almost black. The leaves are the darkest in Nasturtiums. Pkt., 5c.; oz., 15c.

2132 Dwarf Chameleon—Of brilliant shades and diversified markings; some self-colored, others splashed and mottled. Pkt., 5c.; oz., 20c.

2134 Empress of India—A very compact-growing sort, having purplish-green leaves; the flowers are fiery crimson. Pkt., 5c.; oz., 15c.

Dwarf Liliput Nasturtiums

This charming and distinct new class has very small flowers and leaves. In growth it is very compact, bushy and dwarf, being more so in both respects than the Dwarf Nasturtiums. In colors they are most varied and rich. **2152 Mixed**—Pkt., 5c.; oz., 20c.

Queen of Holland (New Liliput Hybrids)—A dainty type of very dwarf growth, making fine compact little bushes only about 6 inches high. The flowers, although smaller than the regular Nasturtiums, are very brilliant in color and are produced in a wonderful variety of shades and combinations, including cream, rose, scarlet, orange, crimson—all beautifully blotched.

2131 Mixed Colors—Pkt., 10c.

Livingston's Glory of the Garden Mixture

This is our best mixture of the dwarf varieties. It is composed exclusively of the most elegant, large-flowered sorts, and the brilliantly colored flowers range through every shade and tint known in this favorite annual. This seed will produce a bed or border gorgeous beyond description.

2130 Glory of the Garden Finest Mixed—Large pkt., 10c.; oz., 15c.; ¼ lb., 50c.

Mixed Dwarf Nasturtiums—We handle such large quantities of Dwarf Nasturtiums that we are able to offer this especially choice mixture at a very low price. You should plant this mixture very liberally.

2150 Choice Mixed—Pkt., 5c.; oz., 10c.; ¼ lb., 25c.

Dwarf Queen Nasturtiums

A gorgeous mixture of all the dwarf or Tom Thumb varieties of the Marble-Leaved Queen Nasturtiums. Containing a great number of named varieties as well as numerous other new hybrids not yet sufficiently "fixed" in color to offer separately. **2123 Mixed**—Pkt., 5c.; oz., 25c.

Mrs. J. K. Astle, Rich Co., Utah, writes: "Your Tall or Climbing Nasturtiums cannot be spoken of too highly, for they provided a gorgeous mass of bloom all Summer long, with little or no care. I am sending another order for Flower Seeds, for I believe your seeds are True Blue."

Glory of the Garden Nasturtium

Nicotiana

(Sweet-Scented Tobacco Plant)—Handsome and well-known hardy annuals that grow easily from seed, forming compact bushes about 3 feet high, which are in continuous bloom throughout the season. Their blooms are tube-shaped, very sweet-scented, and desirable as cut flowers; also fine for pots.

2158 Affinis—A very popular sort; its flowers are pure white and deliciously fragrant. Always in bloom. Pkt., 5c.

2160 Sanderae—This beautiful hybrid Nicotiana forms bushy, much-branched plants 2 feet high, the whole plant laden with flowers from base to summit—literally ablaze with handsome carmine-red fragrant blossoms, hundreds of which are produced on a single plant. Pkt., 10c.

Nigella (Love-in-a-Mist)

A very popular, old-fashioned flower; free-flowering, with finely cut foliage surrounding the curious looking flowers and seed pods. Easily grown from seed.

2163 Mixed—Pkt., 5c.

Ornamental Grasses

Effective and attractive for garden borders and ornamental groups. Also extensively used when dried for Winter bouquets.

1660 Coix Lachrymae (Job's Tears)—Beautiful variety. Has coin-like leaves, and hard, glossy gray colored seeds, which naturally have a hole in them like beads. 2 feet. Pkt., 5c.; oz., 10c.; 2 oz. (enough for a chain), 15c.; ¼ lb., 25c.; lb., 75c.

2170 Eulalia Zebrina (Zebra Grass)—The long dark-green leaves are beautifully striped with yellowish white. Perennial. 5 feet high. Pkt., 10c.

2171 Purple Fountain Grass (Pennisetum)—Beautiful and graceful; is unequaled as an edging to tall-growing plants. Annual. 3 feet. Pkt., 5c.

2172 Mixed Annual Varieties Ornamental Grasses—Pkt., 5c.

Nigella—Love-in-a-Mist

Livingston's Mammoth Pansies

Our Pansy Seeds are grown exclusively for us by the best American and European Specialists. All our strains are from the most noted seed stocks in the world, and we know they cannot fail to give the most unbounded satisfaction to amateur and professional grower alike. Sow in the house, hot-bed, or green house; or as soon as the weather permits, the seed may be sown directly in the garden beds. Pansies thrive best in a rich soil, and cool, moist situation; they do splendidly in partially shaded places. They do not do well under trees, but in some locations where the sun strikes only part of each day the most satisfactory result can be obtained. Seed sown from July to September and the young plants transplanted into cold-frames for the Winter, will bloom grandly very early the following Spring. (Prices by ounce or larger quantities will be quoted upon application.) Free to our customers, leaflet on the culture of Pansies.

Giant Ruffled Masterpiece (Germania)

A remarkable type, the border of each petal being conspicuously curled and undulated, which gives the flower a double or globular appearance. The large blooms are beautifully blotched. 2181—Pkt., 15c.; 2 pkts. for 25c.

Tufted Pansies

Especially adapted for shady places. While the flowers are not so large as in the other varieties of Pansies, their abundance is wonderful, and colors most varied. Hardy.

2231 White, 2233 Yellow, 2232 Blue, and 2230 Mixed, 10c. each per pkt.

Exquisite Orchid-Flowered Pansies

All the delicate shades and tints of the Orchids may be found in these charmingly pretty favorites. Rose, orange, pink, lilac, terra cotta, chamois and other exquisite shades are predominant and please all lovers of the delicate by their refined form and texture. Orchid-flowered Pansies are not as large as some of our Giant strains; but they will appeal by their exquisite coloring and the elegant shape of their flowers. 2179 All Shades Mixed—Pkt., 10c.

Orchid-Flowered Pansy

Mammoth Parisian Pansies

The French Pansies are large, and strongly marked and blotched; in a word they are very attractively "Frenchy." The strain we offer is one of great excellence, the individual flowers being superb, and include many fine shades. 2183—Pkt., 10c.; 3 pkts. for 25c.

Giant German Pansies

The German Pansies are noted for their almost endless variations, which include striped, blotched bordered, veined, and marbled combination, in every possible color and shade. The plants are of compact growth, and flower most profusely and continuously all Summer. 2185—Pkt., 10c.; 3 pkts. for 25c.

Livingston's Giant Pansy Mixture

This splendid mixture is a blended combination of giant-flowering pansies. It contains all colors and will prove a delightful surprise in regard to their great size. 2177 Giant Mixture—Pkt., 10c., 3 pkts. for 25c.; ⅛ oz., 50c.; oz., $2.50.

English Pansies—The old-fashioned "English Face" Pansies. 2191—Pkt., 10c.; 3 pkts. for 25c.

From Our Giant Pansy Mixture

Specimen Flowers
Livingston's Fancy
Pansy Mixture

Madame Perret

A splendid giant-flowering strain, which is of French origin. The flowers are produced most freely, and are of the greatest diversity of colors, comprising all shades of red, from lightest rose to darkest purple. Many are striped. 2189—Pkt., 15c.

Bugnot's Superb Blotched

The flowers of this splendid strain are of the largest size, and produce the handsomest and richest blotched varieties known in Pansies. We recommend this mixture. 2187—Pkt., 20c.; 3 pkts. for 50c.

Bedding Pansies in Separate Colors

For liberal plantings in the garden beds these fine sorts are the most desirable. The plants grow compactly, bushy, and bloom continuously. The bloom is of many beautiful shades, but average smaller than the Giant sorts.

2210 Azure Blue; 2211 Black; 2212 Bright Brown; 2213 Brilliant Red; 2214 Dark Purple; 2215 Dark Red; 2216 Light Blue; 2218 Pure White; 2219 Purplish Violet; 2220 Pure Yellow; 2221 Violet, Wh. Margin; 2222 White, Blk. Center; 2223 Yellow, Blk. Center; 2224 Rosy Lilac—Price, each pkt., 5c.; 6 pkts., 25c.

Collection one each of the above 14 Bedding Pansies, 50c.

Livingston's Fancy Pansy Mixture

In this magnificent mixture of mammoth-flowering pansies the blossoms are borne on long stems well above the foliage and are distinguished for their gorgeous and varied colorings and beautiful markings; of fine substance, velvety texture, perfect form, and giant size, frequently measuring three inches in diameter. The colorings are wonderfully rich and varied; every shade and tint of rose, canary-yellow, black, cream, lavender, garnet, sky-blue and orange are produced in endless variation. An unequaled collection of all the finest types. The best handsomest, and most perfect giant-flowering varieties. 2175 Fancy Mixture—Pkt., 25c.; 3 pkts., 60c.; ⅛ oz., $1.25.

Giant Trimardeau Separate Colors

2194 Gt. Atropurpurea (Rex)—Velvety, royal purple....10c.
2195 Gt. Emperor William—Indigo blue, blotched, black.10c.
2196 Gt. Golden Queen—Pure golden-yellow. Very fine..10c.
2197 Gt. King of the Blacks—Lustrous, jet-black.......10c.
2198 Gt. Lord Beaconsfield—Lavender, heliotrope, purple.10c.
2199 Gt. Peacock (Gloriosa)—Garnet, cream and blue..10c.
2200 Gt. President Carnot—White, large violet, blotches.10c.
2201 Gt. Snow-Flake—Spotless, snow-white ....10c.

Giant Trimardeau, Mixed—These are the largest flowered of all; a most showy class, of robust and very compact growth. Flowers are carried well above the leaves. Mixture of finest colors. 2205—Pkt., 10c.; 3 pkts., 25c.; ⅛ oz., 40c.

Bedding Pansies Mixed

We have taken much pains in composing this mixture and it will make a rich display. Contains all the fine Bedding Pansies named above. 2225 Mixed—Pkt., 5c.; ⅛ oz., 20c.; ¼ oz., 30c.; oz., $1.00.

Our "Giant Six" Pansy Collection

This collection contains one packet (100 seeds) each of the following elegant varieties: Giant Red, Giant White, Giant Blue, Giant Purple, Giant Yellow and Giant Black. 6 packets in all for 25c.

Platycodon Grandiflora
(Chinese Bell-Flower)

A splendid hardy perennial, producing large bell-shaped, white and blue flowers, very showy.
2297 Mixed—Pkt., 5c.; ¼ oz., 25c.

Pyrethrum (Feverfew)

Most attractive hardy Perennials, which have become very popular. Valuable border plants with many stems about two feet high, each surmounted with handsome flowers, in the brightest shades of rose, flesh-pink, crimson, etc.; in bloom a long time, and are splendid as cut flowers. (See Feverfew.)
2362 Single Hybrids—This mixture contains the very largest flowering and choicest varieties. Pkt., 15c.
2364 Golden Feather (Aureum)—Dwarf-growing variety, with bright yellow foliage; largely used for edgings and ribbon work. Usually treated as an annual. ¾ feet. Pkt., 5c.; ¼ oz., 20c.

Bedding Pansy

Annual Phlox

Annual Phlox

For a splendid mass of color and a constant display, the Phlox Drummondii is not excelled by any other annual. It has every desirable quality for this purpose and for beds, edgings and massings nothing can surpass it. Seed may be sown in the open ground any time after danger from frost is past.

Large-Flowering Phlox

This is a magnificent class of these splendid annuals. Flowers are large and brilliant in colors.

2269 Bright Rose—Most pleasing color; a profuse bloomer. Pkt., 5c.; ¼ oz., 30c.

2270 Brilliant Scarlet—Is especially showy in large beds or borders. Pkt., 5c.; ¼ oz., 30c.

2271 Crimson—Popular sort; very brilliant and effective. Pkt., 5c.; ¼ oz., 30c.

2273 Pure White—Pkt., 5c.; ¼ oz., 30c.

2274 Yellow—Distinct. Pkt., 5c.; ¼ oz., 30c.

2267 Prize Mixture of Large Flowering Phlox—Large pkt., 10c.; ¼ oz., 25c.; ½ oz., 40c.; oz., 75c.

Phlox Drummondii—The old-fashioned favorite variety. **2265 Mixed**—Pkt., 5c.; ¼ oz., 15c.; oz., 50c.

Star-Shaped Phlox—Long, pointed petals which give the flowers a star-like appearance; plants grow compact, dwarf. **2278 Mixed**—Pkt., 5c.; ⅛ oz., 20c.

Livingston's Superb Petunias

Petunias are one of the most popular annuals on account of their ease of cultivation and freedom of blooming, succeeding everywhere and giving a constant supply of flowers from June to October. They are also good house plants; flowering freely in a sunny window. Seed can be sown in the open ground early in the Spring or in a hot bed or cold frame, to be transplanted later to beds or borders. Height 1 to 1½ feet.

Large-Flowering Petunias

The blooms are enormous in size and of the richest colors and markings. Varieties listed below are unsurpassed.

2240 Livingston's Superb Single Mixed—A strain of incomparable beauty and luxuriance. Flowers most varied in colors and markings; beautifully ruffled, fringed and of enormous size. Pkt., 15c.; 2 pkts. for 25c.

2244 Ruffled Giants—The flowers of this strain are of extraordinary size and great substance; the edges of the blooms ruffled. Contains the greatest variety of rare colors and combinations. Pkt., 25c.

2246 Livingston's Superb Double Mixed—Our best mixture of all the large-flowering double varieties, including striped, blotched and fringed sorts. Pkt., 25c.

Bedding Petunias

2250 Howard's Star-Shaped—Entirely distinct. The five-petaled blooms have star-shaped markings of blush-pink or white over maroon ground; very fine. Pkt., 5c.

2252 General Dodds—A very fine blood-red variety; grows compactly; very free-flowering. Splendid for beds and borders. Pkt., 5c.

2254 Snowball—A charming, compact-growing variety; grows about 8 inches high and yields in greatest profusion all season its pure satiny-white flowers. Pkt., 10c.

2256 Striped and Blotched—A most beautiful strain of Petunias for bedding and massing. Our mixture contains an endless variety of colors. Pkt., 5c.; ⅛ oz., 20c.; ¼ oz., 35c.

2258 Finest Mixed—A choice mixture of colors and shades; will make a fine display in your garden. Pkt., 5c.; ⅛ oz., 20c.; ¼ oz., 35c.

Large-Flowering Primulas
(Primroses)

The ease with which Primroses can be grown from seed makes them very popular window-plants. For a succession of blooming plants sow the seed from March to May, and again in July or August; in planting, cover the seed lightly, and keep moist. Transplant when the second leaf appears, and keep re-potting the plants as they grow and increase in size. Height, ½ to 1 foot.

2346 Chinese Primrose—Superb Single Mixed—An elegant mixture, embracing all the best large-flowering varieties, and including the finest fringed sorts. Pkt., 25c.

2348 Chinese Primrose—Superb Double Mixed—Splendid strain of the finest large-flowering; fringed varieties. Our mixture includes all the most brilliant colors. Pkt., 25c.

2350 Chinese Primrose—Choice Mixed—This is a very choice mixture, and for general-purpose will be found most satisfactory. Pkt., 15c.

2352 Obconica Grandiflora—Large-Flowering Hybrids—Lovely and profuse blooming Primrose, bearing on long stems large heads of beautiful flowers; white, tinged lilac and rose shades; ever-blooming variety with true Primrose fragrance. Pkt., 10c.

2354 Japonica (Japanese Primrose)—Very bright and showy flowers, borne in whorls on stems 6 to 9 inches long. Choicest colors. Pkt., 10c.

Phaseolus Multiflorus Papilio

2262 New Butterfly Bean—A splendid climbing plant for arbors and trellises equal to the old Scarlet Runner sort as regards productiveness and quality of fruit, but quite distinct in the beauty of its flowers. The flowers are of large size with prettily waved snowy-white wings and salmon-rose standard, these two colors making a most agreeable and striking contrast. Pkt., 10c.; 3 pkts. for 25c.

Petunia—Giants of California. Pkt., 15c.

2242 Giants of California—These Petunias are of great beauty and luxuriance, including fringed and deep-throated sorts in endless variety of colors, veinings and markings. Flowers of enormous size. Pkt., 15c.; 2 pkts. for 25c.

Oriental Poppy. Pkt., 10c.

Perennial Poppies

There are no flowers more ornamental and useful in our gardens than the various varieties of hardy Poppies. Once started they increase in size and beauty each succeeding season.

The Large Oriental Poppy

Perhaps the most popular variety in cultivation, the sturdy plants growing about 3 feet high. Its color, a dazzling scarlet with coal-black blotches, is grand. For gorgeous effect, nothing can equal them in perfectly hardy plants. **2333**—Pkt., 10c.; 1/8 oz., 20c.; 1/4 oz., 35c.

2335 Oriental Hybrids—Splendid hybrids of Oriental Poppy. Enormous flowers, sometimes more than six inches in diameter. Colors include shades of cherry, salmon, darkest red, vivid crimson and innumerable others equally fine. Our mixture contains them all. Pkt., 10c.; 1/8 oz., 25c.; 1/4 oz., 45c.

2336 Trilby—This is one of the most beautiful varieties of the Oriental type. The blooms are of the largest size, and they are produced in great abundance. The color is salmon-pink. Pkt., 10c.

2330 Iceland Poppies (Papaver Nudicaule)—These Poppies are perfectly hardy and in bloom from June until frost; beautiful satin-like flowers, of every shade of yellow, white and orange-scarlet. Plants grow about 12 inches high, forming tufts, from which the flower stems issue most profusely. Very useful for cut flowers. Easy to grow. Pkt., 10c.; 1/8 oz., 15c.; oz., $1.00.

2332 Double Mixed Iceland Poppies—This splendid mixture of double-flowering varieties you will find very superior. Pkt., 10c.; 3 pkts., 25c.

Portulaca

(Sun Plant)

Should be sown in every garden. Scarcely any annual in cultivation makes such dazzling display of beauty as a bed of highly colored, many-hued Portulacas. Plant in dry sandy soil, soon as it becomes warm, with full exposure to the sun.

Large-Flowered Single Mixed—A most elegant mixture; flowers large and of every shade of color. **2340**—Pkt., 5c.; 1/4 oz., 20c.; oz., 60c.

Rose-Flowered Portulaca—From this assortment more than one-half of the plants will produce double flowers; these plants can be transplanted 8 inches apart as soon as they bloom, thus making an entire bed of double bloom. Our mixture contains all best double varieties. **2342**—Pkt., 10c.; 1/8 oz., 75c.

Poppies

The recent development of these old-fashioned flowers has brought them into great and deserved popularity. No flower in our garden affords a more pleasing display of gorgeously brilliant coloring during the blooming season. Poppies of the various varieties grow about 2 feet in height, except as noted.

Double Annual Poppies

2300 Paeony Flowered—Large, showy double globular flowers, almost equal to Paeonies. Our mixture contains the finest colors. Pkt., 5c.; 1/2 oz., 10c.; oz., 15c.

2302 White Swan—Pure snow-white, double and large size. Beautifully fringed. Pkt., 5c.

2304 American Flag—Very beautiful variety. Flowers extra large and double. Snow-white, bordered with scarlet. Pkt., 5c.

2306 Fairy Blush—Immense flowers, perfectly double, 5 inches across; elegantly fringed; pure white, rose-tipped petals. Pkt., 5c.

2308 Carnation Flowered—Splendid large double flowers; showy and beautifully fringed. Mixture is unequaled for dazzling richness and great variety of colors. Pkt., 5c.; 1/2 oz., 15c.; oz., 25c.

2310 "Mikado" (The Striped Japanese Poppy)—Very distinct and beautiful; the large blooms are brilliant scarlet and white, with elegantly curved and fringed petals. Pkt., 5c.; 1/4 oz., 10c.

Livingston's Giant Double Mixed Poppies—A mixture of beautiful double Poppies, including only the improved double, giant-flowering kinds of the richest and brightest colors, as well as the daintiest and softest tints. When grown in masses it is brilliant beyond description. The plants are sturdy, thrifty growers, from 2 to 3 feet high, producing immense flowers, sometimes 4 inches in diameter. Sow the seeds in the early Spring in sandy soil where they are to remain.

2311 Mixed—Pkt., 5c.; oz., 35c.

Single Annual Poppies

2316 Livingston's Giant Shirley Poppies—These are considered by many the most charming Poppies in cultivation. The individual flowers are large and elegant, mostly single blooms, some semi-double and double ones, often measuring from 3 to 4 inches across. The petals are fluted and crinkled and in the sun appear like crumpled satin. The exquisite colors range from purest white to the deepest of blood-red, through all the shades and combinations of pink, rose, crimson and carmine. Pkt., 5c.; 1/4 oz., 20c.; oz., 60c.

2318 Dwarf Shirley—Identical with Giant Shirley except they grow dwarf—not exceeding 18 inches in height. Splendid for beds and borders. Pkt., 5c.; 1/4 oz., 20c.

2321 Danebrog (Danish Cross)—A very showy single variety; brilliant scarlet, blotched with silvery gray. Pkt., 5c.

2323 Tulip Poppies—Large and splendid single flowers of the most dazzling scarlet. The two outer petals resemble a saucer, in which are set two erect petals of the same color. Pkt., 5c.; 1/4 oz., 20c.

2325 New Admiral Poppy—Of surprising beauty. Large, round, smooth edged flowers of glistening pure white, with a broad band of brilliant scarlet around the top. Pkt., 10c.

2327 Livingston's Single Poppy Mixture—Every color ever seen in Poppies, and every conceivable combination of colors is found in this elegant mixture. Pkt., 5c.; 1/2 oz., 20c.; oz., 35c.

Rose-Flowered Portulacas. Pkt., 10c.

Ricinus

(Castor Oil Bean)

One of our best ornamental-leaved annual plants, largely used for the center of beds, being splendidly effective grouped with Cannas, Caladiums, and other tall plants.

2370 Zanzibariensis—A new and distinct class, surpassing in size and beauty all varieties hitherto known. Plants attain great dimensions—12 to 14 feet. Pkt., 5c.; oz., 10c.; ¼ lb., 25c.

2371 Borboniensis—Very large and most showy green foliage; standard variety. 10 to 15 feet. Pkt., 5c.; oz., 10c.

2372 Cambodgensis—Main stem and leaf-stalks shining ebony-black; leaves large and brilliantly colored. Foliage assumes various shades. 5 feet. Pkt., 5c.; oz., 15c.

2373 Gibsoni—Compact-growing variety of branching habit. The large leaves are a deep red. 5 feet. Pkt., 5c.; oz., 10c.

2377 Livingston's Ricinus Mixture—Appreciating fully the splendid effects that a fine array of these desirable foliage plants will make in your garden, we have composed a mixture that for elegant blending is unsurpassed. Pkt., 5c.; oz., 10c.; ¼ lb., 25c.

Roses

(Bloom the First Year from Seed)

Baby Roses, also called **Dwarf Midget, or Fairy Roses**—These beautiful little roses are borne in many flower clusters of double, semi-double and single flowers, and are of all the tints of other roses. Seed should be soaked in warm water a day or two before planting; perfectly hardy, blooming year after year. **2380**—Pkt., (50 seeds), 10c.; 3 pkts., 25c.

Salpiglossis

(Painted Tongue)

The Salpiglossis is one of the most popular and favorite annuals. It is of the easiest culture. Especially is it noted for its beautiful, almost orchid-like blooms. Our mixture is unsurpassed, containing every desirable color and shade of the large-flowering varieties. 1½ feet. **2400 Mixed**—Pkt., 5c.

Salpiglossis, or Painted Tongue. Pkt., 5c.

2401 Brown and Golden Yellow—Rich velvety color, with beautiful veinings that furnish a delightful contrast. Pkt., 10c.

2402 Light Blue and Golden Yellow—A most harmonious color combination. Pkt., 10c.

2403 Purplish Brown Veined Golden Yellow—Handsome in the extreme. The exquisite coloring is beautiful. Pkt., 10c.

Salvia

(Flowering Sage)

Very ornamental plants, for Summer and Autumn flowering; bloom in spikes, and continuing to bloom in the open ground until hard frosts, forming compact bushes, which are literally ablaze with brilliant flowers. While tender perennials, they bloom like annuals the first season from seed. The plants may be started in a box in the house, or in the hotbed, and when the weather becomes warm transplant in the garden. Height 2 to 3 feet. (See illustration.) May be used as a hedge with striking effect.

2384 Splendens Grandiflora (Scarlet Sage)—Gorgeous plants, numerous spikes of intensely vivid scarlet flowers 10 to 12 inches in length. Continues to flower profusely all Summer and Fall. Of easy growth. The most popular Salvia in cultivation. Pkt., 10c.; ¼ oz., 25c.

2386 Bonfire—Plants form healthy bushes about 2 feet high by 2 feet across. Spikes grow erect and stand clear above the foliage, completely covering the plant, and are of a most brilliant, dazzling scarlet. One of the finest sorts. Pkt., 10c.; ¼ oz., 50c.

2388 Silverspot—Strikingly handsome spotted foliage. Leaves rich, soft dark green, with light yellowish spots of various size sprinkled over them, and have a fresh, healthy appearance. Flowers are large, bright red; plants of neat, compact habit. Comes quite true from seed. Pkt., 10c.

2390 Scarlet Dragon—A magnificent free-growing new variety, forming dense, bushy plants, 3 feet high; with clean, light green foliage, and bearing innumerable mammoth spikes of vivid carmine scarlet flowers of extra large size. Splendid for borders, beds and masses, as it is always in bloom and vividly gay. Pkt., 10c.

2392 Goldspot—Leaves bright green, blotched with golden yellow; erect growth, 20 inches high; large scarlet flowers, and lavishly borne. Pkt., 10c.

2394 Coccinea Lactea—A fine, pure white flowering variety. Pkt., 5c.

2396 Patens—Beautiful bright blue. Pkt., 10c.

2398 Zurich—Compact growing sort, forming very handsome, symmetrical bushes, 15 to 18 inches tall, which are completely covered with scarlet flower spikes. A little beauty. Pkt., 10c.

Ostrich Plume—See novelty pages.

Salvia

Mrs. Frank Gregory, Ashtabula, Ohio, writes: "My ruffled Petunias I got of you last year were the finest I ever saw."

Stocks (Gilliflower)

Indispensable for bedding, borders, massing or pot culture.

Large-Flowering Double "Cut and Come Again" Varieties.

2446 Snow White—(See illustration.) Pkt., 10c.

2440 Finest Mixed—This is our very best mixture of large-flowering Stocks. The perfectly double flowers embrace every color and shade. Pkt., 10c.

2448 Giant Perfection Stocks—Long spikes of double flowers. Pkt., 10c.

2450 Fine Mixed Stocks—A choice mixture of various colors and shades. Pkt., 5c.

Sunflower (Helianthus)

A well known family of hardy annual, very showy plants, large flowers.

2454 New Miniature—Beautiful new hybrids; small single flowers in great abundance; colors, creamy white, lemon and orange; indispensable for cutting. Pkt., 5c.; ¼ oz., 20c.

2456 Globe of Gold—Globe-shaped, double yellow flowers. Pkt., 5c.

2460 Livingston's Mixed Sunflowers—A great variety of single and double varieties. Every shade of yellow is included. Pkt., 5c.; ½ oz., 10c.; oz., 15c.

Sensitive Plant

A pretty and curious annual plant; the leaves and foot-stalks close and droop at the slightest touch, or in cloudy, damp weather. 1½ feet. **2430**—Pkt., 5c.

Smilax

Charming tender perennial climber for house or greenhouse. **2435**—Pkt., 5c.

Ten-Week-Stock Snow White. Pkt., 10c.

Stokesia Cyanea

(Cornflower Aster)—A valuable hardy perennial, bedding plant. Plants large, 18 to 20 inches high, with Bachelor Button-like, light lavender-blue flowers, which are several inches in diameter. Are produced from July until late in October. Very easily grown in almost any situation. **2436**—Pkt., 10c.

Shasta Daisies

A hardy perennial plant; blooms more abundantly each season; multiplied by division of roots or sowing seed. They bloom for several months in great abundance. The flowers are large and graceful, with three or more rows of pure white petals.
2433 Selected Seed—Much superior to original strain. Pkt., 10c.

Schizanthus or Butterfly Flower

Popularly called the "Poor Man's Orchid." It grows from a foot to eighteen inches tall, with fine fern-like foliage, begins to flower early and produces masses of oddly marked and queerly shaped blooms in various shades of blue, purple and pink and some pure white.
2427 Schizanthus Mixed—5c. per packet.
2428 Schizanthus Wisetonensis—A new large-flowering type—20c. per packet.

Scarlet Runner-Bean

Ornamental climber. Bright scarlet sprays of bloom, followed by edible beans. **2429**—Pkt., 5c.; ¼ lb., 15c.

Scabiosa

(Sweet Scabiosa, Mourning Bride, Pin-Cushion Flower, Egyptian Rose, etc.)—The seed can be sown any time in the Spring after danger from frost is past. The plants grow about 2½ feet high, and come into bloom early in June, continuing without interruption until the hard frosts of Autumn. The exquisite double flowers (see illustration) are borne on very long stems, and when cut keep in perfect condition for the best part of a week.
2404 Livingston's Improved Large-Flowering Scabiosas, Finest Mixed Colors—A very fine mixture, containing all the finest large-flowering double sorts. All colors. Pkt., 5c.

2406 Azure Fairy—Exquisite sky-blue. Pkt., 10c.
2408 Fiery Red—Very striking; double; fiery scarlet. Pkt., 5c.
2410 Black Prince—Very large; double; almost black. Pkt., 5c.
2412 Snowball—Double white flowers; fine for bouquets. Pkt., 5c.
2414 Golden Yellow—Very fine color. Pkt., 5c.

2416 Pompadour — Claret-purple, edged white. Pkt., 5c.
2418 Flesh—Pkt., 5c.
2419 Rose—Pkt., 5c.
2420 Lilac—Pkt., 5c.
2421 Cherry Red and White—Pkt., 5c.
2422 White and Lilac—Pkt., 5c.

Collection Scabiosa, above 11 separate colors, 50c.
2426 Hardy Scabiosa Caucasica—Grand hardy perennial, 3 feet high; large lilac-blue flowers; splendid for cut flowers. Pkt., 10c.

LARGE FLOWERING SCABIOSA

Sweet Peas

This flower is more popular than any other annual and each year we see new colors and shades developed, so that we can now procure an almost endless variety and with the introduction of the Spencer type we have a new departure, distinct in every way.

We are pleased to announce that the Sweet Pea crop is much better this season than for the past three seasons.

Our customers will no doubt appreciate the reduction in many of the prices; also the collections of the various types will be found fully up to standard as to the matter of shades, as well as to quantity, in the packets.

New Orchid-Flowering or "Spencer" Sweet Peas

These new Sweet Peas are distinguished for their gigantic size, frequently measuring two inches across; the bold, erect standard, which is uniformly waved, crimpled and fluted in exquisite fashion; the charming blendings of harmonious colors, the exceedingly long flower stems, which make them unexcelled for cutting; the great profusion of flowers and the large number of flowers on the stem, usually three to four. So superior is this new type in every respect that we believe it is certain to supersede the old grandiflora kinds just as fast as new colors appear and become fixed.

How to Grow Fine Sweet Peas

The general opinion is that Sweet Peas being common and hardy can be planted anywhere, which accounts for a lot of failures. There is no reason why every one should not have fines. If they will observe a few simple rules. First of all plant early, just as soon as the ground can be dug and is not sticky. Dig deeply. If you are growing sweet peas every year, try and prepare your ground in the Fall, and dig 18 inches deep, mixing manure thoroughly in the subsoil. The surface soil in which the seed is sown should not contain manure. If you start in the Fall you will find you can sow earlier in the Spring. If you can't secure manure, use bone meal or commercial fertilizers containing phosphate and potash. Cover the ground an eighth of an inch with these and then dig in and mix thoroughly with the soil. Sow the seed three inches deep if on sandy soil, or two if in clay. Sow thinly unless you have the courage to pull them out after they come up. You can't have fine flowers through the season when plants are very thick. Two to three inches apart, or better, four inches if you want big flowers. Cultivate as soon as they are up and keep cultivating. Stake them as soon as the rows show plainly. For the first month they scarcely make any growth above ground, but don't need water unless the season is very dry. Later on, when they are showing vigorous growth, a thorough watering twice a week will help wonderfully, if there is not sufficient rain. Don't plant them alongside a house, under trees or close to a board fence and expect much from them. They need an open space.

This Great Collection of Superb Spencer Sweet Peas --- Seven Liberal Packets for 25 Cents, postpaid

Astha Ohn

Finest lavender Spencer Sweet Pea grown. Comes remarkably true to type, producing the elegant, bold, wavy flowers in greatest profusion. 2584—Pkt., 10c.

Captain of the Blues Spencer

Purplish maroon standard and bluish-purple wings with veins of rosy purple make this exquisite sort one of the finest in our collection. The immense flowers are of true Spencer, type, well waved and crinkled. 2620—Pkt., 10c.

Othello Spencer

Deep velvety maroon. By far the finest of the dark-colored Spencers. Of very large size and beautiful form. 2623—Pkt., 10c.

White Spencer

Without doubt the largest and most magnificent White Sweet Pea ever introduced. The vines are almost completely covered with mammoth flowers. The flowers are borne 3 to 4 on a stem and are of splendid substance. It is without a rival among White Sweet Peas. 2590—Pkt., 10c.

King Edward Spencer

Undoubtedly the largest and best scarlet Sweet Pea to date. Each stem carries from 3 to 4 enormous flowers. Wings carmine-scarlet, reverse side rosy carmine. The beautiful blossoms are carried on long, stiff stems. 2583 —Pkt., 10c.

Countess Spencer

Of perfect form, remarkable size and exquisite color. The flowers are often 1½ to 2 inches in diameter, with both standard and wings charmingly waved and fluted. The coloring is an exquisite soft rose-pink, daintily tinted with silvery white. 2570—Pkt., 10c.; oz., 25c.

Helen Lewis

This superb variety is a grand gigantic orchid-flowering seedling of Countess Spencer. The orange-rose wings roll and fold; the standard is reflexed, and is of an intense rich crimson-orange. 2580—Pkt., 10c.; oz., 25c.

The Above Great Collection of Superb Spencer Sweet Peas --- 7 Liberal Packets for only 25c., postpaid.

Spencer Sweet Peas—(Continued)

Blanche Ferry Spencer

The popular old "painted lady" pink and white Sweet Pea in magnificent new form. 2591—Pkt., 10c.; oz., 25c.

Mrs. Routzahn Spencer

May be described as buff or apricot, suffused with delicate pink which deepens to a rose near edges of wings and standard. Usually four to a stem. 2613—Pkt., 10c.; oz., 25c.

Florence Morse Spencer

Extremely large flowers of finest wavy form and good substance. Resembles Countess Spencer, but has an exquisite light pink edge around each petal. Fine, stiff stems usually 4 flowers to a stem. 2572—Pkt., 10c.; oz., 25c.

Senator Spencer

The combination of color in the flowers is charming—a deep claret or chocolate, striped and flaked on a ground of light heliotrope. Both standard and wings are extra large, wavy and drooping. Flowers are usually borne four to the stems. 2621—Pkt., 10c.; oz., 25c.

Apple Blossom Spencer

Is a lovely form of the old fashioned Apple Blossom Sweet Pea. 2612—Pkt., 10c.; oz., 25c.

2615 **Dainty Spencer**—White, with exquisite rose-pink edges. Of uniformly large size and elegant shape. Pkt., 10c.; oz., 25c.

2622 **Aurora Spencer**—Very large and of true "Spencer" type. The ground color is creamy white, which is finely flaked and mottled with orange-salmon. Pkt., 10c.; oz., 25c.

2614 **Beatrice Spencer**—White, tinted with soft pink and buff on standard, while the wings have prominent blotches, of a brighter pink near base. Pkt., 10c.; oz., 25c.

2610 **Primrose Spencer**—Both standard and wings are of beautiful, soft primrose or creamy yellow color. Flowers are very substantial and in a class of their own in both color and size. Pkt., 10c.; oz., 25c.

Spencer Seedlings Mixed

All of the best-named sorts, also many rare new hybrids in lavender, blue, striped, mottled, purple, maroon and many other shades are included in this superb mixture. All flowers are of extremely large size, typically frilled and waved, and very lovely. 2630—Pkt., 10c.; oz., 25c.

Eight Best Grandiflora or Large Flowering Varieties for Only 25 Cents Postpaid

The greatest bargain in "grandiflora" Sweet Peas on record. Full-sized packets, finest sorts, lowest price consistent with top-notch quality. Order to-day—before you forget where you saw this offer.

2467 **Dorothy Eckford**—An exceptionally fine white variety as popular as the new "Spencer" type on account of its beautiful hooded flowers, borne three and even four on very long stems, making it of exceptional value to the florist.

2474 **Mrs. Collier**—Flowers are extra large, coming in threes and fours on a long stiff stem and of a rich primrose tint, entirely free from any trace of pink. Richer in coloring than any other primrose variety. Can be described as a primrose Dorothy Eckford.

2493 **Phenomenal**—Flowers silvery-white, faintly suffused with soft pink, and beautifully edged with rich purple, after the style of Maid of Honor, but much larger in size.

2499 **King Edward VII.**—The largest and best bright crimson scarlet.

2526 **Brilliant Blue**—Dark indigo blue.

2483 **Prima Donna**—Lovely soft pink, hooded form, vigorous grower.

2505 **America**—Brightest blood-red striped, on white ground, superb.

2515 **Lady Grisel Hamilton**—Beautiful silvery lavender.

PRICE: Livingston's "Grandiflora" Collection of 8 Magnificent Sweet Peas, as described above, for only 25 cents, postpaid.

All the Best Named Grandiflora Sweet Peas

The varieties listed below are the cream of all known sorts. Only those are included in our collection which produce flowers of the finest form and largest size. Every shade and color amongst Sweet Peas will be found. All inferior varieties have been discarded.

For the convenience of our customers we have arranged the varieties in tables according to color.

FREE—If requested with order, our pamphlet of cultural directions telling **How to Grow Perfect Sweet Peas.**

Prices for Any Sweet Peas Named Below

5c per packet—Enough for a single row 5 feet long.

Any 6 packets for 25c.

15c. per oz.—Enough for a single row 15 feet long.

40c. per ¼ lb.—Enough for a 60-foot row.

White

2465 New White Wonder—Flowers pure white of giant size, and borne in greatest abundance, usually 4 to 6 on a long, stout stem.

2466 Blanche Burpee — Large; pure white; fine form, grand flower.

2467 Dorothy Eckford—A grand white. The stems are extra long and stiff and usually carry three flowers of grand size, substance and form. (See illustration.)

2468 Emily Henderson — Large, pure white, profuse, early and continuous flowering.

Creamy Yellow and Primrose

2473 Hon. Mrs. E. Kenyon—The most desirable of all **Primrose** Sweet Peas. Grand, large flowers, splendid form.

2474 Mrs. Collier—Flowers are extra large, coming in threes and fours on a long stiff stem and of a rich primrose tint, entirely free from any trace of pink. **Richer** in coloring than any other primrose variety. Can be described as a primrose Dorothy Eckford.

2475 Stella Morse—Has a faint tinge of pink underlying the cream, producing a **true** apricot shade; beautiful for bunching.

Blush and Light Pink

2478 Dainty—Crystal-white, with pink flush, deepening to a pink edge.

2479 Jennie Gordon—Standard bright rose, shaded cream; wings creamy, suffused rose.

2480 Lovely—Soft shell pink; exquisite shade; large size.

Pink and White

2484 Blanche Ferry—The popular pink and white; always reliable.

Rose and Pink

2488 Prima Donna—Lovely soft pink; hooded form; vigorous grower.

2489 Prince of Wales—Very elegant rich carmine rose; a grand flower.

Blue and White

2493 Phenomenal — Flowers silvery-white, faintly suffused with soft pink, and beautifully edged with rich purple, after the style of Maid of Honor, but much larger in size.

Maroon and Claret

2495 Black Knight—A very rich dark maroon, veined black; the darkest of all.

2496 Shahzada—Intensely dark maroon, with a tint of purple in standard and inner portion of wings.

Red and Scarlet

2499 King Edward VII.—The largest and best bright crimson-scarlet.
2501 Salopian—Rich deep crimson-red; enormous flower; elegant sort.
2500 Queen Alexandra—An **intense** scarlet sort, with bold expanded flowers of finest form. It is very free flowering, with long, strong stems. The flowers do not burn in the sun.

Blue and Purple

2526 Brilliant Blue—Dark, indigo-blue.
2529 David R. Williamson—This new variety is brightly effective. The large standard is of a rich indigo-blue, the wings are lighter in shade.
2530 Romolo Piazzani—A grand **blue** Sweet Pea. The color is almost a true violet-blue self; the standard is only slightly hooded; grand flowers.

Named Grandiflora Sweet Peas—Continued

Lavender and Light Blue

2513 Admiration—A grand large flower of beautiful form, self-colored in a delicate shade of rosy lavender.

2514 Flora Norton—A very beautiful rich lavender, entirely free from any mauve or pinkish tinge. The flowers are large and of fine form; one of the most delicate and pleasing shades for florists' use as a cut flower.

2515 Lady Grisel Hamilton—Beautiful silvery lavender.

2516 Mrs. Walter Wright—This new giant-flowering variety is a beautiful shade of mauve, clear and bright, with wings of a bright coerulean blue, shaded slightly with mauve.

PRICE—Any of above-named Sweet Peas, pkt., 5c.; oz., 15c.; ¼ lb., 40c.

Orange and Salmon

2522 Henry Eckford—The nearest approach to an orange-yellow in Sweet Peas; a beautiful color. Medium large and open form.

2523 Miss Wilmott—Enormous bold, upright flowers on stout stems. Wings and standard are of richest orange-pink, delicately shaded rose.

Striped and Variegated

2505 America—Brightest blood-red striped white.

2506 Aurora—Orange-salmon, flaked and striped white.

2507 Prince Olaf—Large flowers striped and mottled bright blue on white ground. Very free bloomer.

Our Sweet Pea Mixtures for 1916

Most people like as big a variety of Sweet Peas as they can get. To buy a dozen separate packets and mix them would be far more expensive than to buy an ounce of our Special Mixture, and even then the packets would not contain nearly the assortment of colors found in this mixture. We make up these mixtures ourselves, using the best and most popular sorts in pleasing proportion as to colors and shades.

Livingston's Special Mixture

This superb mixture is our special pride. During the several years we have sold it, it has been our constant aim to improve and perfect it. The different kinds and sorts contained in this mixture are grown separately, so that we have an opportunity to choose only the largest and most beautiful varieties. These we mix ourselves in proper proportions for the most brilliant effect. It embraces the finest American and Eckford varieties, as well as the latest novelties, and will produce a great abundance of giant flowers of beautiful colors. Some are edged, mottled, blended, flaked and striped. Without exception, this is the very finest mixture it is possible to make. We recommend that our customers buy these seeds by weight and plant liberally.

2540 Special Mixture—Large pkt., 10c.; oz., 25c.; ¼ lb., 60c.

Livingston's Gilt Edge Mixture

This is a very superior mixture, made up of over 50 of the finest named varieties; all bright colors.

2542 Gilt Edge Mixture—Pkt., 5c.; oz., 15c.; ¼ lb., 35c.

Fine Mixed

This mixture, for the price, will be found very satisfactory. It contains a great variety of choice colors and shades.

2543 Fine Mixed—Pkt., 5c.; oz., 15c.; ¼ lb., 25c.

> Sweet Pea "Nitragin" adds to the size of the bloom and to the length of stem. In ordering be sure to mention Sweet Pea Nitragin as there are other kinds. For full particulars, see Page 75.

Sweet William (Dianthus Barbatus)

A very beautiful class of easily grown and very hardy plants of extreme richness and diversity of colors, deliciously sweet scented. For cut flowers they are not surpassed. Hardy biennial. Height 1 to 1½ feet.

Holborn Glory

This strain is a large-flowered selection of the Auricula-Eyed section, but most beautiful and admired of all Sweet Williams. The individual flowers and trusses are of extraordinary size, and the range of color, all showing a clear, white eye, is superb. **2640**—Pkt., 10c.

Sutton's Scarlet

The color of this variety is an intense scarlet similar to a Grenadin Carnation. **2642**—Pkt., 15c.

2643 Double Mixed—This mixture you will find of very superior quality; containing all colors and shades. Pkt., 5c.; ¼ lb., 20c.

2646 Single Mixed—A very choice assortment of all the best single-flowering varieties. Pkt., 5c.; ¼ oz., 15c.

2648 Double and Single Mixed—This mixture is made by blending the double and single-flowering varieties. Pkt., 5c.; ¼ oz., 15c.; oz., 50c.

SWEET WILLIAM

Livingston's Mammoth Verbena.—Pkt., 10c.

Thunbergia

Rapid-growing Annual Climber, with pretty buff, white and orange flowers of various shades, with a dark center or eye. Adapted for vases, hanging baskets, trellises, etc. 2654 Mixed—Pkt., 5c.

Valeriana

(Hardy Garden Heliotrope)—Showy plants; grow in any garden soil; do well in the shade. Hardy perennial; grows 2 feet high and blooms the first season from seed. Fine for bouquets. Bright rose, red and white varieties. 2658 Mixed —Pkt., 5c.

Vinca

(Periwinkle)—Free-flowering, bushy plants, with glossy foliage and beautiful circular flowers. In sunny situations they bloom all Summer; if potted before frost, will bloom in Winter; very easily grown, blooming profusely the first season from seed. A very fine mixture of all colors. Half-hardy perennials. 1½ feet high. 2680 Mixed—Pkt., 5c.

Wild Cucumber

(Echinocystis)—A rapid-growing annual climber. Has beautiful leaf and pretty, fragrant white flowers. 2695—Pkt., 5c.; ½ oz., 10c.; oz., 15c.

Xeranthemum

(Everlasting Flowers)— Very desirable. Easy to grow. Leaves covered with silvery down. Hardy annual. 2 feet. A very fine mixture of colors. 2697 Mixed—Pkt., 5c.

Mrs. J. van E. Barry, Elliott, Fembuland, South Africa, on Mar. 12, 1913, writes: "Last year I tried some of your sample Sweet Pea and Nasturtium Seeds. Planted them in July. The month before that we had no rain, and, July being our first planting month, I thought I would risk it. We had no rain since June then, the first shower only came during the last week in December; all that time I had to water the above mentioned seeds with stagnant water. They were splendid; everybody admired them and they stood the terrible drought very well. I was the only person who had lovely flowers during the seven months of drought in this town."

Livingston's Mammoth Verbenas

If it were possible, it would seem to us that Verbenas are becoming more popular every year. The plants thrive in any good garden soil, and if grown from seed are much more vigorous than if started from cuttings. Verbenas will flower perfectly from seeds. Height 1 to 1½ feet.

2675 Helen Willmott—This new variety is a distinct color in Verbenas, being a bright salmon rose with a white eye. Pkt., 15c.

2662 Mammoth Defiance—Bright, rich scarlet; small leaves. Pkt., 10c.

2663 Mammoth Blue Varieties—Showy, distinctive; fine for edgings. Pkt., 10c.

2664 Mammoth Striped Varieties—Beautiful; a rich collection. Pkt., 10c.

2665 Mammoth Pink Shades—Many very brilliant shades of pink. Pkt., 10c.

2666 Mammoth Pure White—Large trusses of purest white flowers. Pkt., 10c.

2667 Mammoth Cloth of Gold—Golden yellow foliage; crimson flowers. Pkt., 10c.

2668 Mammoth Purple—Deep royal purple. Pkt., 10c.

Collection, one each of above 7 Mammoth Verbenas, 50c.

2670 Livingston's Mammoth Mixed Verbenas—Our strain of these elegant mammoth-flowering Verbenas will make beds and borders in the garden of the greatest brilliancy. These are our best Verbenas, and for enormous flowers of rich and superb colors are unsurpassed. (See illustration.) They bloom most profusely. Our mixture contains every desirable color and shade. Pkt., 10c.; ¼ oz., 25c.; ¼ oz., 40c.; oz., $1.00.

2672 Fine Mixed—A very satisfactory assortment, containing many fine colors and shades. Pkt., 5c.; ¼ oz., 15c.; ½ oz., 25c.; oz., 75c.

Violet

(Viola Odorata)—Sweet-scented Violets are easily grown from seeds; and if you can plant them in a cool and moist situation, so much the better. All varieties are of great beauty.

2682 Sweet-Scented—Old-fashioned Blue Violet. Pkt., 10c.

2684 The Czar—Largest flowering, deep blue. Pkt., 10c.

2686 Finest Mixed—Blue and white sorts. Pkt., 10c.

Wallflower

Well-known and deliciously fragrant half-hardy biennials; the large spikes of bloom are of most beautiful colors. Height 1½ feet.

2690 Large-Flowering Single Mixed—Pkt., 5c.

2692 Large-Flowering Double Mixed—Pkt., 10c.

Mammoth-Flowering Zinnias

Double Pompon Zinnias. Pkt., 5c.

Livingston's Superior Zinnias

One of our most stately and showy border plants; a strong grower, and therefore succeeds well, even if the ground is not very rich. Excellent for cut flowers, and continuously in bloom. Height 1 to 3 feet.

Livingston's Mammoth Flowering Prize Zinnias

These splendid large-flowering Zinnias (see illustration on page 116) represent the very highest perfection in this flower, and for perfect doubleness, mammoth size, as well as the wonderful variety of colors and shades, are unsurpassed by any strain in cultivation. We offer the following splendid separate colors and our elegant mixture.

2700 **Mammoth Crimson**   2704 **Mammoth Pure White**
2701 **Mammoth Dark Purple**   2705 **Mammoth Rose-Pink**
2702 **Mammoth Flesh-Pink**   2706 **Mammoth Golden Yellow**
2703 **Mammoth Lilac**   2707 **Mammoth Scarlet**

Above 8 sorts, each 5c. per packet; ¼ oz., 25c.; oz., 75c.

2710 **Livingston's Mammoth Flowering Prize Mixture**—A gorgeous mixture containing many new and rich hues. Pkt., 5c.; ¼ oz., 20c.; oz., 60c.

Double Pompon

(See illustration.)—These Zinnias grow 2 feet high and are sturdy and bushy. They are also sometimes called "Lilliput," on account of their beautiful little flowers, which are very double and cone-shaped. 2727 **All Colors Mixed**—Pkt., 5c.

Improved Dwarf Zinnias

This strain, not growing quite so high as Livingston's Prize Zinnias, is especially desirable for borders, edgings and small beds. The individual flowers are equally large. 2714 **Improved Dwarf Mixture**—Pkt., 5c.; ¼ oz., 20c.; oz., 60c.

New Double Fringed

A very fine new type. The petals of the perfectly formed double flowers are more or less deeply cut or fringed, giving them a more graceful appearance than the usual form. The plants are of compact habit, about 30 inches high, and have all the free-flowering merits of the family. We offer three separate colors:

2717 **White.**   2718 **Deep Carmine.**   2719 **Bright Rose.**

Each, packet, 10c.

Collection—A packet of each of the 3 Double Fringed Zinnias, 25c.

Wild Flower Garden, or Children's Garden

Especially adapted for producing a display in large borders, or sowing along woodland walks, railroad embankments, for hiding an unsightly fence, stump, etc. Nothing in the way of flowers delights children more than this WILD GARDEN, chiefly because they can be allowed to pick their own bouquets without stint. Sow in drills 2 feet apart, or even broadcast. Cover lightly and keep the soil from drying out until started. 2740 **Our Extra Choice Mixture**—Large pkts., 10c.; ½ oz., 15c.; oz., 25c. Ask for Special Price by the Pound.

Livingston's Rainbow Collection of Choice Annual Flowers, 50c.

Consists of One Full Sized Packet Each of the following grand annuals, and is sent free by mail for Fifty Cents. At regular prices it would cost you $1.00.

Asters, Semple's Giant Branching, Mixed; Bachelor's Buttons, Giant Flowering Imperialis; Candytuft, Mixed Colors; Cosmos, Mammoth Perfection Mixed; Dianthus Pinks; Marigolds, French; Mignonette, Sweet; Nasturtium, Giant Pansy, Mixture; Petunia, Blotched and Striped; Phlox, Livingston's Special Mixed; Poppies, Livingston's Giant Double Mixture; Portulaca, Mixed; Scabiosa, Livingston's Large Flowering Mixed; Sweet Alyssum; Antirrhinum, New Giant Flowering; Sweet Peas, Gilt Edge Mixture; Zinnia, Livingston's Prize Mixture.

18 packets for only 50 cents.

Bright Array Collection, 25c.

A most brilliant flower garden for a very little money. One full sized packet each of the following 8 "Easy to Grow" Flowers for 25c.:

Sweet Alyssum; Asters, Peony-Flowered Perfection; Candytuft, Mixed Annual Sorts; Nasturtiums, Tall Climbing; Pansies, Giant Trimardeau; Phlox Drummondii; Sweet Peas, Gilt Edge Mixture; Zinnias, Prize Mixture.

Striped, or Zebra

A very pretty strain with striped flowers. Colors vary on each plant; presents a beautiful and curious appearance. 2721—Pkt., 5c.

Curled or Crested

A fine strain, with large double flowers of perfect form; petals twisted, curled and crested into fantastic and graceful forms. 2723—Pkt., 5c.; ¼ oz., 25c.

Tom Thumb, or Double Miniature

Charming, perfectly double, small-flowering class; 10 inches high; bloom profusely. Fine for borders. 2725 **Mixed Colors**—Pkt., 5c.

Have You a Hardy Garden?

So much interest is being displayed in the hardy perennial flowers at the present time that a few words here regarding them may not be amiss. You will find throughout our List Seeds of many of the most popular sorts. Perennials are slower in starting than the annuals, so that care should be taken that the ground does not dry out. The ideal place to start them is in a cold frame, where the soil can be kept constantly moist, and, when the young plants appear they can be protected from heavy rains. Some varieties bloom the first year from seed if they are sown early, but it is not until the second year that you get the best results, and from that on for several years these beautiful plants increase in value, affording color in the garden at a season when few, if any, annuals are blooming, and at the same time furnishing fine material for house decoration, as most of these varieties are excellent as cut flowers. Coreopsis Lanceolata, Gaillardia Grandiflora, Shasta Daisy, and a few others are not reliable unless they are divided and reset in the early Fall after flowering, but such varieties as Delphinium or English Larkspur, Pyrethrum Hybridum, Oriental Poppy, Columbine and Sweet William may be depended upon for years. It is so much cheaper to grow them than to buy the plants.

The Growing of Summer-Flowering Bulbs

The Caladium Esculentum or Elephant Ear is readily grown if one bears in mind that the beauty of the plant lies in its large, sub-tropical foliage and to obtain a rank growth one must provide rich soil and an ample amount of water. If these are given, a single plant will grow to a height of six feet with mammoth leaves, four by three feet. Give each plant a bucket of water every day that it does not rain and about once a week add a teaspoon full of nitrate of soda to the water. Take up the bulbs in the Fall after the leaves are frozen; cut off the tops and store the bulbs in a cool place free from frost.

Cannas are very generally used throughout the country as bedding plants, where large beds are planted or bold, sub-tropical effects are required. There are no plants which adapt themselves so well to our varied climate and with the introduction of many new forms of flower and foliage, we have today in the Canna probably the most satisfactory bedding plant grown. From a 3-inch pot plant set out after danger of frost is past we can get a six-foot plant by Fall, with quantities of brilliant flowers. Then, when the frost has killed the tops, cut them off and dig the roots. Do not shake the soil off, but put the roots in a box with what soil that sticks to them and store in a cool, frost-proof place until Spring, when, if you have a place for it you can start the roots into growth, or about the middle of May set the roots out in the open ground. The roots will stand dividing and each new shoot will make a good, large plant, if you want to increase your stock.

When it comes to Summer flowering bulbs, the Gladiolus is the most popular and effective of all, useful alike for garden decoration and as cut flowers. The bulbs can be planted from the middle of April on, setting them six inches deep, if the soil is a loam and mellow, or four inches in stiff clay. The bulbs can be planted right up to the first of June and will, of course, flower late in this case. When frost has killed the tops, dig up the bulbs and cut stalks off about two inches above the bulbs; then place where they can dry off for a couple of weeks; after this rub off the old bulb at the base of the new growth, also the balance of the stem and store in a cool frost-proof place. Save all the small bulblets which you find at the base of the bulb; sow them the following Spring like peas and the second year from planting they will flower. Handle these small bulbs same as you do the larger ones.

Lilies are harder to grow than other bulbous flowers, but are so beautiful one can't do without them. The bulbs should be set at least six inches deep and in a partially shaded place. If the soil is sandy, so much the better, but they must never be put where water will stand, and if you mulch them in the Fall with a good foot of leaves or straw, removing it soon as the frost is out in the Spring, you will find the Lilies will do very much better.

Livingston's Superb Cannas

The Canna is one of the most beautiful of all Bedding Plants

We make a specialty of Cannas at our "True Blue" Nurseries and the fields are much admired. No other plant is better adapted to this country, and nothing which costs so little excels them for masses and beautiful foliage, as well as the abundance of dazzling bloom in many shades.

Plant outdoors about the middle of May, if the weather is warm and settled, than the dormant roots. We send out plants only, as we find they give better satisfaction than the dormant roots. We send free on application an illustrated leaflet on the cultivation and care of Cannas.

At the single and dozen prices we forward Cannas postpaid. If you need large quantities of Cannas, ask for special quotations.

New Cannas { Gustave Gompper, see page 15.
Firebird, see page 15.

Kate F. Deemer

Very peculiar sort, in that the flowers, when opening, are of a rich shade of yellow; changing, as they unfold, to a beautiful red at the throat, while the rest of the flower becomes almost white. Very interesting and attractive. 5 feet. Each, 20c.; doz., $2.00.

Loveliness

A bright ruby red bloom, with large, erect heads on strong stems. Flowers of perfect form and substance. 3 feet. Each, 20c.; doz., $2.00.

Panama

The orange-red petals of this magnificent variety have a broad rich golden-yellow edge, making the large blooms and heads very striking. 3 feet. Each, 35c.; doz., $3.50.

Patrie

A beautiful light crimson variety, growing about four feet in height. A fine bedding variety. Each, 25c.; doz., $2.50.

Gladiator

A variety that has been listed for years, but is still one of the best in its class. It is a fine yellow bedding sort with red spot on each petal. Fine green foliage. The bloom stands sunshine and storm better than almost any other variety. Blooms from early to late and looks well throughout the season. 5 feet. Each, 15c.; doz., $1.50.

Charles Henderson

A fine crimson bedding variety growing to about four feet in height. Each, 15c.; doz., $1.50.

King Humbert

This is certainly the King of all bronze-leaved Cannas. It produces giant flowers of a brilliant orange-scarlet and these combined with its beautiful bronze foliage have made this variety the sensation of the past few years. It is a hybrid of the Orchid-flowering and French or Crozy type, and has all the merits of both. Either as specimen plants or in beds this beautiful variety shows its superiority over all other kinds, and we hope all our customers will order some plants of King Humbert, knowing that in so doing they will be getting the best bronze-leaved variety on the market today. Each, 15c.; doz., $1.50.

Canna
King Humbert

Cannas---Continued

Mlle. Berat

This is a very free flowering variety, and perhaps represents the nearest approach to a true pink. On account of its luxuriant growth, this Canna lends itself most effectively to massing and to background work. Height about 5 feet.

Wintzer's Meteor

The almost solid mass of deep, dazzling crimson bloom produced is spectacular. One of the best red Canna on the market and a magnificent bedding variety. 5 feet. Each, 25c.; doz., $2.50.

Mont Blanc

This variety is almost pure white. Has large, handsome green foliage. Blooms on strong stems well above the foliage. 3½ feet.

New York

A bronze-leaved, Orchid-flowered variety, with very intense brilliant carmine flowers of great beauty. A strong grower; 6 to 7 feet.

President Myers

Fine large flowers of a rich shade of cherry-carmine; foliage distinctly bronze in color. The plant is of a sturdy, robust growth, attaining a height of about 5 feet.

Professor Romberg

A brilliant rich, fiery red, flowers of medium size in large trusses held well above the bronzy foliage; 3½ to 4 feet. 20c. each; $2.00 per doz.

Queen Charlotte

Rich crimson-scarlet with wide gold border on every petal; a profuse bloomer; broad green leaves. 3½ feet.

Richard Wallace

A pleasing canary yellow with exceptionally large flowers, which are carried well above the foliage; one of the best yellow bedders. 4½ feet.

Rubin

Flowers ruby carmine; very rich and glowing; foliage dark bronzy green; great bedding sort. While the flowers of this variety are not large they are produced in profusion, and are intensely rich and glowing, and, combined with the dark foliage, make it one of the best bedding varieties. 3 feet.

Giant Flowering Canna, Burbank

Burbank

Green foliage. The flowers are gigantic in size. Toward the inner part the petals show fine crimson spots; all the rest of the flower is of a rich canary-yellow. 5 feet.

Souvenir d'Antoine Crozy

Large full spikes; rich crimson flowers, bordered with golden yellow. The colors are intense, giving a very striking and ornamental effect. 3 to 4 feet.

Dr. Budingen

One of the most brilliant scarlets, both the individual flowers and the trusses being of large size; bronze foliage; 4 feet.

Madame Crozy

Bright scarlet, gold border to each petal. Foliage green. A well known and popular variety. 3½ feet.

Florence Vaughan

Large yellow flowers, dotted with bright red. Very broad, bright green leaves. It still remains one of the most popular as well as one of the best types of yellow Cannas. 5 feet.

Express

Flowers are bright scarlet, with broad petals and compact truss; blooms freely until frost. A splendid variety. 3 feet.

Duke of Marlborough

One of the finest of the very deep crimsons; fine individual blooms in large trusses, and exceptionally free-flowering and attractive. 4 feet.

Venus

Vigorous growing sort with erect stems and magnificent trusses of large size and perfect form. Petals are oval, exquisitely colored and variegated; warm rose pink, mottled near center with creamy white edges. A superb variety.

Wyoming

Purple foliage, giant orchid-flowered orange colored, large round petals. This is a particularly useful and attractive bedding variety. Its richly colored foliage serving to admirably set off the striking shades of its massive spikes of flowers. It is a very free bloomer and we can not too strongly recommend it. 6 feet.

PRICE—Any of the above, except as noted, 15c each; $1.50 per doz.

Dahlias

The Dahlia is one of the most important Summer and Autumn flowers. Commencing to flower in July, they are a perfect blaze of bloom until stopped by frost. Especially fine for cut flowers.

It is one of the easiest of all flowers to cultivate. Deep and thorough stirring of the soil during the early growth of the plant is indispensable, but later in the season frequent surface cultivation only, should be given. Plant in an open, sunny situation, at least where the sun reaches them the greater portion of the day. It is a rank feeder, and should have well-enriched soil; keep free from grass and weeds. Water regularly in dry weather. Plant the bulbs four inches below the surface of the ground, laying the bulb on its side. Don't stand on end with the crown out. Do not plant until the ground has become warm. As soon as the frost has killed the foliage the roots should be carefully taken from the ground, and the soil shaken from among them; must be stored away in a cool place, not too dry, but secure from frost.

NOTE—We fill all orders with strong, divided, dormant roots. All prices are prepaid, except where noted.

Peony-Flowered Dahlias

This is the newest type of Dahlias and is remarkable for the large size of its flowers and its vigorous growth. It is fine in the garden or for cut flowers. If you want something fine, try this new type, which is just as easy to grow as any other variety.

Duke Henry—Brilliant red. Large broad petals.

Queen Emma—A grand variety, having flowers of a peculiar shade of pink.

Queen Wilhelmina—Immense fluffy flowers; pure white. A remarkably chaste and beautiful flower.

Souv. Franz Liszt—A dark purple maroon, veined with white. The blooms are very large and stems long.

Any of the above, 20c. each; $2.00 per dozen.

Century Dahlias

These are the very latest and best form of Single Dahlias. They are remarkably strong growers and produce immense flowers on long stems, making them of exceptional value either in the garden or for house decoration. The varieties we list are the finest of the "Centuries."

White Century—A big snowy white bloom; very fine.

Rose Pink Century—A great improvement over Pink Century. A wonderfully vigorous grower producing immense flowers on 3-foot stems, making them fine for cutting.

Golden Century—A new one and a prize winner. Pure golden yellow, of large size, and especially fine for cut flowers on account of its size, long stems and good keeping qualities.

Maroon Century—The darkest of all, being a deep maroon shading to black. A very rich and effective color.

Cardinal Century—A rich cardinal red of large size and very brilliant. The best single red.

Twentieth Century—This is the original "Century." Early in the season it is an intense rosy crimson shading to white at the tips and base of the petals.

Any of the above, 20c. each; $2.00 per dozen.

Dahlias in Separate Colors

These are named varieties of a very high grade, many of which we have too few of to catalogue them separately. They are fit for any collection and contain many sorts especially suitable for cut flowers. We offer them in shades of crimson, pink, yellow, variegated and white. 15c. each, postpaid. 10c. each; $1.00 per dozen; $7.50 per 100, by express, purchaser paying charges.

New Peony Flowered Dahlia

Pompon Dahlias

These are a miniature form of the show and fancy Dahlias, having the same round, ball-like form, but being much smaller. The plants are also much smaller, but no type produces as many flowers. The plants are literally covered and as the blooms can be cut in sprays they are valuable as cut flowers. We offer several of the most distinct.

Klein Domitea—A golden terra cotta color; very free bloomer.

Sunshine—Rich vermillion scarlet. Very fine color and flowers are produced on long stems.

Snowclad—A snowy white and remarkably free bloomer.

Raphael—Dark maroon with quilled petals.

Little Beauty—Soft, silvery pink. Rightly named.

May Clift—Bright purple.

Any of the above, 15c. each; $1.50 per dozen.

Decorative Dahlias

Standard Varieties

Henry Patrick—Pure white flowers; large and fine.

Dr. Gates—Beautiful shell pink; long stems, and fine for cutting.

Catherine Duer—A bright crimson scarlet; very fine and wonderfully popular in the East.

Clifford W. Bruton—A standard yellow variety; large and perfect.

Grand Duke Alexis—White edged with latender; very pretty and a satisfactory grower.

Blue Oban—A soft lavender, nearest to blue in Dahlias.

Minnie McCullough—Very fine; a soft golden yellow tipped with bronze red. A perfect flower produced on long stems.

Sylvia—Deep pink, of large, perfect form on long, stiff stems. One of the best for the garden or for cutting.

Yellow Duke—Canary yellow; very large flowers on long stems.

Zulu—A popular variety called the "Black Dahlia," being a very dark maroon.

Lyndhurst—The brightest vermillion and the best of its color for cutting. An early, free and continuous bloomer with long stems.

Frank L. Bassett—Very free bloomer, and a rich color, being a purplish blue.

Any of the above standard Dahlias, 15c. each; $1.50 per dozen.

Decorative Dahlia Jack Rose

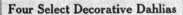

Four Select Decorative Dahlias

Jack Rose

The color is the same as the celebrated rose Genl. Jacqueminot, but a shade darker and richer. To be successful with Jack Rose give plenty of room, pinch back and grow to the single stem branching system, every branch should be disbudded and your plants will produce 25 to 50 blooms on stems 24 to 30 inches long. Price, 20c. each; dozen, $2.00.

Delice

The most popular variety. Its beautiful soft, yet lively color, a glowing rose pink, together with its perfect shape, stout, stiff stems which hold the flowers well above the foliage, and the fact that when cut, it retains its freshness for a long time, makes this one of the most valuable sorts. The florist and all Dahlia growers will make no mistake in planting this variety, as we could not get enough flowers to supply the demand. Price, 20c. each; dozen, $2.00.

Princess Victoria Louise

A giant decorative Dahlia, of most approved form. The color is pure cerise, being nearly the shade of the American Beauty Rose. The plant is a strong, vigorous grower, of branching habit, and produces the flowers in the greatest profusion on slender stems. Roots, 25c. each; $2.50 per dozen.

Admiral Togo

A very distinct and striking new decorative Dahlia, large size, and perfectly double. Color, bright wine red, margined velvety maroon. Roots, 25c. each; $2.50 per dozen.

Manzanita—A clear, rich lavender. The purest of its color with long stems and substance which makes it valuable for cutting.

Empress Josephine—A very strong grower producing on long stems, light pink blooms lightly penciled with purple and of great substance. The flowers are large and of perfect form.

Gaiety—A superb variety; vivid scarlet heavily marked with pure white. Away above the average of its type. The stems are long and flowers produced freely.

Manitou—A flower which is always very double and uniform in outline and of immense size—sometimes 8 inches in diameter. The color is a rich amber bronze, with a shading of pink.

Mrs. J. Gardner Cassatt—A new pink variety which has attracted much attention for its beauty of form and color and great freedom of bloom. The flowers are immense and borne on long stems. It is a beautiful rose color.

Mme. V. Dael—An immense flower which is proving a favorite with all and is entitled to first place amongst the lighter colors, being a shell pink. While being very large, yet it is not coarse and the stems are long and wiry. It is certainly a choice variety.

Umatilla—A Dahlia of superior merit on account of its remarkably long stems and good keeping qualities. In color it is a deep blood red.

Any of the above Dahlias, 25c. each; $2.50 per dozen.

Dahlia Red Hussar

Show and Fancy Dahlias

The "show" Dahlias are of ball shape with full, round, regular form and cupped or quilled petals of solid color. The "Fancy" Dahlias are very similar to the "Show" except that they are spotted, tipped, penciled or striped, two or more colors, or the tips of petals are lighter than the ground color of the flower.

Princess Victoria—The finest pure yellow show Dahlia; great bloomer, with long stems.

Drear's White—A pure white, of large size and a beauty.

J. T. West—Yellow; heavily tipped with rich, rosy purple.

Harlequin—A flower of perfect form; rich velvety crimson, tipped with white.

Miss Cornell—White tipped with rosy purple.

A. D. Livoni (Show)—A standard variety and a beautiful rose pink; great bloomer and fine in every way.

Kaiser Wilhelm (Fancy)—One of the finest deep yellow, tipped with cherry red.

Jamaica (Show)—A dark purple shading into maroon. One of the darkest colors.

Red Hussar (Show)—Brilliant cardinal red; one of the very best show Dahlias. See illustration.

Ethel Schmidt (Fancy)—White suffused with pink and pencilled with crimson; very free bloomer with long stems.

Arabella (Fancy)—A beauty; soft primrose yellow, tipped with pink.

Above sorts, 15c. each; $1.50 per dozen, postpaid.

Show Dahlias of Special Merit

Alice Emily—The color is a rich yellow, edged red, always a pleasing and striking combination. A popular cut-flower and excellent for exhibition.

Bonton—Large, absolutely full, and of round-regular form, the petals reflexing to the stem. Color, deep rich crimson. A free bloomer on long stems.

John Walker—The flowers are of large size, pure white, and are produced on long, slender stems, beautifully formed, and full to the center, the outer petals reflexing to the stem. It is an early bloomer.

May Lomas—A beautiful fall Dahlia of large size, and always full to the center. White, suffused soft lavender, edged blue. This edging is the nearest pure blue found in Dahlias.

Price of above, 20c. each; $2.00 per dozen, postpaid.

Cactus Dahlias

This type has become wonderfully popular of late years. We have endeavored to list some of the most meritorious of the new varieties and the best of the Standard kinds.

Mrs. Ferdinand Jeffries—The flower is irregular; its long petals are curved and twisted, giving the flower a shaggy appearance. Color, deep velvety red.

Charm—Petals long and regular, delicate salmon rose, changing to pale pink; often pink edged with salmon rose.

Charles Clayton—The color is a most intense red, so vivid as to dazzle the eye. Flowers are large in size and are produced freely.

Ventura—Yellow, shading to amber and pink. A very free bloomer.

Olive Tracy—Clear canary yellow, a delicate color, produced on long stems, making it a valuable variety for cutting.

T. G. Baker—Very large, finely formed. The best clear yellow cactus Dahlia.

Liberty—A fine variety of beautiful form, rich velvety maroon, tipped with crimson.

Thomas Parkins—Large flowers of a bright terra cotta, strong grower, with long stems and fine for cutting.

Kriemhilde—Deep rosy pink. Good keeper.

Mont Blanc—A fine white variety with long, stiff stems.

Standard Bearer—Bright, clear scarlet; very free bloomer.

Burbank—A vivid vermilion scarlet; tall grower and late bloomer; long stems. 15c. each; $1.50 per dozen.

J. B. Briant—Golden yellow, with a slight shade of pink on tips of petals.

Mrs. H. J. Jones—A clear scarlet with band of white running through each petal. 15c. each; $1.50 per dozen.

Princess—A beautiful soft pink flower of largest size.

Pius X—An exceptionally fine white cactus.

Countess of Lonsdale—The best cactus Dahlia, all things considered. A very free bloomer, fine stems and good color —a blending of amber and salmon pink.

Dainty—Most fittingly described by its name. The dainty coloring baffles description, but may be partly described as a lemon base, shading to an exquisite rosy pink at the tips. 15c. each; $1.50 per dozen, postpaid.

Any of the above, except as noted, 20c. each; $2.00 per dozen, postpaid.

Gladioli

Probably these are, on account of their hardiness, wide range of brilliant colors and their peculiar adaptability as cut-flowers, the most popular of all the Summer flowering bulbs. By taking care to make plantings at 10 day intervals through April, May and June, they will bear a succession of splendid spikes of bloom from late July until October. The great reduction in prices on all varieties offered, bring them within reach of all.

America

This is a variety to grow by the thousands and the soft lavender pink tint of its blossoms and their lasting qualities never fails to recommend it to private grower and florist alike. To any one who has never grown it, we cannot too strongly recommend this sort. Each, 5c.; doz., 40c., postpaid. By express, not prepaid, doz., 30c.; 100, $1.50; 1000, $12.00.

Augusta

Flowers pure white with blue anthers. One of the older varieties and the first really successful white to be introduced. Each, 5c.; doz., 45c., postpaid. By express, not prepaid, doz., 35c.; 100, $2.00; 1000, $17.50.

Baron Hulot

The best blue variety. A very dark, violet blue, bordering on purple, with wide open flowers well placed. Each, 8c.; doz., 70c., postpaid. By express, not prepaid, doz., 60c.; 100, $4.00.

Brenchleyensis

Intense fiery crimson, scarlet; an old type but a very popular variety. Each, 5c.; doz., 70c., postpaid. By express, not prepaid, doz., 35c.; 100, $2.00; 1000, $16.00.

Chicago White

A pure white of comparatively recent introduction; lavender markings in throat. Each, 8c.; doz., 70c., postpaid. By express, not prepaid, doz., 60c.; 100, $4.00.

Klondyke

A fine light yellow with blotches of vivid crimson in the throat. A good grower and makes a beautiful bouquet. Each, 6c.; doz., 55c., postpaid. By express, not prepaid, doz., 45c.; 100, $3.00.

Mrs. Francis King

A magnificent and most effective variety for window store or home decoration. The strong, sturdy flower stalk stands very erect, bearing long, showy, broad spikes of brilliant scarlet vermilion. The flowerets are unusually large with 6 to 8 open at one time, thus making a very lasting cut flower. Each, 5c.; doz., 45c., postpaid. By express, not prepaid, doz., 35c.; 100, $1.75; 1000, $16.00.

Mrs. Frank Pendleton

A new sort exquisitely colored. See Specialty pages for fuller description. Each, 20c.; doz., $2.10, postpaid. By express. not prepaid, doz., $2.00; 100, $15.00.

Niagara

A beautiful cream shade, and a variety of great merit. See Specialty pages for fuller description. Each, 10c.; doz., $1.00, postpaid. By express. not prepaid. doz. 90c.; 100, $7.00.

Panama

A beautiful soft pink. For fuller description see Specialty pages. Each, 10c.; doz., $1.10, postpaid. By express, not prepaid, doz., $1.00; 100, $7.50.

Peace

A very large new white, of exceptional merit. See Specialty pages for fuller description. Each, 18c.; 2 for 35c.; doz., $1.85, postpaid. By express, not prepaid, doz., $1.75; 100, $13.00.

Princeps

Scarlet crimson with deeper shading toward the throat; lower petals marked with large white blotches. Flowerets are remarkable for their size and beauty of coloring. Each, 6c.; doz., 55c., postpaid. By express, not prepaid, doz., 45c.; 100, $3.00.

Livingston's "True Blue" Mixed Gladioli

This splendid mixture is a blending of high-grade named varieties and embraces a great and pleasing range of colors. We heartily recommend it. Each, 5c.; 6 for 25c.; doz., 40c.; 100, $2.00, postpaid. By express, not prepaid, doz., 30c.; 100, $1.50; 1000, $12.00.

Livingston's Superb Special Seedlings

A brilliant collection made up of an assortment of exceptionally high grade, but unnamed seedlings of the richest combinations of shades. Our customers may rest assured that this mixture contains excellent and unusual values and will insure for them a wide range of colors, shades and types, which cannot be secured in any other collection. Each, 8c.; 6 for 40c.; doz., 70c.; 100, $4.00, postpaid. By express, not prepaid, doz., 60c.; 100, $3.75; 1000, $32.00.

Gladioli Francis King

Bulbs By Parcel Post
Gladioli Bulbs weigh about 7 pounds per 100, and if wanted by mail, include enough to cover postage in your remittance.

Lilies

Plant bulbs in the Spring as soon as frost is out of the ground. Select a well-drained spot, dig the soil deep and make it fine.

Lilies thrive best in rather sandy soil and no manure should be put where it will touch the bulbs. Partial shade is best for all varieties and plenty of water is required during growth, although the bulbs must not be planted in low places where water stands. Set the bulbs at least five inches deep

Auratum (Gold Banded)—Flowers pure white, thickly studded with crimson spots, while through the center of each petal runs a clear gold band. Mammoth bulbs, each, 25c.; doz., $2.50, postpaid.

Speciosum Rubrum, or Roseum—Light rose, heavily shaded and spotted rosy-crimson. First size Bulbs, each, 5c.; 2 for 25c.; doz., $1.50. (Weight, 3 lbs. per doz.) Extra size Bulbs, each, 20c.; 2 for 35c.; doz., $2.00. (Weight, 4 lbs. per doz.)

Speciosum Melpomene—Darker shade than the above, heavily spotted with crimson. Each, 15c.; 2 for 25c.; doz., $1.50. (Weight, 3 lbs. per doz.)

Speciosum Album—Large, fragrant, pure white flowers, with a greenish band running through the center of each petal; height, 3 to 4 feet; bloom at midsummer. Each, 20c.; 2 for 35c.; doz., $2.00. (Weight, 4 lbs. per doz.)

Tigrinum Splendens—The old-fashioned Tiger Lily; hardy anywhere; beautiful orange-red flowers, spotted with black; blooms in August; about 4 feet high. Each, 15c.; 2 for 25c.; doz., $1.50. (Weight, 1½ lb. per doz.)

Caladium

Plants attain a height of from 4 to 6 feet, the leaves being veined with different shades of green; when massed alone or with Cannas, they produce a striking and beautiful effect. They are of easy culture, and will grow in almost any garden soil, but if especially large plants are wanted they should be planted in a well-enriched soil and given water in abundance throughout the season. The bulbs may be kept over Winter by taking up in the Fall when frost kills the foliage; leave some soil on the roots, dry gradually in an airy, shady place for several days, then pack in a shallow box in a dry sand or soil, store in a dry cellar where it does not freeze.

CALADIUM PRICES
Prices by Mail, Postpaid

5 to 7 inches in circumference.Each, 10c.; 5 for 45c.
7 to 9 inches in circumference.Each, 20c.; 5 for 85c.
9 to 11 inches in circumference.Each, 25c.; 5 for $1.25
10 to 12 inches in circumference.Each, 40c.; 5 for $2.00

By Express, not Prepaid

5 to 7 inches in circumference.10 for 80c.
  100 for $5.00.
7 to 9 inches in circumference.10 for $1.25
  100 for $7.50.
9 to 11 inches in circumference.10 for $2.50
  25 for $5.75.
10 to 12 inches in circumference.10 for $3.75
  25 for $8.50.

LILIUM AURATUM

Tube Roses

One of the most delightfully fragrant and beautiful Summer-flowering bulbs. Its waxy-white flowers are the sweetest-scented that grow. The growing plant is fond of light and heat and should not be planted outside before May 1.

Our Tuberoses are grown and cured with the greatest possible care, and all are flowering size. For large, perfect flowers we recommend the larger sizes.

Double Dwarf Pearl Tuberose—Flowers, large size and very double. Extra size bulbs, by mail, postpaid, each, 7c.; 4 for 25c.; 65c. By express, not prepaid, doz., 50c.; 100 for $3.00. First size bulbs, by mail, postpaid, 2 for 10c.; 6 for 15c.; doz., 25c. By express, not prepaid, doz., 20c.; 25 for 35c.; 50 for 60c.; 100 for $1.00.

Cinnamon Vine

Perfectly hardy. Attains a height of from 15 to 25 feet. Brilliant glossy foliage and an abundance of fragrant flowers. Each, 5c.; 6 for 25c.; doz., 40c., postpaid.

Maderia Vine (Climbing Mignonette)

Rapid-growing vine; easy to grow; light green leaves; bears small, white, feathery, fragrant flowers; free from insect pests of all kinds. Each, 5c.; 6 for 25c.; doz., 40c.; 100, $2.25, postpaid.

Farm, Garden, Fruit, Flowers, BOOKS Vegetables, Poultry, Etc.

Books are sent at purchaser's expense, except those marked postpaid. Shipping weight will be found noted in each instance where the book weighs over 8 ounces and your remittance should be sufficient to cover the postage. See page 2 for Parcel Post Rate Table.

FARM AND GARDEN

Asparagus: How to Grow for Market or Home Use. 174 pages, 5x7 inches, handsomely illustrated. Cloth, 50c. Weight 1 lb.

Broom Corn and Brooms. How to raise Broom Corn and Make Brooms on a small or large scale. Cloth, 50c. 1 lb.

Cabbage, Cauliflower and Allied Vegetables. By C. L. Allen. 5x7; 128 pages. Illustrated. Cloth, 50c. 1 lb.

Celery Culture. By W. R. Beattie. Illustrated. 5x7; 143 pages. Cloth, 50c. 1 lb.

Smith's Corn Book. Tells how to raise a hundred bushels per acre on worn soil. Price, $1.00. 1 lb.

Clovers and How to Grow Them. By Thomas Shaw. Treats on the growth, cultivation and treatment of Clovers as applicable to all parts of the United States and Canada. Illustrated. 5x8; 337 pages. Cloth, $1.00. 2 lbs.

Forage Crops. By Thomas Shaw. An exhaustive work. Illustrated. 5x7; 287 pages. Cloth, $1.00. 2 lbs.

Forcing Book. The cream of all information on forcing vegetables under glass. 266 pages, 5x7. Cloth, $1.25. 2 lbs.

Farming with Green Manures. 5x7; 249 pages. Cloth, $1.00. 2 lbs.

Garden Making. By Bailey. The beginner is shown how easy it is to raise Flowers, Fruits and Vegetables and beautify one's home grounds. 417 pages, 256 illustrations. New edition, $1.50. 2 lbs.

Gardening for Pleasure. By Henderson. $1.50. 2 lbs.

Gardening for Profit. A standard work, valuable as a reference book. Henderson. $1.50. 2 lbs.

Ginseng. Kains. Its cultivation, harvesting, marketing and market value. Illustrated. 5x7; 144 pages. Cloth, 50c. 1 lb.

Hints and Helps for Young Gardeners. Hemenway. A very practical treatise for beginners in gardening. 35c., postpaid.

How to Make Home and City Beautiful. Hemenway. $1.00. 1 lb.

How to Make a Flower Garden. Very practical and suggestive, having been written from actual experience. Many lists of flowers and shrubs for special purposes and seasons are given, with directions how to grow each. 8x11; 370 pages; 200 fine half-tone illustrations. Price, $1.75. 3 lbs.

Landscape Gardening Applied to Home Decoration. By Maynard. 338 pages, 5x7. Illustrated. Cloth, $1.50. 2 lbs.

Landscape Gardening. By F. A. Waugh. Treats general principals which govern the art of producing pictures with plants. Contains many excellent suggestions applicable to common gardening. 152 pages; illustrated. Cloth, $1 lb.

Money in the Garden. A very practical work on vegetable gardening. 268 pages, 5x7. Cloth, $1.00. 2 lbs.

Mushrooms: How to Grow. 14-page booklet. 10c., postpaid.

Mushroom Culture, Robinson's. Illustrated. 172 pages. Cloth, 50c. 1 lb.

Mushrooms: How to Grow. Falconer. The best work on this subject published in America. 169 pages, 5x7. Cloth, $1.00. 1 lb.

New Onion Culture. By T. Greiner. A complete guide for growing Onions for profit. 5x7; 111 pages. Illustrated. Cloth, 50c. 1 lb.

Onion Book. By 17 Successful Growers. Greatest value for the price. Paper binding, 20c., postpaid.

The Pruning Book. By Bailey. A complete and practical book on the pruning and training of all kinds of trees and shrubs as applied to American conditions. 539 pages, 4½x7. Cloth, $1.50. 2 lbs.

The Potato. By Samuel Fraser, of Cornell Agricultural College. Contains full instructions on cultivation, spraying, harvesting, marketing, etc. 75c. 1 lb.

Picturesque Gardens. A magnificent book, beautifully illustrated, treating all forms of ornamental gardening. By Henderson. 168 pages. 10x12. Cloth, $2.50. 3 lbs.

Principles of Vegetable Growing. By Prof. Bailey. Gives the simplest directions for growing commonest things. Tells how to plant, prune, train and care for flowers, fruits, vegetables, bushes and trees. 250 pages, with many marginal cuts. Price, $1.50. 2 lbs.

Rhubarb Culture. New. How to grow in hotbed or field. Half-tone illustrations. 130 pages, 5x7. Cloth, 50c. 1 lb.

The Farm and Garden Rule Book. Bailey. This is a revised and very much enlarged edition of the Horticulturist's Rule Book, covering farm practice as well as gardening. $2.00. 3 lbs.

The Gold Mine in the Front Yard. How to improve your home grounds, be it small or large. Practical guide to the amateur in floriculture. 280 pages, 5x7¼. Cloth, $1. 2 lbs.

Tomato Culture. By Will W. Tracy. Practical treatise on the Tomato. 5x7; 149 pages. Illustrated. Cloth, 50c. 1 lb.

The Gardenette. A complete garden guide; tells how to grow choice vegetables by the celebrated Sandwich System, how to start early, thrifty plants without a hotbed; how to grow melons, cucumbers, etc., by the new Post Hole Method; how to stimulate quick germination, and induce vigorous growth; how to grow and blanch 1000 fine celery heads on one square rod, on any kind of soil, and other new and valuable methods of gardening, not idle theories, but successful facts. Finely illustrated. 60c., postpaid.

FRUITS, FLOWERS, BULBS, ETC.

Bulbs and Tuberous Rooted Plants. By Allen. Complete directions for their successful culture. 5x7; 311 pages. Illustrated. Cloth, $1.50. 2 lbs.

Best Method of Heating Greenhouses. 13 essays. 25c., postpaid.

Carnation Culture. By Lamborn. Tells the whole story. Third edition. Illustrated. $1.50. 1 lb.

Commercial Rose Culture. Eber Holmes. The most recent book on growing roses. Very complete and a valuable book. $1.50. 1 lb.

Commercial Violet Culture. Of great value to commercial or amateur growers. 224 pages, 4½x7. Cloth, $1.50. 1 lb.

Flowers, and How to Grow Them. Of especial value to amateurs. By Eben E. Rexford. Cloth, 50c. 1 lb.

Fuller's Small Fruit Culturist. Beautifully illustrated. 287 pages, 5x7. Cloth, $1.00. 2 lbs.

Fuller's Grape Culturist. Take the palm for practical value. 282 pages, 5x7. Cloth, $1.50. 2 lbs.

Greenhouse Construction. Manual on building, heating, ventilating, arrangement, etc. 218 pages, 5x7. Cloth, $1.50. 2 lbs.

Greenhouse Management. A manual for florists on forcing flowers, vegetables, etc., in greenhouse. 128 cuts, 400 pages, 5x7. Cloth, $1.50. 2 lbs.

Home Floriculture. By Eben E. Rexford. New; elegantly illustrated. 300 pages, 5x7. Cloth, $1.00. 2 lbs.

Nursery Book. By Bailey. Illustrated. 365 pages, 4½x7. Cloth, $1.50. 2 lbs.

American Apple Orchard. By F. A. Waugh. A strong, practical and explicit work on the culture of the greatest of American fruits. Best book on the subject published. Illustrated. 5x7; 226 pages. Cloth, $1.00. 2 lbs.

Bush Fruits. By F. W. Card. A treatise on the Raspberries, Blackberries, Dewberries, Currants, Gooseberries, and other shrub-like fruits. 536 pages. 5x7. Cloth, $1.50. 2 lbs.

Principles of Fruit Growing. By L. H. Bailey. A comprehensive treatise on the growing of fruit trees, with suggestions as to best methods of selecting, planting, pruning, fertilizing, spraying and harvesting. 516 pages. Cloth, $1.50. 2 lbs.

Practical Floriculture, Henderson's. A standard work. Illustrated. 325 pages, 5x7. Cloth, $1.50. 2 lbs.

The Book of the Daffodil. Bourne. A very complete and practical treatise, giving all varieties and types with full cultural directions. $1.00, postpaid. 1 lb.

Tulips. New book by the noted English authority, Rev. Joseph Jacobs. Contains 8 photographic illustrations in accurate colors. 65c. 1 lb.

The Daffodil. New book on Narcissi, by Rev. Joseph Jacobs. A companion volume to his work on Tulips, and contains, beside much valuable text, 8 photographic plates in natural colors. 65c. 1 lb.

FERTILIZERS AND MANURES.

Fertilizers. Voorhees. Probably the best book on the subject. Enters into the analysis of fertilizers and their uses, also the proper kinds to be used on various crops. A very fine book. $1.00. 2 lbs.

Manures: Methods of Making. By Bommers. Gives process to improve farm manures. Paper, 25c., postpaid.

POULTRY AND LIVE STOCK.

Standard of Perfection. A complete description of all recognized varieties of fowls. 6x9; 300 pages; illustrated. Cloth, $2.00. 2 lbs.

Pets of the Household. How to care for them in health and sickness. Plain and practical. 25c., postpaid.

The Biggle Books.

Biggle Garden Book. 130 pages. 50c.
Biggle Horse Book. All about horses. 128 pages. 50c.
Biggle Cow Book. All about cows. 144 pages. 50c.
Biggle Berry Book. All about berries. 144 pages. 50c.
Biggle Poultry Book. All about poultry. 160 pages. 50c.
Biggle Swine Book. All about swine. 144 pages. 50c.

Profusely illustrated. Cloth, each 50c.; any 3 for $1.40. All Biggle Books are sent postpaid, at the prices quoted.

The Cement Worker's Handbook. By W. H. Baker. Tells the whole story. A most valuable little book to have handy. Fourth Revised Edition. 50c., postpaid.

Spraying Crops. By Prof. Weed. Why, when and how. Fully illustrated. 150 pages. Cloth, 50c. 1 lb.

Canning and Preserving. By Mrs. Rohrer. Tells how to can and preserve fruits and vegetables. Gives best methods of making jellies, marmalades, butters, syrups, catsups, etc. 5x7; 80 pages. Cloth, 50c. 1 lb.

Raffia Basket Making. By T. Vernette Morse. Profusely illustrated. 5x7; 30 pages. Paper, 25c., postpaid.

Prices Net—When ordering goods from this page to be mailed, ask postmaster for amount of postage to remit

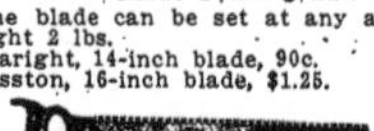

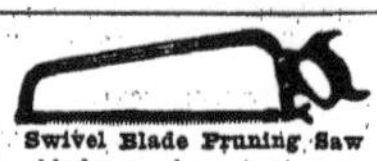

Swivel Blade Pruning Saw

The blade can be set at any angle. Weight 2 lbs.
Searight, 14-inch blade, 90c.
Disston, 16-inch blade, $1.25.

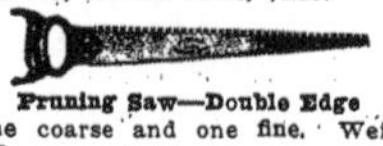

Pruning Saw—Double Edge

One coarse and one fine. Weight, 2 lbs.
19-inch blade, 75c.
26-inch blade, $1.25.

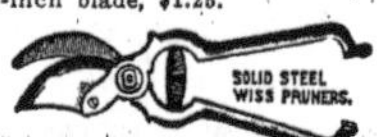

Guaranteed. Weight, 2 lbs. 9-inch, $2.00; 10-inch, $2.25.

Common—Very strong. Best steel blade and excellent spring. 60c.; weight, 1 lb.

Keen Cutter Pole Pruner—10 ft., $1.00; 12 ft., $1.25.

Send for Special Pruning Tool Catalog.

Cahoon Hand Broadcast Seeder

For sowing any grain or grass seed. Sows at a common walking gait 4 to 8 acres per hour. A saving of labor and one-third of the seed is effected by this machine. Reliable in all respects. (See illustration.) Price, $3.50; weight, 9 lbs.

Little Giant Seeder

Strongest, Lightest and Easiest Running

Best and cheapest crank Seeder made in the quality of work done and durability. Will not get out of order nor be affected by dampness or the

weather. Distributes all kinds of fertilizer, land plaster, ashes and seeds. We have sold it for years with good satisfaction. No. 1 (Fiddle-Bow), $1.25; weight, 5 lbs.; No. 3 (Crank), $1.50; weight, 6 lbs.

Hot-bed Sashes

Best Cypress—3½x6 ft., unglazed for 4 rows 8x10 glass. Each, $1.25; 10 for $12.

Our sales of Hot-bed Sashes are increasing each season, so satisfactory do our customers find them.

Columbus Corn Sheller

Shells any size ear from popcorn to large field corn. May be fastened to a board or on top of the fence. Always ready. (See illustration.) By freight or express, $1.25.

The New Christy Garden Weeder h the famous scalloped cutting edge as the Cristy Bread Knife. Each, 20c.; weight, 1 lb.

Hazeltine's Hand Weeder—Blade solid steel, tempered, ⅞-inch wide and ⅛-inch thick, sharpened on all edges. Each, 20c.; weight, 1 lb.

Excelsior Weeder—Very useful for weeding seed beds, stirring soil in hot-beds, cold frames, etc. Each, 10c.; weight, 1 lb.

Lang's Weeder—Doz., $2.25; each, 20c.; weight, 1 lb.

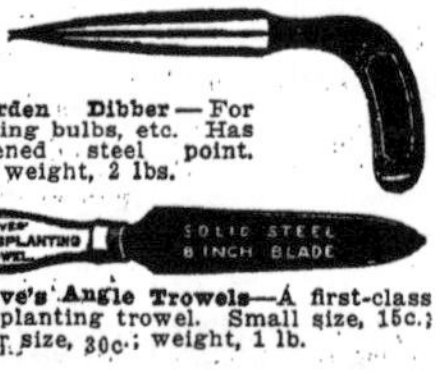

Garden Dibber—For planting bulbs, etc. Has hardened steel point. 30c.; weight, 2 lbs.

Cleve's Angle Trowels—A first-class transplanting trowel. Small size, 15c.; larger size, 30c.; weight, 1 lb.

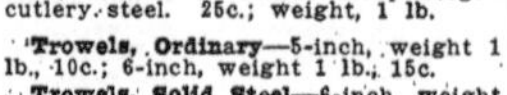

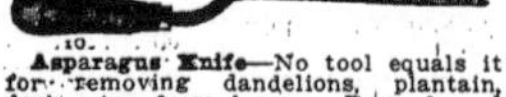

Asparagus Knife—No tool equals it for removing dandelions, plantain, dock, etc., from lawns. Drop forged cutlery steel. 25c.; weight, 1 lb.

Trowels, Ordinary—5-inch, weight 1 lb., 10c.; 6-inch, weight 1 lb., 15c.

Trowels, Solid Steel—6-inch, weight 1 lb., 25c.

Van Reyper's Glazing Points

Per box of 1000, 60c.; weight, 1 lb. Lots of 500 and over, per box, 55c. **Pinchers** for driving, 60c.; weight, 1 lb.

Siebert's Glazing Points

⅝-inch size, 1200 to lb., per lb., 40c.; ⅞-inch size, 800 to lb., per lb., 40c.

Wood Pot Labels

Painted Pot Labels—Best made. Put up in packages of 1000 each.—

4 x⅝ inch	per 1000	$0 70
4½x⅝ inch	"	80
5 x⅝ inch	"	95
6 x⅝ inch	"	1 20
10 x⅝ inch	"	2 50
12 x⅝ inch	"	3 00

Wood Garden Stakes

For Labeling			Painted	
8x ⅞-inch.	Per 100	45c	Per 1000	$3 70
10x ⅞-inch.	"	60c	"	4 80
12x1⅛-inch.	"	75c	"	6 00

McWhorter Fertilizer Distributer—For the practical and superior distribution of all commercial fertilizer. It distributes the fertilizer in a furrow, beside the growing crop, as a top dresser or as a broadcaster to any extent up to a uniform spread of over 2 feet, without removing or adding any part or loosening a bolt, and in any quantity from a few pounds to 40 or more pounds to the 100 yards of row. (See illustration.) Price, $10.00.

Out O' Sight Mole Trap

Best Mole Trap ever offered, and only has to be tried to be appreciated. Can be used in hot-bed under sash. The secret of mole catching is a good trap and to know their habits. Full directions with each trap. (See cut.) Each, $1.00; weight, 2 lbs.

Plant Bed Cloth

A protecting Cloth of Waterproof Fiber; excellent substitute for glass, late in season. All pieces are a yard wide and contain from 40 to 60 yards each. Heavy grade, per yard, 15c.; weight, 7 oz., by the piece, 40 to 60 yds., per yd., 13¼c. Medium grade, per yd., 10c.; weight, 3¾ oz.; by the piece, 40 to 60 yds., per yd., 9½c. Light grade, per yd., 5c.; weight, 1½ oz.; by the piece, 40 to 60 yds., per yd., 4½c.

Clipper Grain and Seed Cleaner

No. 1, for general use, has 8 sieves (7 zinc), cleans grain and seeds of all kinds. Each, $20.00.

Send for Special Catalog of Clipper Mills.

Neponset Paper Pots

Are made of tough waterproof fiber paper unbreakable and the best pot made for starting plants in hot-beds or greenhouses and for shipping and marketing. For lightness and cheapness they have no equal.

	Per 100	Per 1000	No. in Crate
2¼ inches	$0 25	$2 42	1000
2½ inches	30	2 78	1000
3 inches	45	3 82	1000
3½ inches	60	5 24	1000
4 inches	80	6 60	500
5 inches	1 20	10 96	500
6 inches	1 65	14 68	500

Poultry Supplies

Incubators, Brooders, Bone Cutters, Grit, Shell, Bone, Medicines, Lice Killers, Fountains, Leg Bands, Etc.

Send for Special Catalog.

All prices on this page are for the goods f. o. b. Columbus, O., and subject to market change.

Fertilizers

Ask for special quotations on ton lots.

BONE MEAL—10 lbs., 40c.; 25 lbs., 75c.; 50 lbs., $1.25; 125 lbs., $2.60.

ARMOUR'S 2-8-1—10 lbs., 40c.; 25 lbs., 75c.; 50 lbs., $1.00; 125 lbs., $2.40.

ARMOUR'S 3-8-1—10 lbs., 40c.; 25 lbs., 75c.; 50 lbs., $1.25; 125 lbs., $2.60.

NITRATE OF SODA—10 lbs., 90c.; 25 lbs., $2.00; 50 lbs., $3.50; 100 lbs., $6.00.

SHEEP MANURE (Pulverized)—10 lbs., 40c.; 25 lbs., 75c.; 50 lbs., $1.25; 100 lbs., $2.00.

BARWELL'S PLANT GROWER—Odorless, highly concentrated soluble food for house plants: ½ lb. box, 20c.; 1½ lbs., 35c.

Insecticides, Fungicides, Etc.

ARSENATE OF LEAD (Powdered)—Mixes with water almost instantly—one pound goes as far as two to three of paste—remains in suspension much longer. We have given a three-year test to the brand we carry and consider it unequalled. ¼ lb., 25c.; lb., 40c.; 5 lbs., $1.50; 10 lbs., $2.75; 25 lbs., $6.00; 50 lbs., $10.50; 100 lbs., $20.00.

APHINE—For destroying aphis (plant lice) on roses, sweet peas, nasturtiums, etc. A fine article: ¼ pt., 25c.; ½ pt., 40c.; 1 pt., 65c.; 1 qt., $1.00; 1 gal., $2.50.

BLACK LEAF 40—A concentrated solution of Nicotine Sulphate. For black aphis and sucking insects of this class: 1 oz., 25c.; ½ lb., 75c.; 2 lbs., $2.50; 10 lbs., $10.75.

BORDEAUX MIXTURE—1 gallon makes 50; 1 qt., 40c.; 1 gal., $1.00; 5 gal., $4.50.

FISH OIL SOAP—1 lb., 20c.; 2 lbs., 35c.

FUNGINE—Excellent for fungous diseases of all kinds: ½ pt., 35c.; 1 pt., 50c.; 1 qt., 75c.; 1 gal., $2.00.

HAMMOND'S SLUG SHOT—Non-poisonous; the best powder insect destroyer for potato bugs and all insects that chew: 1 lb., 10c.; 5 lbs., 35c.; 10 lbs., 55c.; 25 lbs., $1.25; 50 lbs., $2.45.

TOBACCO DUST—Valuable in combating the striped cucumber beetle when used with Slug Shot: 2 lbs., 10c.; 10 lbs., 40c.; 100 lbs., $3.50.

TOBACCO STEMS—For fumigating and mulching: 100 lbs., $1.25; 500 lbs., $5.00; 1 ton, $15.00.

VERMINE—For destroying ant, worms, maggots, etc., in the soil. Dilute 1 part to 400 parts water and soak soil: ¼ pt., 25c.; ½ pt., 40c.; 1 pt., 65c.

WEED KILLER (Target Brand)—Keeps paths and roads free from weeds and grass: 1 qt., 40c.; ½ gal., 65c.; 1 gal., $1.00.

SEND FOR SPECIAL INSECTICIDE CATALOG—It is free and it contains valuable information about spraying, etc., as well as a more complete list of insecticides.

Garfield Knapsack Sprayer

(See illustration below)

Made entirely of brass and copper. Tank holds 4 gallons, has 4 feet bent rubber hose, brass pipe 15 inches long and Combination Vermorel Nozzle attached. Without Agitator, price, $11.00; with Agitator, $12.00.

Garfield Knapsack Sprayer

Myers' Little Giant Bucket Spray Pumps

(See illustration)

Constructed entirely of brass, which is not affected by the poisons used in spraying fruit trees, vines and shrubbery. Is so arranged that the labor of pumping is all done on the downward stroke of the piston and nothing on the up, which has the effeet of holding the pump down. The footrest steadies the pump. Will throw a solid stream 50 feet and are very useful for washing windows and buggies, sprinkling lawns, flowers, etc. Price, with Rubber Hose, $3.00. With 8-foot Extension Rod, $3.50.

Myers' Little Giant Bucket Spray Pump

The "Perfection" Sprayer

This high pressure type is larger and much more powerful than anything in its class, and is as near burstproof as it can be made. The barrel is 7½ inches in diameter, 20 inches high. The pump is 1¾-inch seamless brass tubing. The valves are METAL. The top is fastened like the best makes of fire extinguishers. The hose is 5-ply. The nozzle is of the Automatic type. Capacity of Sprayer, 3¾ gallons. Weight, 9½ lbs. All Sprayers tested to 60 lbs. before leaving factory. This Sprayer handles whitewash, water, paints, Bordeaux mixtures, etc., perfectly. For whitewash and all heavy mixtures it is necessary to use a No. 2 Cap in nozzle, which is furnished with Sprayers.

Price: All Brass, $7.50; Galvanized, $5.

Perfection Sprayer

The "Auto-Spray"

Works automatically for 6 to 15 minutes, according to the nozzle opening. It may be started in 15 seconds by a few strokes of the plunger.

The "Auto-Spray" has a capacity of four gallons, and when properly charged contains three gallons of solution and one gallon compressed air. Eight to twelve strokes of the plunger will compress the air, and two pumpings will discharge the entire contents. Three gallons of solution or one charge will easily cover one-half acre of potatoes or other similar crop. Galvanized Iron Tank, with Auto-Pop Nozzle, $5.00; Solid Brass Tank, with Auto-Pop Nozzle, $7.20.

Auto-Pop Spray Nozzle—In operation a lever is moved by simply closing the hand, thus opening the valve and allowing the lever it closes itself automatically, hence the spray is in perfect control. Each, $1.25.

Extension Rods for Auto-Spray, 2 ft. long. Each, 50c.

The "Auto-Spray"

Continuous Sprayer

ALL BRASS, $1.00
Brass Ball Valve

Will handle fly oils and disinfectants as well as the regular spraying materials giving a fine and effective spray. An extra nozzle cap is furnished for spraying under the side of the foliage.

Lowell Sprayer

BRASS TUBES
Zinc Can Screw
75 cents

Simple and cheap for spraying shrubs and plants with water or insecticides. Each, 75c. Cannot be mailed.

Send for our Special Catalog of Latest Improved Spray Pumps, Nozzles, Pruning Tools, etc. You will receive the benefit of our experience by having placed before you thoroughly tested honest goods at the right prices.

S, indicates Seeds.
B, Bulbs.

INDEX

R, Roots.
P, Plants or Shrubs.

Special Notice with Reference to Nursery Stock

Our customers will notice that, with few exceptions, all plants, shrubs, and trees have been eliminated from this Cat alog. We found it increasingly difficult to satisfy the exacting requirements made in many states by laws regulating the sale of live plants. The cost of the licenses required for selling nursery stock in many states makes it impossib to do business there. Considering the wide distribution which this Catalog receives, the long distances plants often hav to travel and the exorbitant transportation charges arising for the customer, we thought best to discontinue the handlin of nursery stock in connection with our mail-order business. Order heavy plants, shrubs and trees from reliable nu series in your immediate neighborhood is the sincere advice of

THE LIVINGSTON SEED COMPANY.

Names for Livingston's Seed Annual. We hope you like TRUE BLUE SEEDS well enough to wish to introduce them into those families of your acquaintance whom you know and all of by SEEDS, BULBS, Etc. If so, kindly write their Names and Post Office Addresses on the blank lines below. We would be glad to send them a copy of this Seed Annual free. When convenient, if you would say a good word for our stocks we would be very much obliged to you.

POST OFFICE	Rural Route or Street Number	STATE

PRICES

AN ORDER FOR LIVINGSTON'S SEEDS, BULBS, ROOTS, ETC.

From _____

P. O. _____

State _____

DON'T FORGET
TO PLACE A
2-CENT STAMP
HERE.

The Livingston Seed Co.,

"FAMOUS FOR TOMATOES"

COLUMBUS,

OHIO.

THE LIVINGSTON SEED CO., Columbus, Ohio, U.S.A.

WE DELIVER FREE IN THE U.S. TO ANY POST OFFICE, RAILROAD EXPRESS OFFICE OR FREIGHT STA-
TION IN THE U. S., AT OUR OPTION, ALL SEEDS IN PACKETS,
OUNCES, ONE-FOURTH POUNDS, POUNDS AND TWO POUNDS OF OUR OWN
PUT-UPS, ALL OTHER PLANTS, BEANS AND CORN, BULBS AND
PURCHASES PAY TRANSIT CHARGES on quantities larger than those named above, as well as on Farm Seeds, Tools,
Implements, Insecticides, Etc. UNLESS OTHERWISE NOTED IN CATALOGUE.
ALL ORDERS FOR POTATOES, PLANTS, or other perishable goods, are carefully looked and filled in rotation as soon as
the weather will permit. If shipped earlier they are at buyer's risk. For full instructions about ordering, etc., see Di-
rections on Page 2 and 3 of this Seed Annual.

THE LIVINGSTON SEED COMPANY
give no warranty, express or implied, as
to description, quality, productiveness, or
any other matter of any seeds, bulbs or
plants we send out, and we will not be in
any way responsible for the crop.

☞ **PLEASE WRITE YOUR NAME AND ADDRESS PLAINLY AND IN FULL IN THE BLANKS BELOW**
EXTRA ORDER SHEETS AND RETURN ENVELOPES WILL BE SENT YOU ON APPLICATION

Date..............

Name..............

Post Office..............

Box..........R. F. D. No..........

Street No...........

Ship to (Station)...........

By (Express or ....
PLEASE W

Ship by { MAIL / EXPRESS / FREIGHT

FOR BEST RESULTS IN YOUR PLANT GARDENS

LIVINGSTON'S "TRUE BLUE" GARDEN, FIELD, and FLOWER SEEDS ARE THE SELECTED STRAINS AND THE BEST IN THE WORLD.

THE LIVINGSTON SEED CO. COLUMBUS, OHIO.

LIVINGSTON'S FAMOUS TOMATOES and FAMOUS STRAINS OF ONIONS

LIVINGSTON'S "TRUE BLUE" BULBS, POTATOES and VEGETABLE ROOTS

THE AMOUNT ENCLOSED		DO NOT WRITE HERE
Express Money Order, $..........		No. ....
P. O. Money Order, $..........		Date received ....
Bank Draft - - $..........		Checked by ....
Stamps - - - $..........		Wrapped by ....
		Date sent ....
	$..........	P. ....

	Do not write in this column	PRICES	
		Dollars	Cents

Livingston's Four Finest New Vegetables

Peter Pan Peas
New—Immense Dark Green Pods

A fine new, early dwarf variety of English origin. The plant is very robust and grows to a height of 1½ feet. It is a heavy cropper, producing long, dark green pods, well filled with peas of excellent quality (see illustration). This new variety is sure to become popular with those wishing a large podded dwarf variety. Pkt., 15c.

Sweet Corn
Livingston's Early Sugar

This is a remarkably fine early variety; a heavy cropper, producing quite large ears for so early a variety. The ears have such a thick husk that they are seldom bothered by worms. This corn at roasting ear stage is pure white and it is of exceptionally fine quality. Pkt., 10c.; ½ lb., 15c.; lb., 25c.; 2 lbs., 50c., postpaid. By express, not paid, ½ pk., 60c.; pk., $1.10; bu., $3.75.

Chinese Cabbage (Pe Tsai)
Also known as Celery Cabbage, Odorless Cabbage, etc.

An annual introduced into this country from Chontung, China. This new vegetable belongs to the Cabbage family but resembles somewhat a stalk of Celery; it is as tender as head lettuce and is in great demand for numerous dishes, such as salads, cole slaw, and may be served raw. When cooked it has the taste of Cabbage, but has a much milder flavor. Pkt., 10c.; ½ oz., 20c.; oz., 30c.; ¼ lb., $1.00; lb., $3.75.

Sweet Salad Pepper

This new heart or top shaped variety is of the Spanish or Pimento type, large, smooth and very thick meated. The flesh is very firm, sweet and is of fine texture. Pkt., 10c.; ½ oz., 25c.; oz., 40c.; ¼ lb., $1.50.

For full description of the above varieties, see Novelty Pages.

We offer a collection of one packet each of the four fine new vegetables offered above for only 35c. postpaid.

Peter Pan Peas.

Choice New Dahlia
Delice

A very popular variety. We have grown this variety at our True Blue flower gardens for the past two seasons and consider this Dahlia one of the best of its kind. Its beautiful soft, yet lively color, a glowing rose pink, together with its perfect shape, stout, stiff stems which hold the flowers well above the foliage, and the fact that when cut, it retains its freshness for a long time, makes this one of the most valuable for cutting or decorative sorts in the garden. The florist and all Dahlia growers will make no mistake in planting this variety. Price, 20c. each; dozen, $2.00.

Other new varieties of Dahlias are offered on novelty pages, and for complete list and full description, see pages 121 and 122

Lightning Source UK Ltd.
Milton Keynes UK
UKHW022208021218
333278UK00006B/488/P

9 780260 691484